Ple *Elizabeth Macarthur*

Michelle Scott Tucker lives on a small farm in Victoria with her husband and children. She owns and operates a management consulting company. *Elizabeth Macarthur: A Life at the Edge of the World* is her first book.

Elizabeth Macarthur

A LIFE AT THE EDGE OF THE WORLD

MICHELLE SCOTT TUCKER

t

TEXT PUBLISHING MELBOURNE AUSTRALIA

textpublishing.com.au

The Text Publishing Company
Swann House
22 William Street
Melbourne Victoria 3000
Australia

First published by The Text Publishing Company 2018.

Book design by Imogen Stubbs.
Typeset by J&M Typesetting.
Index by Mary Russell.
Cover images: Joseph Lycett 'The residence of John McArthur Esqre. near Parramatta New South Wales', National Library of Australia; Elizabeth Macarthur (reputedly), 1785–90, watercolour on ivory miniature, State Library of New South Wales.

Printed and bound in Australia by Griffin Press, an accredited ISO/NZS 14001:2004 Environmental Management System printer.

ISBN: 9781925603422 (paperback)
ISBN: 9781925626469 (ebook)

A catalogue record for this book is available from the National Library of Australia.

This book is printed on paper certified against the Forest Stewardship Council® Standards. Griffin Press holds FSC chain-of-custody certification SGS-COC-005088. FSC promotes environmentally responsible, socially beneficial and economically viable management of the world's forests.

For Tim, Charlie, Will and Ashlee,
with all my love.

Contents

Author's Note

Many excerpts from original letters and journals are included throughout this biography. Idiosyncratic spelling, use of ampersands, underlining and capitalisation have been left unamended, to the extent possible to still allow for easy reading.

During Elizabeth Macarthur's life, she and her family spelled Macarthur in a variety of ways including M'Arthur and MacArthur. The family later came to consistently prefer Macarthur, which I have used throughout.

Many historians refer to the area that would become Camden Park as Cowpastures. John Macarthur, in his letters to Elizabeth, refers to Cow Pastures, so that is the usage I have followed.

While the standard convention is to refer to a biographical subject by his or her last name, there are so many Macarthurs discussed throughout the text that to do so would be unnecessarily confusing. My references to 'Elizabeth' and 'John' are therefore made in the interests of clarity, rather than as the result of over-familiarity.

Family Tree

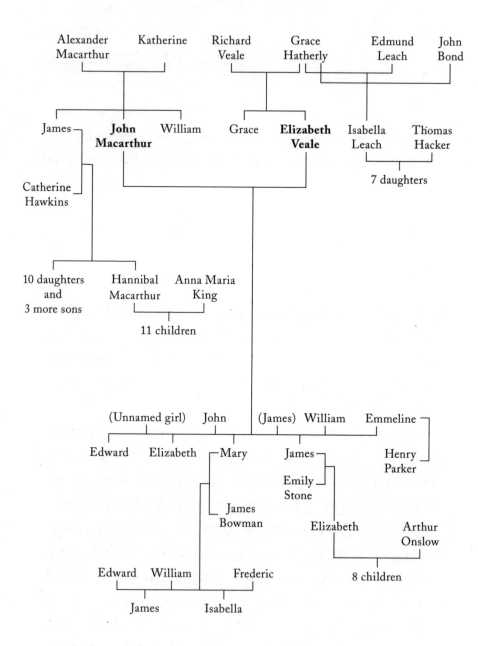

1

The Lost Comforts of Home

This ship arrived...and came timely to prevent very great distress.
ELIZABETH MACARTHUR TO BRIDGET KINGDON, 7 MARCH 1791

Convict ship *Scarborough* was no place for a gentleman's daughter. Elizabeth Macarthur was cold, pregnant and bone-weary. The Southern Ocean pummelled the ship with storm after storm and her soldier husband and infant son were both grievously ill. Elizabeth prayed.

Somewhere on that roaring sea, exhausted by her nursing duties, and constantly pitched and tumbled, Elizabeth was 'thrown into premature labour, & delivered of a little Girl who lived but for an hour.'[1] There was no one on *Scarborough* to help. No other women were on board, and the ship's surgeon was unlikely to have been sober, let alone skilled. We only know of the nameless baby's existence from a single line in a letter Elizabeth wrote to her mother, many months later. There is no record of a shipboard funeral, no record of where the small bundle wrapped in weighted canvas was delivered to the sea, and no record of Elizabeth's grief. All we have—all Elizabeth had—is that single tragic hour.

Weeks later, on the final days of June 1790, *Scarborough* and her Second Fleet sister ship *Neptune* limped into Port Jackson. Within the immense harbour dense green-grey scrub grew down to the water's edge, interrupted by rocky headlands, reedy swamps and some bright sandy crescents. Thin columns of smoke flagged the presence of local inhabitants, discomfortingly close, in the newcomer's eyes, to the settlement at Sydney Cove.

Elizabeth gathered her family close. Eighteen-month-old Edward had survived the voyage, albeit sickly and undersized. Husband John had, since they left their Cape Town stopover some two months before, been 'attack'd with a violent, & very alarming Fever; it continued to rage until every sense was lost, & every faculty but life destroyed'.[2] But he could now walk unaided and was able to see for himself the destination he'd chosen for his family.

In October of the previous year, a month before boarding the ship, Elizabeth wrote to her mother about what she had read of Britains's newest colony. 'We learn that Wheat which has been sown flourished in a manner nearly incredible, and that the Settlers are making rapid progress in building; so that by the time our Corps arrives everything will be made comfortable for their reception.'[3] Nothing was further from the truth. All reports of the colony that had filtered back to London were written within months of the First Fleet's arrival in January 1788. These accounts were full of optimism and hope and based on little evidence. The grim reality, though, was clear to those eyeing the shore from *Scarborough*'s deck.

On the evening of Monday 28 June 1790, the *Neptune* and *Scarborough* transports anchored off Garden Island, well inside the harbour. The following morning a cable was run from each ship's capstan to the shore, fastened to a sturdy tree, and then the ship was winched to its anchorage. As she approached the much-vaunted township Elizabeth can only have despaired. Town was in fact too grand a term for the motley collection of huts and tents, tree stumps and rutted, muddy tracks. Many of the marines she could see onshore were without shoes, their faces gaunt, the remnants of their uniforms too large for their emaciated frames. The Macarthurs had risked everything to come here—there could be no going back.

The thirteen hundred or so colonists were teetering on the edge of starvation. Attempts at growing crops had largely failed and the foodstuffs brought in the holds of the First Fleet ships were now at least three years rancid and running low. Governor Phillip had introduced strict rationing, and theft of food was punishable by death. Many convicts were too weak to work (indeed some were said to have died of starvation), and those remaining made meagre progress building the roads, houses, stores and offices that would eventually turn the campsite into a town. Few colonies in the British Empire were as abject and miserable as the settlement Sydney Cove.

When *Lady Juliana*, the first ship of the Second Fleet, was sighted three weeks earlier on 3 June, the colony's reaction was predictably ecstatic. 'Every countenance was instantly cheered, and wore the lively expressions of eagerness, joy, and anxiety,' wrote bureaucrat David Collins, 'the whole settlement was in motion and confusion.'⁴ Watkin Tench, a marine officer and diarist, opened the door of his hut 'and saw several women with children in their arms running to and fro with distracted looks, congratulating each other, and kissing their infants with the most passionate and extravagant marks of fondness...My next door neighbour, a brother-officer, was with me, but we could not speak. We wrung each other by the hand, with eyes and hearts overflowing.'⁵

With her cargo of some two hundred female convicts, *Lady Juliana* brought valuable commodities—news and women. Governor Phillip was less than thrilled with the practical uselessness of the latter ('many of them appeared to be loaded with the infirmities incident to old age'⁶), but was deeply relieved when, two weeks later the store ship *Justinian* arrived. The survival of the colony was ensured, at least in the short term, and he immediately ordered that the full food ration be restored. The news, however, was just as much appreciated. Letters from home 'were torn open in trembling agitation', wrote Tench. 'News burst upon us like meridian splendour on a blind man. We were overwhelmed with it: public, private, general, and particular. Nor was it until some days had elapsed, that we were able to methodise it, or reduce it into form.'⁷ There was King George's illness and his happy return to health; the French revolution; and the fate of HMS *Guardian*, fully laden with stores, which should have arrived three months earlier but had struck an iceberg in the Southern Ocean. But the colonists also learnt of the imminent arrival of three more transports—a thousand more hungry convict mouths to feed and nowhere to house them. Elizabeth Macarthur's *Scarborough* was one of these ships.

Scarborough and her captain, John Marshall, had made the trip with the First Fleet two years before. Marshall had left behind his Newfoundland dog, Hector. Now, the dog was so pleased to be reunited with its master that it leapt into the water and, to the delight of onlookers, swam out to the ship.[8] Governor Phillip's welcome was somewhat less warm. Even having longed for the arrival of ships from home for so long, the existing colonists found it hard to muster enthusiasm for *Scarborough*, *Neptune* and (a few days later and carrying a broken mast) *Surprize*. As well as convicts, these three ships carried the incoming soldiers and officers of the newly formed New South Wales Corps. Governor Phillip's marines were to be sent home, replaced by army men. This was to cause much ill-feeling. Marines, despite often looking and acting like soldiers, were in fact part of the Royal Navy, and routinely took orders from their ship's captain. Soldiers, however, operated within a completely separate arm of the English defence forces and answered only to their own superior officers. As a career officer in His Majesty's Royal Navy, Phillip knew the difficulties of combined army and navy operations: the jealousies, the divided councils, the arguments over precedence. Even though Phillip was not now commanding vessels at sea, the maintenance of sound discipline remained a matter of life or death for them all—only now the main danger lay in being overthrown by the convicts rather than by a rogue wave.

Governor Phillip presumably met the incoming officers and received them formally at Government House—a grand name for the only two-storey building in the settlement. Phillip was introduced to his new subordinates: Captain Nicholas

Nepean, the Corps' commanding officer in the absence of the Regimental Commander; Nepean's second in command Captain William Hill; and the lieutenants, including John Macarthur, and Macarthur's twenty-three-year-old wife Elizabeth, the only officer's wife to make the journey.

The Macarthur family was allocated a hut after the senior officers Nepean and Hill had chosen theirs. Exactly who had to move out of the hut in order to accommodate the Macarthurs, or their feelings about doing so, is not recorded. Nor are Elizabeth's thoughts about her new home. John Macarthur's superior officer, Captain Hill, did however, record his own thoughts about the situation, in a letter to a friend in England:

> Here I am, living in a miserable thatched hut, without kitchen, without a garden, with an acrimonious blood by my having been nearly six months at sea, and tho' little better than a leper obliged to live on a scanty pittance of salt provision, without a vegetable, except when a good-natured neighbour robs his own stomach in compassion to me.[9]

Then began the urgent task of unloading the convicts. The ships spewed forth a cargo of filth and misery. 'The landing of these people was truly affecting and shocking,' wrote the Reverend Johnson, first chaplain of the settlement, 'great numbers were not able to walk, nor to move hand or foot; such were slung over the ship side in the same manner as they would sling a cask or box or anything of that nature. Upon their being brought up to the open air, some fainted, some died upon deck, and others in the boat before they reached the shore.' Johnson went aboard the *Surprize* and was appalled. Many of the men had neither bedding nor clothes, and they were 'unable to turn, or help themselves'. Johnson tried to speak to them as he passed along 'but the smell was so offensive I could scarcely bear it'. He then boarded the *Scarborough* to again go down among the convicts, but Captain Marshall dissuaded him. 'The *Neptune*,' wrote Johnson, 'was still more wretched and intolerable and therefore never attempted it.'[10]

Of the one thousand or so convicts sent out in the Second Fleet, 273 did not survive the journey. Those who died after their ships entered Port Jackson were flung overboard, and their unweighted corpses washed up on the shore. Governor Phillip was furious with the captains, wrote one of the convict women of the *Lady Juliana*: 'I heard him say it was murdering them.'[11] Phillip's dispatches back to England were, however, far more circumspect. Nearly half the convicts were landed sick: 'Some creeped upon their hands and knees, and some were carried upon the backs of others.'[12] The rest were lean and emaciated.[13]

The hospital could hold no more than eighty, at a pinch, so tents were hurriedly erected. Each one held up to four men who lay on the damp ground with a single blanket to share, although the strongest would often take it for himself. Reverend Johnson continued to be dismayed. 'Some were exercised with violent fevers, and others with a no less violent purging and flux. [Many] were covered over almost with their own nastiness, their heads, bodies, cloths, blanket, all full of filth and lice.'[14] The store ship *Justinian* contained the materials for a portable field hospital, but it comprised 602 pieces of wood and copper, and it took nearly six days to erect. It probably made no difference. Antiseptics and sanitary hospital practices would not be widely adopted for almost another hundred years so the hospital was in reality little more than a marquee staffed by ill-qualified surgeons and inexpert convict nurses. Of the 486 convicts listed sick, 124 would die in hospital.[15] The rest took weeks and months to recover, if indeed they ever did.

By way of comparison, six per cent of the convicts aboard the First Fleet died on the journey, the Third Fleet lost nine per cent and within ten years the death rate aboard convict transports was consistently around two per cent. The Second Fleet masters responsible for the inexcusable conditions on their ships blithely proceeded to set up shop almost as soon as they arrived. Articles of 'grocery, glass, millinery, perfumery, and stationery'[16] were offered at extortionate prices and, according to a disgusted Tench, were eagerly bought up by the colonists.[17]

These were Elizabeth's first days in the colony—filled with horror, dashed hopes and despair. What a bad bargain she had made, trading solace and safety in England for a precarious and unpredictable future on the edge of the world. For this she had left behind her family and friends—and a daughter out there in her ocean grave. It would be a rare individual who did not think about the lost comforts of home.

2

An Ill-advised Marriage

*In the little friendly meetings that we have in
Sydney 'the banks of the Tamar' is a general toast—
Many of the Officers having friends and connexions in
Devon & Cornwall, the remembrance is pleasing to all.*

ELIZABETH MACARTHUR TO HER MOTHER, 18 MARCH 1791

Elizabeth Veale was born in 1766 and raised in the village of
Bridgerule, in Devon in England's southwest. It was then home
to some fifty families.[1] Elizabeth's father, Richard Veale, was
a farmer, and her mother Grace, nee Hatherly, was a farmer's
daughter just nineteen years old when Elizabeth was born.[2]
Elizabeth's father is variously described in surviving public documents as Richard Veale yeoman farmer; as Mr Richard Veale;
or as Richard Veale Esq.[3] The terms Mr and Esquire indicate
that at the very least Veale thought himself a gentleman and
that others (or at least the record keepers) did so too. Elizabeth
and her family belonged within the boundaries of polite society.

The Veale's farm, 'Lodgeworthy', lies, to this day, just south
of Bridgerule on the eastern banks of the Tamar River, and
was within sound, if not sight, of the five bells in the tower of
Bridgerule's Anglican church of St Bridget. The Veales' nearest

neighbours across the fields were the Reverend Kingdon and his young family. The eldest Kingdon child, Bridget, was born shortly after Elizabeth and the pair were, as Bridget would later note, 'from childhood brought up together as intimate friends'.[4] Georgian Bridgerule was a place that might be familiar to readers of *Pride and Prejudice* or *Sense and Sensibility*. Jane Austen, only nine years younger than Elizabeth, lived in Hampshire, about 300 kilometres away, and her fictional Bennets, or Dashwood sisters, might just as easily have lived in Elizabeth's real-life Bridgerule.

In the winter of 1772, when Elizabeth was almost six years old, her two-year-old sister died. With the coming of spring Elizabeth's father died too, aged only thirty-two.[5] Lodgeworthy, the family home, passed to a John Veale, probably an uncle, and soon after was sold.[6] Elizabeth and her mother, Grace, seem to have remained living nearby, possibly with Grace's father John Hatherly[7] and then with her mother's second husband, but Elizabeth continued to spend her time with the well-to-do Kingdons. The Reverend John Kingdon and his family were kind people who would become lifelong and very useful friends to Elizabeth and her family. Elizabeth was most likely educated at the Bridgerule vicarage with Bridget, probably by the Reverend (himself an Oxford man) and, when she could find the time, Mrs Kingdon. Bridget was the first of eleven Kingdon children, including eight boys. Elizabeth was possibly welcomed as much for offering an extra pair of useful hands as for her company.

Bridgerule in the late eighteenth century was a provincial backwater with little to differentiate it from a hundred similar villages. Except, that is, for the presence of Elizabeth Veale. In

Bridgerule Elizabeth gained the principles, skills, opinions and prejudices that she would carry with her to New South Wales and that she and her husband would contribute to the beginnings of the new colony. Bridgerule formed Elizabeth's social and moral blueprint. The rules of society played out in Bridgerule every bit as strongly as they did in the drawing rooms of aristocratic Londoners. Knowing one's place and, more importantly, keeping to it was an unwritten rule that underpinned village life. It is little wonder that Elizabeth would later find the concept of egalitarianism—where a convict emancipist might be accorded the same social standing as free settlers—utterly abhorrent.

Elizabeth, her parents and the other Bridgerule inhabitants were deeply connected to their community. Throughout England, outsiders (those from another parish or region) were listed in official documents as 'strays'. Most families lived in the same region for generations. The Bridgerule villagers were deeply familiar to Elizabeth, each person known at least as an acquaintance and more likely as a servant, merchant, tradesman or friend. Genteel families like the Veales and the Kingdons were deeply conventional and overtly focused on family and church. Outward behaviour was a key marker of social merit and the genteel eschewed vulgarity, insincerity and—worst sin of all—display.[8] Yet for all their emphasis on the rewards of heaven, the gentlefolk of Georgian England maintained a steely gaze on the rewards of this earthly life. While the aristocracy had finances enough to be able to haggle over the merits or otherwise of an individual's breeding, members of polite society kept their focus largely on the one thing that mattered most: money. It was the element that would underpin many of the most important decisions in Elizabeth's life.

It's not clear how Elizabeth Veale met John Macarthur, a 'stray' from another parish. John was the second son of Plymouth draper, Alexander Macarthur, who provided slops (coarse fabric for clothing) for sailors.[9] The family business operated from premises in Fore Street, then the busiest thoroughfare near the naval wharves.[10] John's father had spent time in America and the West Indies before settling, with his wife and eldest son James, at Plymouth Dock (now Devonport). John was born several years later, in 1766.[11] According to family legend, his mother Catherine was a woman 'of great beauty and accomplishments' who married Alexander 'in opposition to the wishes of her family'.[12] The fifteen-year gap between John and his older brother suggests a sad string of miscarriages or infant tragedies. One more brother, William, lived to be baptised in 1770, but died as an infant. John's mother died in 1777, when he was only ten or eleven.[13] In 1782 James, at the age of thirty and having taken over the family business, married brewery heiress, Catherine Hawkins. James's occupation is listed in the marriage register as a mercer.[14] A mercer dealt in fine fabrics; so James had by this time clearly improved the family business. Catherine's father advanced various sums of money to the couple and perhaps some of that money made its way to young John Macarthur.[15] Within six months of his brother's marriage, John, in the manner of many second sons, joined the army.[16]

With £400, teenage John was able to buy a commission of the lowest officer rank—ensign—in one of the lowest-ranked regiments. He joined an independent company of militia comprising, as its commanding officer Major Fish admitted, men 'mostly old and unfit for service' with their purpose being to defend England against incursion by the French.[17] Overseas service was not then part of John Macarthur's prospects. But at this early stage, he was not seeking a glorious military career—John Macarthur was seeking honour. Even as a lowly ensign in the lowest of regiments, his purchase of the King's commission elevated him to the status of officer and gentleman. He could put his socially dubious mercantile background behind him and step out into the world as a man among men—gentlemen, of course. Or so he hoped. As is common among those whose footing on the social ladder is not quite as firm as they might wish, John remained throughout his life very touchy about the subject of his honour. In the absence of money or family connections, it was honour upon which his status as a gentleman absolutely depended.

John Macarthur took up his commission in October 1782, just as the American war was ending. During the winter, his regiment was moved to Barnstaple, a small port on the north Devon coast. Then, in April 1783, with his services no longer required, Macarthur was pensioned off on half pay.[18] He had no desire to return to Plymouth and he remained in north Devon. His son would later record that he lived near the market town of Holsworthy 'at a farmhouse, on the borders of Cornwall and Devonshire. There he took a lively interest in the various rural occupations going on, hunted, being a bold and accomplished horseman, and spent much time in the perusal of such books as he could obtain'.[19] Given that an ensign on half pay couldn't have afforded a lifestyle that included hunting he must have had another source of income, possibly as a schoolmaster—Elizabeth would much later write that John met one of Bridget's younger brothers at a grammar school.[20] Or he might have supplemented his income by buying, breeding and selling horses, as he would later do successfully in New South Wales. In either occupation—schoolmaster or horsemaster—he soon found cause to visit the nearby village of Bridgerule.

Exactly how John and Elizabeth first met is unclear, but they certainly had much in common. Both were articulate and intelligent. Both were members of the Anglican Church: an important connection in a time when some were beginning to lean towards Protestant dissent.[21] In outlook, both were conservative and provincial. Both, too, had a lost a parent at an early age, although that was hardly unusual. And they must have exclaimed to discover their birthdays were only one day apart: John was born on 13 August and Elizabeth the following day.

Years later Elizabeth advised Bridget, using her marriage to John Macarthur as an example, to 'look out for good sense in a husband. You would never be happy with a person inferior to yourself in point of understanding.'[22] Elizabeth clearly believed she was John's intellectual, as well as his romantic, match. Bridget, with the clear-eyed vision of hindsight, wrote back to Elizabeth saying that 'it was ever my opinion that Mr M would make an excellent husband, if he met with a woman whose disposition and accomplishments suited him, in that respect how fortunate, and how fortunate for you, that you met with a man possessed of good sense and sensibility.'[23]

It appears that Elizabeth and John's formal engagement occurred in the English spring of 1788. A man about to be married surely needed more than half pay to live on and so Ensign Macarthur resumed his commission and returned to full pay in

May. He paid almost £100 to move to a regiment then stationed in Gibraltar (although John never joined it there). It seems likely that his path was smoothed by Kingdon connections.[24] At around the same time Elizabeth sold some land (presumably an inheritance) to a local gentleman for the sum of £340, providing herself with a dowry roughly equivalent to a year's income. [25]

Both aged twenty-two, they were young to be marrying, particularly John. He had very little to offer his bride except castles in the air. Most grooms, in contrast, waited to marry until their careers were established and they could afford to support a family. The average marriage age for a man of Macarthur's class and circumstance was mid- to late-twenties.[26] It was typical of Macarthur's impetuosity to act first (propose), then deal with the consequences later (try to find a more lucrative posting). It was an impetuosity he would demonstrate throughout his life. In the circumstances, Elizabeth should have refused John Macarthur. Through her Kingdon connections she could reasonably have expected to do better. A miniature portrait thought to be of Elizabeth, painted around the time of her engagement, shows a fair-skinned beauty with hazel eyes and curled dark hair. Her modish, décolleté empire line gown reveals more than just a magnificent bust—the portrait reveals a status-conscious woman aspiring to be far more than a farmer's daughter.[27]

Any eighteenth-century woman's decision to marry was one of the most important of her life and a prudent and considered choice was of the essence if she were 'not to be the architect of her own misfortune'.[28] However Elizabeth was certain that few of her friends 'thought that either of us had taken a prudent step. I was considered indolent and inactive; Mr Macarthur too proud and haughty for our humble fortune or expectations.'[29] The villagers, then, did not approve of the match.

Macarthur was tall, by the standards of the day, but not especially handsome and his proud manner, as described by Elizabeth, was not immediately appealing. Throughout his life he was either loved or loathed. Portraits show a man with small dark eyes above prominent cheek bones, a sharp nose, full lips and a fine head of thick wavy hair swept back from his forehead.[30] His sons would later point out that his features were marked by smallpox. But he was eloquent, well read, and could be charming when he chose to be. Clearly Elizabeth was in love and, besides, the Macarthur men appear to have had a certain knack for capturing brides above their station.

The clearest indicator of their engagement is to be found in the baptismal register of St Bridget's. In May 1788, John and Elizabeth stood together as godparents to the Kingdons' eleventh and last child, a daughter.[31] A fond Mrs Kingdon knew Elizabeth would soon be leaving to start a household of her own and so offered her a double honour and loving bond by also naming the baby Elizabeth, though she would be known as Eliza. In the face of the village's objections to Elizabeth's fiancé, the Kingdons were offering her an important gesture of love and support. The baptism became a public affirmation of the Kingdons' support for the couple's intentions as well as a formalisation of their engagement.

The Reverend Kingdon officiated at the subsequent wedding ceremony, held on a Tuesday morning in early October 1788.[32] A morning ceremony was often followed by a celebratory breakfast but it was not usual to issue invitations or to expect friends and family to travel from afar. Elizabeth's mother and younger half-sister, resident in Bridgerule, were probably present at St Bridget's but John's father and brother, resident in Plymouth, were more likely not. Mrs Jane Kingdon, the Reverend's wife and John Bond, a church functionary, stood as witnesses. John Bond himself get married four years later—to Elizabeth's mother, who had been twice widowed by that stage. John Macarthur's name in the church register is followed by the title Esq., although no other male name is (even those whose listed occupation was 'gent'). Maybe the title was bestowed by the Reverend in honour of Macarthur's military commission. Or perhaps the kind Reverend was simply happy to pander to a young man's vanity on his wedding day.

The next few months were anxious ones for the newlyweds. They probably set up home in the farmhouse where John had been living but John was absent without official leave for all but two months of his term with the 68th or Durham Regiment of Foot at Gibraltar.[33] The army had never been a vocation for John, more a means to an end, and he was now determined to sell his commission. The secretary of war, though, had other plans for Ensign Macarthur, stating in reply to a query from John's commanding officer that 'His Majesty does not allow officers to be brought from the half-pay for the purpose of selling entirely out' and 'if Macarthur was unwilling to go to Gibraltar he must return to half pay, receiving no more than the sum he had lately paid out.'[34] As soon as Macarthur saw the letter he set off for London to petition the secretary directly. Such a journey—some 400 wearisome kilometres by coach—should have been unremarkable but a foolhardy Elizabeth, heavily pregnant with her first child, went along too.

Travelling from Devon to London on turnpiked roads, travellers could take as many as four days. Poor Elizabeth spent uncomfortable hours bumping along in a coach, subject to the vagaries of March weather. And on 16 March 1789, at a public house in Bath called the White Hart, far from the assistance of friends and family, Elizabeth gave birth to a healthy baby boy: Edward Macarthur.[35] John and Elizabeth had been married for just five months.

It is possible that Elizabeth, in deciding to travel to London, was herself unaware of how far advanced her pregnancy was. Or perhaps in convincing others that hers was a wedding-night baby she also half convinced herself. I wonder, though, if she was running away. In the early eighteenth century, a verbal commitment was considered legally valid, ensuring that a proposal, once accepted, was as binding as the marriage itself. An engaged couple may well have considered themselves as good as married and so consummated the union with impunity. However, in 1753 Lord Hardwicke's Marriage Act was passed. From 1754 only the church wedding, not the verbal spousals, was legally binding.[36] It was now over thirty years later, and having been raised in such proximity to the vicarage, Elizabeth must surely have known that an engagement was not a marriage and that her feminine honour and her family's honour—that concept apparently so dear to her fiancée's heart—was dependent upon her pre-marital chastity. While a gentleman's honour depended upon his actions and reliability, a gentlewoman's honour was solely dependent upon public recognition of her virtue.[37] Pre-nuptial conception was dangerous enough in 1773, some fifteen years prior to Elizabeth's engagement, for the popular *The Lady's Magazine* to warn its readers to be especially on their guard against seduction between the spousals and the wedding.[38] Not for the last time would John's standards in regard to honour reveal themselves to be subject to the vagaries of self-interest.

The Macarthurs may have avoided the immediate disapproval of the village by travelling on to London, as soon as was practicable after Edward's birth. In April John was in London, petitioning the secretary of war. He wrote three times asking to sell his commission, with the secretary's unchanging response growing more curt each time. The Macarthurs felt keenly their lack of influence and connections. John might well have styled himself a gentleman, but in this instance the twenty-two-year-old ensign had neither the resources nor the clout to enable his desires to come to pass. It looked like he was off to Gibraltar after all.

In frustration, John scoured his mind for any other military patrons who might promote his cause—and found one. The undersecretary in the Home Office, Evan Nepean, was an acquaintance of John's older brother James.[39] Nepean was responsible for appointments in New South Wales. He had just arranged for his own younger brother, Nicholas Nepean, to form a company within the newly minted New South Wales Corps. Evan Nepean certainly had a vested interest in attracting bright young officers like John Macarthur to a posting that was far from attractive. He would have emphasised the opportunities available to those men of ambition who were early on the scene. Not only was John offered a place, but also a promotion and a financial incentive in the form of a recruiting bonus for every man he enlisted.[40] Thus Lieutenant Macarthur, his wife and their infant son were soon installed at Chatham Barracks, readying themselves for departure to Port Jackson. Just as he was to do time and again in the future, John had managed to turn a difficult situation to his own advantage.

For John, travelling to New South Wales was the least worst alternative and offered some hope of material advancement. More puzzling, though, are Elizabeth's reasons for accompanying him to the end of the earth. Was it love—or something more? The young couple had become engaged on the assumption that John would resign his commission and that they would create a home in England. Yet here was John only a year later—or rather a wedding, a baby and a year later—deciding whether or not to embark upon a military career; whether or not they should all set sail for an infant colony on the other side of the world. They may as well have contemplated a trip to a colony on Mars.

The First Fleet had sailed for Botany Bay from John's home town of Plymouth nearly two years earlier, generating enormous fanfare and public interest.[41] At the end of March 1789, First Fleet ships began to arrive back in England. A total of six published accounts of the new colony, written within the first few months of arrival, found an eager and widespread audience. The first to be published in book form—*A Narrative of the Expedition to Botany Bay*—was by marine officer Watkin Tench, who would later become a good friend of Elizabeth's. His book was an immediate success and went through three editions by the end of 1789, was pirated in Dublin and was translated into Dutch, French and German. Governor Phillip's early reports to government were also published, in parts, between July and December 1789. As the officially sanctioned account, this book was also highly successful.[42] These early reports were uniformly optimistic and Elizabeth had clearly done some reading.

Elizabeth avoided returning to Bridgerule. She wrote to her mother from London, describing the positive things she had read about the new colony. She admitted she had at first found John's New South Wales proposal to be 'terrific and gloomy'; it made her feel 'timid and irresolute…[and I] suffered myself to be blinded by common and vulgar prejudices'. But she soon came around to become 'a warm advocate for this scheme' and felt she would 'be greatly disappointed if anything happens to impede it'. Elizabeth said she regretted leaving her mother but tried to console her by pointing out that 'if we must be distant from each other, it is much the same whether I am two hundred, or far more than as many thousand miles apart from you'. How consoled her mother actually felt by that thought is a moot point. Elizabeth's rationale for the change of heart was purely economic: 'We have every reasonable expectation of reaping the most material advantages.'[43] But it wasn't only the money that talked.

John was no doubt articulate and persuasive in his arguments for taking the whole family to New South Wales. It would certainly be more comfortable for him if Elizabeth came along. But surely the village of Bridgerule was talking too—who could resist counting the months between the October wedding and the March birth? If Elizabeth were to return, she faced the weight of community censure, the sly smiling whispers seasoned by the hint that perhaps Macarthur had left her behind deliberately, even as family and neighbours cooed at her baby. After all, except for the Kingdons, Elizabeth's friends in the village never approved of the match in the first place. The tightly knit village community that could be so comforting could also be achingly claustrophobic. Elizabeth, in the space of less than a year, had begun to experience a wider world—Bath, Plymouth, even London. At Chatham Barracks she had made new friends and joined the community of officers' wives. To stay behind would be to turn her back on adventure, on a once-in-a-lifetime chance to leave the physical and social confines of Bridgerule. But worst of all to the young and passionate Elizabeth, to stay behind would be to lose for years—perhaps forever—her newfound friend, confidant, lover and husband. So she embarked on what would be the longest, hardest and most terrifying journey of her life.

3

Honour and a Small Victory

*I took leave of my friends in London and accompanied
by Mr McArthur, hired a Gravesend boat from Billinsgate,
which conveyed us to the Neptune.*

OPENING SENTENCE OF ELIZABETH MACARTHUR'S
SHIPBOARD JOURNAL, UNDATED

Many sailors believed beginning a voyage on a Friday brought
bad luck and they went to great pains to avoid doing so. The
Macarthurs, with eight-month-old Edward and his nursemaid,
stepped into their Gravesend boat on a cold and wet Friday,
13 November 1789. A Gravesend boat was a small sailing vessel,
six metres long, used to carry passengers and cargo up and down
the Thames. The rear half of the boat was covered in a large
canvas tilt that was stretched over a curved frame, not unlike
the covered wagons of the American west.[1] Here Elizabeth sat,
out of the rain and looking at riverside London, wondering if
she would ever see it again.

From the bustle of the fish markets at Billingsgate to the
Neptune's anchorage downriver at Longreach was a trip of about
twenty-eight kilometres. As the little river boat approached the
Neptune, it was dwarfed by the ship's bulk. While not nearly as

large as His Royal Majesty's ships-of-the-line or as considerable as some of the East India Company's merchantmen, *Neptune* was still a substantial ship, the biggest of all the First and Second Fleet transports. As the waterman rattled his boathook and drew alongside the *Neptune*, the Macarthurs couldn't help but notice the stench. Even with only some of the convicts as yet on board, and probably none of the livestock, the ship already housed upwards of a hundred people. Every day their refuse and bodily wastes were discarded overboard, to surround the anchored ship until the tide turned.

In a ship of the *Neptune*'s age the bilge (the lowest compartment of a ship) contained a ballast of sand and gravel. *Neptune*'s bilge, like that of every other ship, was also designed to be a collection point for water draining from the decks above. Water used to swab the decks, or which entered through small leaks in the hull, or which accumulated on deck during a storm—all was channelled to the bilge, and then manually removed via the bilge pumps. As the water travelled down through the ship, the shipboard detritus was carried with it: food scraps; cockroaches; dead cats, rats and mice; excrement; urine; vomit; blood. All slopping about in the bilge, captured in the ballast, for years at a time, the foul smell permeating the ship.

The smell was worst in the lowest, or orlop, deck. Here the bulk of the cargo, livestock and male convicts were housed. The *Neptune*'s orlop was about twenty-three metres long and about eleven metres at its widest point. Into this orlop were to be crammed hundreds of men. His Majesty's Royal Navy officially allocated hammock space of a mere fourteen inches (thirty-five centimetres) width per sailor—convicts were probably not treated as generously.

The convicts slept shoulder to shoulder on wooden platforms in an airless partitioned space without portholes, and were shackled by the wrists or ankles, usually paired with and chained to another convict. According to many witnesses but denied by the *Neptune*'s captain, most of the male convicts remained shackled for the entire voyage and had little opportunity for exercise. Three large tubs on the orlop deck were used 'to ease nature' but crew would later testify that these were 'frequently overset by accident or negligence'.[2] In standard practice, the ship's crew was housed in the forecastle, the area between the central mainmast and the bow. At the rear was the quarterdeck, raised above the rest and enclosed by a rail. This deck was for officers only, and their accommodation was built into the area below.[3] On the *Neptune*, carrying some forty soldiers and two officers of the New South Wales Corps, additional accommodation was probably incorporated into the level immediately below the open deck.

The master of the *Neptune*, Thomas Gilbert, had already sailed out to New South Wales, as commander of the First Fleet transport *Charlotte*. A merchant seaman, Gilbert's title as captain was only an honorary one. In the complex social hierarchy of Georgian England, before the Napoleonic Wars elevated the status of those serving in the English Navy, army officers generally had social precedence over their naval equivalents. In turn, officers of the Royal Navy had precedence over the often genteel captains of the East India Company.[4] Merchant seamen like Gilbert—of dubious background and regardless of their maritime skills—had little or no social standing. These social nuances played themselves out, dangerously, during the first weeks that the Macarthurs were on board.

The Macarthurs settled with their baggage into the cabin they were to share with Captain Nicholas Nepean. The nursemaid and baby Edward may well have bunked in with them too, while John's personal servant, who would have been a private soldier, quartered with his regimental colleagues. Here was a valuable opportunity for the Macarthurs to establish a strong relationship with Captain Nepean. He and John were the only officers of the New South Wales Corps on board the *Neptune*; each of the Second Fleet vessels *Surprize* and *Scarborough* carried another two officers. In total, the officers on the Second Fleet were in charge of nearly a hundred soldiers (seven of whom had embarked with their wives and children) and about a thousand convicts.[5] Seventy-eight female convicts (plus their dozen children and babies) were all accommodated on the *Neptune*, as were some 420 convict men.[6] Three women married to convicted men also gamely accompanied their husbands on the *Neptune*. In total, the *Neptune* would carry about 650 people—convicts, soldiers, and crew—to New South Wales.

The Macarthurs found themselves in influential company on the largest ship of the Second Fleet, in their small berth beneath the raised cabins of the quarterdeck. Perhaps they congratulated each other on their good fortune. John's formal duties were relatively light and involved supervising the soldiers—he was to have little direct interaction with the convicts.[7] The day after the Macarthurs boarded, the *Neptune* moved downriver to Gravesend, where she took on stores, before sailing into the English Channel.[8] Elizabeth played sightseer, being 'much struck with the formidable & romantick appearance of the Cliffs of Deal & of Dover'.[9] But it would be only a few days before her troubles began.

Captain Nicholas Nepean very quickly concluded that sharing a cabin with Lieutenant John Macarthur (and his wife, his infant and the nursemaid) was not going to make for a pleasant voyage. Nepean moved to the upper cabin in the raised area beneath the quarterdeck, leaving Elizabeth to note sarcastically in her journal that he had adopted 'the truly generous maxim "every man for himself"'. Nepean gave permission for his half of their cabin to be sectioned off and used as additional space for 'female Convicts, leaving the other half to us'.

John Macarthur's protestations to Nepean fell upon deaf ears and Elizabeth wrote that 'a slight partition was erected which was thought fully sufficient to separate us from the set of abandoned creatures that were to inhabit the other part'.[10] The Macarthurs, landlubbers both, were unaware that the practice of rearranging cabins, partitioning off areas as required, was commonplace within ocean-going ships, particularly on overcrowded vessels like the *Neptune*. And in light of the carpenter's need to erect and dismantle partitions quickly and as required, the thinness of the partitions was similarly commonplace. Privacy at sea was a very rare commodity. John Macarthur, however, continued to complain about the cabin—this time to the first mate, Nicholas Anstis. When the message was passed on to *Neptune*'s master, Captain Gilbert, he was furious—about the complaint itself and that it hadn't been made to him directly.

On the Saturday that Elizabeth was admiring the Dover cliffs, Macarthur ducked into the upper cabin to raise the partition problem with Nepean again. The stench and noise of the convict women were unbearable. Captain Gilbert happened to come in at that instant, so Nepean raised the matter with him then and there. Gilbert, every bit the cantankerous old Jack Tar, flew into a passionate rage. John Harris, an Irishman in his early thirties and the Corps' surgeon's assistant, had befriended John Macarthur and was witness to the ensuing altercation.

Harris later produced a statement detailing Gilbert's behaviour. 'Rome was not built in a day,' fumed Captain Gilbert to Macarthur, nor did he understand people 'making mountains out of molehills.' He was sure Macarthur meant to be troublesome and he threatened to write to the War Office and have him turned out of the ship.[11] Macarthur recklessly stood his ground, calling the Captain an 'insolent fellow' and pointing out that he'd spoken to Nepean, not Captain Gilbert. Again, Macarthur's inexperience told. By long custom a captain was, in his little wooden world, second only to God. The soldiers and convicts were to Gilbert no more than passengers and cargo. With all the grizzled contempt of an experienced mariner for a callow army lieutenant, Gilbert shoved Macarthur aside and strode off. Nepean was forced to restrain a livid Macarthur, urging him not to do anything extreme now that the ship was underway to Plymouth.[12] Seething, Macarthur managed to hold his peace for the next few days. Elizabeth's views on the matter are not recorded.

With a fine wind driving them down the channel, all expected to be in Plymouth by Tuesday morning. However Gilbert mistakenly sailed much further west than he'd planned and spent the rest of the week beating back against a headwind.

Finally, on the morning of Friday 27 November, the *Neptune* moored safely in Plymouth Sound. No sooner had the fore and aft anchors settled in the seabed when Macarthur (having kept his promise not to do anything while the ship was underway) mounted the quarterdeck and, in front of everyone, called Gilbert 'a great scoundrel', rebuking him for his 'ungentleman-like conduct.'[13] Gilbert barked that he 'had settled many a greater man' and that he would see Macarthur ashore. As John had no doubt intended, Gilbert challenged him to a duel.

At four o'clock that afternoon, the duel combatants met on shore at Plymouth Docks, at the Fountain Tavern on Fore Street. The Dock was then a separate town from Plymouth itself, situated about three kilometres further north towards the mouth of the Tamar. Like many a thriving port city in the late eighteenth century, Plymouth and its surrounds was a mix of squalor and new buildings, of poverty and prosperity, with a transient population that wouldn't have looked twice at the pistol-carrying soldiers and sailors from the *Neptune*.

It was John Macarthur who had named the tavern as their meeting place—it was in the same street as his family's drapery business[14] and presumably he stepped in to say goodbye. Surgeon Harris seconded Macarthur; a Plymouth man did for Gilbert. From the tavern the men moved to the Old Gun Wharf, about a kilometre away. Gilbert and Macarthur stood back to back, before they stepped out the regulation number of paces, turned, raised their pistols and fired. They both missed, although John's bullet left a hole in Gilbert's coat. The seconds conferred and reloaded the guns. The protagonists fired again—and missed again. Although none of Macarthur's problems was resolved, honour was satisfied and the business was considered done.[15]

The duel was reported in several London and provincial newspapers.[16] Duelling was illegal but widely accepted, and it was not successfully banned in the British army until the 1840s. A gentleman's career progression, credit risk, social standing and character all depended upon his honourable reputation: many were prepared to fight to the death to maintain it. The formalised choreography of the duel allowed a public demonstration of bravery, which usually resulted in a bloodless outcome. With each man taking ten measured paces, the combatants finally stood about twenty metres apart. They stood side-on to reduce the size of the available target and the smooth-bored duelling pistols themselves were notoriously inaccurate. Thus no one was surprised when John Macarthur and Thomas Gilbert, honour fully restored, lived to fight another day.[17]

Elizabeth didn't find out about the duel until the men returned to the *Neptune* that evening. She wrote in her journal that the more she thought about it over the next months, the stronger her feelings became to the point where she trembled to consider the 'unhappy consequences that might have arisen'—death for John, and a penniless widowhood for herself and her fatherless infant. But that particular evening Elizabeth notes that she had 'many disagreeable circumstances then pressing on my mind' and she didn't consider the duel as seriously as she later would.[18] One such circumstance was probably her recent discovery that she was pregnant again, though it was not something she ever mentioned in her journal.

Elizabeth's journal is almost the only record of the Second Fleet voyage to survive, although the last pages of the manuscript are torn and some of the text is illegible. Even the ships' logs are lost to us. One of the sailors on the *Lady Juliana* wrote a memoir of his travels thirty years later but his ship had left well before Elizabeth sailed on the *Neptune*. Elizabeth's journal is regularly derided for its narrow focus. She completely ignored the plight of the convicts, except as their presence discomforted her. She discussed little of shipboard life, or the other soldiers, sailors and passengers on board. Her focus is exclusively on her family and she leaves out the monotony and the worst of the horrors. The journal was not a personal diary for Elizabeth's eyes only, but an artefact clearly meant for her children, her friends and family. In fact, the journal was discovered, in 1888, among the papers of Elizabeth's youngest daughter. The invisible convicts and servants, the absence of detail about her own squalid shipboard living conditions, her failure to mention her own pregnancy are all absolutely in keeping with Elizabeth's sense of the demands of propriety.

Most of what we know about the *Neptune*'s voyage is the result of a campaign, launched in London upon the return of the Second Fleet, and the subsequent murder trial of the *Neptune*'s master, that brought to public awareness the onboard treatment of the convicts. The First and Second Fleets were early examples of government outsourcing. Nine of the eleven ships of the First Fleet were provided by a contractor, William Richards junior. From the point of view of the Home Office, equipping the First Fleet had been outrageously expensive. Contractor Richards, despite the success of the first voyage, was largely overlooked for the Second Fleet (he did, however, provide the *Lady Juliana*). Instead Camden, Calvert and King, also private shipping contractors, were engaged by Treasury and the Navy Board to transport convicts, soldiers and stores to New South Wales. Specialists in the African slave trade, they offered three ships and their crews at a bargain price.

The contractors were paid £17.7.6 for each convict embarked. Crucially (and unlike the slave trade) there was no financial incentive to ensure those convicts arrived safe and healthy at their destination. A convict who died en route in fact offered the contractors a better profit margin than did a convict who had to be fed all the way to New South Wales. The Navy's per-head payment method gave the contractors reason to squeeze on board as many convicts as possible. And their contract provided only vague instructions ('as you shall find necessary, in which you will be guided by circumstances'[19]) about stopping along the way for rest and fresh food. In selecting convicts for transportation, little or no effort was made to identify and dispatch the skilled artisans or labourers Governor Phillip had asked for. Many were already infirm or unwell. The vast majority of the Second Fleet convicts came from the floating hulks, and were selected only on the basis of time served.

The *Neptune* was scheduled to remain at least several days in Plymouth Sound. The day after the duel, Saturday 28 November, saw the embarkation of a further three hundred or so convicts. Livestock (to provide the officers with fresh meat during the voyage) and other provisions were also probably hoisted aboard at this stage. Captain Cook's *Endeavour*—two-thirds the size of the *Neptune* and carrying only ninety-four people—had sailed twenty years earlier with a menagerie that included two greyhounds, three cats, seventeen sheep, four pigs, twenty-four chickens, hens and other birds and a milking goat. Given that the *Neptune* was also carrying cargo destined for the colony, her menagerie was likely to have been at least as big and possibly also included cattle. Every inch of space on and within the ship was spoken for.

Rather than remain on board among the cacophony of loading, Elizabeth decided to take the sixty-five kilometre trip north to her family's home in Bridgerule. On Sunday 29 November Elizabeth, baby Edward and the nursemaid 'took a Post Chaise & reached Launceston that night—& the next morning about eleven O'Clock I arrived at my Mother's'.[20] It was a visit tempered with sadness, with Elizabeth's impending departure for New South Wales casting a pall over the short reunion. Elizabeth must have divided her brief visiting time between her mother, her half-sister Isabella and her dearest friend Bridget Kingdon. Elizabeth wrote that she was 'not much enlivened by the short interview I had had with my friends, & considerably depressed with the Idea of parting with my only surviving parent, perhaps, for ever'.[21] She could only stay in Bridgerule for two nights, as the *Neptune* was due to sail early on the morning of Thursday 3 December.

During Elizabeth's absence, more trouble brewed on the *Neptune*. A dispute arose over who had ultimate authority over the convicts: Nepean, the army officer ordered to guard them, or Gilbert, the master of the ship ordered to convey them to New South Wales. On Saturday 28 November, Nepean decided to take charge of the convicts, 'as Capt'n Gilbert has usurp'd too much power over him and his soldiers without right'.[22] The same problem had already arisen aboard the *Surprize*, with Captain

Hill of the New South Wales Corps complaining to the Home Office that while his instructions were to guard the convicts, to prevent them from gaining possession of the ship or from escaping, the master of the *Surprize* 'does not think my power extends so far as to be in possession of the Keys, or ordering just as many up daily as I think I can guard.'[23]

Given their ambiguous orders and the unclear lines of command, the dispute between the army officers and the ships' captains was inevitable. Nepean outranked Gilbert, officially and socially. Yet on board the *Neptune* Gilbert's word was necessarily law and the ordering of the ship—including the movement of convicts above and below decks—was very much his concern. Brawls and brouhaha between the services, in the ranks as well as in the corridors of power, were commonplace. But the relatively small altercation that was about to take place on the *Neptune* would, in the new colony, be re-enacted and enlarged over and again as the army, in the form of the New South Wales Corps, effectively took over from the navy, in the form of Governor Phillip and his marines.

While Gilbert was on shore, Nepean ordered the first mate Nicholas Anstis (who seems to have been considered a soft touch by the army men) to hand over the keys to the convict compartments. Anstis gave Nepean the keys. Nepean then went on shore himself, leaving orders for his sergeants to use the keys as necessary and then leave them with Lieutenant Macarthur. That night, when Gilbert returned and discovered what had happened, he indignantly demanded the keys from Macarthur, who refused to give them up. Over the next few days letters were written, demands were made, locks were changed, and keys were passed reluctantly back and forth.

On Tuesday 1 December, Nicholas Nepean wrote to his brother Evan, seeking to have Gilbert removed. He described Gilbert as 'the greatest scoundrel that was ever created' and went on to note that 'his insolence to me has been so extraordinary that words can hardly convey you an Idea of his Infamy'. Nepean went on to accuse Gilbert of subverting his authority and inciting mutiny 'and that unless he is removed I fear worse consequences must ensue.'[24] Nepean then returned ashore, once again leaving Macarthur and Harris in charge of the keys.

Gilbert also remained on shore until Wednesday afternoon when he boarded the *Neptune* accompanied by three friends. The four men spent the afternoon and early evening drinking in Gilbert's cabin. At some point in the evening Gilbert politely sent Macarthur ashore, asking him to collect Captain Nepean because the ship was ready to sail at three o'clock in the morning, on the next tide. John obliged, planning also to meet Elizabeth as she returned from Bridgerule. Gilbert's request, however, was a malicious one: he had not the slightest intention of sailing that evening, having previously ordered half a dozen hogs to be sent on board the following day.

While Macarthur was gone there was a fracas among the convict women, who were noisy and violently abusive, forcing Harris to place the ringleader in irons. Gilbert yelled down the hatchway 'several vulgar phrases', wanting to know 'who was that below making such a Rackett, damning his eyes'. Upon discovering Harris, Gilbert was furious, theatrically demanding to know who had given Harris authority to command the ship. Harris replied that he was obeying his officer's directions. Then, casting fuel on the fire, Harris added 'and let me see who would hinder me'.[25] Gilbert flew down the ladder and grasped Harris' shirt front, damning Harris and Nepean together. Gilbert then turned on the soldier standing guard, grabbed him by the neck, damned him and asked what right had he there. The soldier stood his ground, asking Gilbert 'not to shove him on his post or he would run him through' and noting that he had private orders which he had no right to explain to Gilbert.[26] At this, Gilbert melodramatically bared his chest to the soldier and dared the man to run him through, according to his orders. The soldier—bemused, bewildered or simply belligerent—failed to run Gilbert through, but we can guess as to how tempting he may have thought the offer. Gilbert finally left only to return shortly afterwards to continue taunting the soldier before he and his cronies holed themselves up in Gilbert's cabin with a dozen loaded muskets. There they calmed down and had some time to reflect. A short time later Gilbert, leaving his friends in the cabin, prudently slipped away to shore. It was to this 'scene of uproar and confusion' that Elizabeth, accompanied by John Macarthur and Captain Nepean, returned.[27]

Elizabeth had spent much of the day travelling from Bridgerule. Exhausted as she was, on the basis of Gilbert's malicious message she was obliged to travel out to the *Neptune* right away. She arrived on board with John and Nepean at about midnight, to be met by a dishevelled Harris. No sooner had Harris described the evening's events than Nepean sent him off to brother Evan with an ominous note, hastily scrawled: 'There is a Mutiny in the Ship'. With Gilbert gone, his friends in the cabin surrendered their arms to Nepean and went ashore. Poor

Elizabeth noted in her journal that she didn't manage to crawl into her cot until about three in the morning. The fact that *Neptune* remained anchored in Plymouth Sound for another week was further salt to her wounds. She needn't have hurried back from Bridgerule after all.

During the time the *Neptune* remained in Plymouth, Gilbert and Nepean were, separately, busy rounding up support on shore. A number of senior officials and naval officers found themselves asked for advice and assistance. Evan Nepean, naturally, was very much involved, as were the contractors who owned the *Neptune*. A flurry of letters criss-crossed between them. The result was that even though Gilbert was largely considered to have been in the right, he was to be removed before the *Neptune* departed for New South Wales. Nepean's powerful patrons had prevailed. But Nicholas Nepean seems to have been told in no uncertain terms about the limits of his power, as his subsequent actions—or lack of action—would demonstrate.

On Thursday 10 December Gilbert sailed the *Neptune* eastward to Portsmouth, tiresomely retracing his earlier passage through the English Channel, made mere weeks before. Several convicts died on the way and were carelessly buried at sea; four corpses were later found floating back to shore. A further sixteen convicts, according to one account, would die before the ship left Portsmouth.[28] It seems reasonable to assume that these convicts were unwell before their embarkation. And those that died so early in the piece cannot possibly have been the only ones who were sick or chronically diseased before they boarded the Second Fleet transports. Yet even that being the case, pre-existing illnesses cannot account for the eventual inexcusable death rate among the *Neptune*'s convicts. Almost one-third, or a total of 158 of the *Neptune*'s convicts (including eleven of the women), would die before the ship reached New South Wales—nearly one for each day at sea.

Gilbert anchored in Stokes Bay on Sunday 13 December. Waiting there, ready for sea, were the *Neptune*'s sister transports, *Scarborough* and *Surprize*. Soon after arriving in Portsmouth Thomas Gilbert left the ship for the last time. Captain Donald Trail, formerly of the *Surprize*, was moved onto the *Neptune* to become its new master. First mate Anstis found himself promoted to captaincy of the *Surprize*. Surgeon's mate Harris, John Macarthur's friend and supporter, was moved to the *Surprize* too. Elizabeth wrote that she was 'heartily glad' to see the back of Gilbert and she and John congratulated themselves with the thought that 'such another troublesome man could not be found'.[29]

But Elizabeth and John were wrong. 'Experience however soon taught us a very disagreeable truth,' continued Elizabeth in her journal. 'Mr Trail's character was of a much blacker dye than was ever in Mr Gilbert's nature to exhibit.'[30]

4

From the *Neptune* to the *Scarborough*

*I wrote to you from Portsmouth that we had a Lady going out with us;
the wife of Captain Trail; she appeared a very agreeable woman, but
her husband proved himself a perfect sea monster.*

ELIZABETH MACARTHUR TO HER MOTHER, 20 APRIL 1790

In Elizabeth's journal of the voyage she names only those who,
in her eyes, were at the top of the ship's hierarchy. *Neptune*'s
new master, Donald Trail, a Scotsman aged forty-four, was
an experienced mariner and navigator. He had been an officer
in the Royal Navy, at one stage serving under Nelson. Nelson
would later describe Trail as the 'the best Master I ever saw
since I went to sea'.[1]

The differences between the blustering Gilbert and hard
man Trail were, as Elizabeth noted, at the level of character.
Gilbert, although in a position of authority, received very little
respect from the officers of the New South Wales Corps. They
challenged him at every turn. Few men were as keen to take on
Trail. He was a stern disciplinarian, and his shipboard authority was absolute. Trail's willing contribution to the culture of
systematic cruelty and avarice of each of Camden, Calvert

and King's Second Fleet transports ensured they were places of brutishness and savagery. Upon the eventual return of the *Neptune* to England, Trail and his first mate, William Ellerington were brought to trial for the murder of the *Neptune*'s Portuguese cook, John Joseph.

The murder allegedly took place off the coast of China, where the *Neptune* sailed after leaving New South Wales. During the 1792 trial, witnesses told how the cook was beaten by Ellerington with a lump of wood and with rope. Trail then ordered that the cook be flogged, using a lash unusually and cruelly knotted and 'too severe for anybody but a Sodomite'. After two strokes Trail complained the work was not being done properly by the boatswain's mate and ordered another man to take over the flogging. When the cook's back was 'all over blood and mangled' he was cut down and lay on the deck, unable to walk. Ellerington walked over and kicked him 'as hard as he could' in the side. Then he threw him down a 'ladder and struck him several times with his fist and put him in Irons for three or four hours'.[2] The man died three weeks later. The judge and jury were unconvinced of a connection between the beating and Joseph's death and both Trail and Ellerington were acquitted. Trail went on to have a long and prosperous maritime career.

Accompanying Trail on the *Neptune* was his wife, who Elizabeth thought 'appeared a very agreeable woman'.[3] Fifty-year-old naval agent Lieutenant John Shapcote joined the ship while the *Neptune* was anchored at Portsmouth, to ensure that the convicts were transported in accordance with Camden, Calvert and King's government contract. Subsequent events would, however, show him to be at best unwell and distracted from his duties and at worst an ineffective lackey. Trail, his wife and Shapcote, along with Captain Nepean, 'lived together' in the upper cabins and, to Elizabeth's dismay, she and John 'seldom benefited by their society'.[4]

Elizabeth herself pinpoints the true reason for her and John's exclusion. With the new master on board, John continued to complain about the partitioning of their cabin and the unsavoury presence of the convict women. The Macarthurs' cabin had two means of accessing the open deck. One passage led straight through the upper cabin and onto the quarterdeck, while the other common passage to the deck was now rendered totally dark and was, wrote Elizabeth, 'always filled with Convicts & their constant attendants, filth and Vermin'.[5] The only concession that John Macarthur could eventually obtain was an assurance that the passage through the upper cabin to the quarterdeck would always be open for his family and their servants to use. The outcome of this dispute was, explained Elizabeth, a studied 'coldness between Capt'n Nepean, the Master of the Ship & Mr McArthur'.[6] Macarthur stopped speaking to Nepean and Trail, and they to him, except when forced to in the performance of their duties.

Excluded from polite society, such as it was, Elizabeth and John appear to have made no effort to find friends elsewhere. The ship's surgeon and mates, employees of Camden, Calvert and King, may have been likely candidates but they don't rate a mention in Elizabeth's journal. Nor, more surprisingly, does the assistant surgeon, D'Arcy Wentworth—a genteel, handsome and popular young man who had become something of a London celebrity. The twenty-seven-year-old Irishman boarded the

Neptune at Portsmouth, having come straight from the Old Bailey where for the fourth time he had been tried and acquitted of highway robbery.[7] Wentworth's well-connected relations seem to have arranged his passage on the *Neptune*, perhaps deciding that some time on the other side of the world might do him (and them) some good.

The *Neptune* remained anchored at Portsmouth for more than three weeks. During this time a formal search of the convicts' quarters revealed almost one hundred knives and other metal items, such as tin pots, that could potentially be crafted into knives. This, as well as a fear of gaol fever contagion, was considered reason enough for many of the convicts' personal boxes, bags and belongings to be tossed overboard. Any meagre store of clothes or mementos of home were gone in an instant. Trail would later claim that Shapcote had ordered the property overboard, while *Neptune* seamen attested to Trail giving the order.[8] Who it was that gave the order hardly mattered to the convicts. The conditions of their new internment were rapidly becoming clear.

If the convicts hadn't already learnt survival skills while on the hulks, they were forced to pick them up fast. Those that made it to New South Wales were observed on arrival by the Reverend Johnson:

> When any of them were near dying, and had something given to them as bread or lillipie (flour and water boiled together), or any other necessaries, the person next to him or others would catch the bread &c. out of his hand and, with an oath, say that he was going to die, and therefore it would be of no service to him. No sooner

would the breath be out of any of their bodies than others would watch them and strip them entirely naked. Instead of alleviating the distresses of each other, the weakest were sure to go the wall.[9]

It seems safe to assume that the convicts' behaviour on board each of the Second Fleet transports differed little from the behaviour Johnson recorded.

The Macarthurs' shipboard Christmas—little Edward's first—was likely cold, cramped and lonely. Elizabeth doesn't mention it in her journal. She does note, though, that she 'made it a practice every fine Evening to…walk or sit with Mr M' on the stern gallery, a small balcony at the rear of the ship opening off the upper cabin.[10] The fresh air, the ocean view and the company of her husband made for a pleasant interlude from the stale confines of their partitioned cabin. Elizabeth was 'much pleased with the variety of different Fish & seabirds which every day presented themselves.'[11] Unfavourable winds delayed the fleet's sailing until 5 January, but again the weather was against them and they didn't truly get underway until Sunday 17 January 1790. By then Elizabeth had been on board the damp and dismal *Neptune* for two months, without leaving English waters.

As soon as they were at sea, the crew demanded access to the female convicts. The men claimed that Trail had promised in Portsmouth that 'they should have the Women among us'.[12] Trail denied having made any such promise. Subsequently, each time a crew member was found to have had illicit contact with the women (and at one stage Trail found that a partition between the carpenter's berth and the women's compartment had been secretly removed), Trail had the man flogged. Such floggings occurred with sickening regularity. To a large extent the seamen were used to such treatment—floggings were a standard method of exerting discipline at sea—but Trail seems to have been particularly brutal. In 1791 ten *Neptune* crew members, a mix of senior and ordinary seamen, made sworn statements before the London Guildhall in which they complained of frequent beatings and inhuman cruelty.

While Trail denied his crew contact with the convict women, he was far more lenient with his officers. Naval agent Shapcote was 'constantly attended' by a convict woman and it was she who, many months into the voyage, would report his sudden, late-night death. D'Arcy Wentworth too had a convict companion, who would much later become his wife. She conceived a child on the voyage and the baby grew up to be the well-known explorer, colonist and society figure William Charles Wentworth.[13]

The fine weather that had carried the Second Fleet down the English Channel and south past the French coast lasted only a few days. Near the Bay of Biscay, Elizabeth records, the wind shifted and 'it blew exceedingly hard, and now for the first time I began to be a coward. I could not be persuaded that the Ship could possibly long resist the violence of the Sea which ran mountains high.'[14] By the following night the storm abated and morning dawned a perfect calm.

At about this time Elizabeth notes that her 'poor little Boy was taken very ill' and that her unnamed servant 'was attack'd with a Fever that reigned among the Women Convicts'.[15] Baby Edward's illness could be attributable to almost anything but the servant probably had typhus. Spread by infected lice, typhus was common in the cramped environments of ships and gaols. The ship's surgeon, William Gray, had very little to offer. Medical qualifications (or even rudimentary expertise) were unnecessary for the role, and his supply kit included so-called medicines: oil of tar, essence of malt, spice, barley, oatmeal, sugar and wine. And neither invalid was likely to have been helped in any way by the shipboard diet.

A surviving copy of the contract of transportation lists the rations to be provided for each soldier and convict. Over a period of seven days each soldier was to receive seven pounds of bread (equivalent to a small loaf each day); four pounds of beef; two pints of pease (a form of split pea soup or porridge); six ounces of butter; seven pints of beer or three and a half pints of rum; two pounds of pork; three pints of oatmeal and twelve ounces of cheese. The male convicts received substantially less (and no cheese or alcohol); the women less again.

Camden, Calvert and King's directions to Captain Trail stipulated that Shapcote and Nepean were 'to be accommodated in a respectable and comfortable manner at your table, without any expense to themselves whatever', but these contractual niceties were not extended to junior officers and their wives.[16] Customarily, the junior army officers and the ship's senior crew would buy in their own stores and so eat moderately well: better than the ordinary soldiers and seamen but not as well as the captain, but only for as long as the extra purchases lasted. The problem facing Elizabeth at each meal was not, however, the nutritional value of the food or even the quantity (although that was an issue too). It was the quality. Food at sea was always poor but on the *Neptune* it was abysmal. Even crew members, well-accustomed to a poor diet at sea, found cause to complain, later claiming they were kept on a very 'short allowance of bad provisions'.[17]

All the food was stored below decks in conditions that were either cold and damp or, in the tropics, hot and damp. Mould and decomposition were inevitable. As well, it was not uncommon for provisions to be up to several years old before they were even loaded onto a ship. Surgeon Lind wrote that in his experience naval food consisted of 'putrid beef, rancid pork, mouldy biscuits and flour'.[18] A surgeon on board Captain James Cook's second voyage remarked that 'our bread was…both musty and mouldy, and at the same time swarming with two different sorts of little brown grubs…Their larvae, or maggots, were found in such quantities in the pease-soup…that we could not avoid swallowing some of them in every spoonful we took.'[19] And this was on board the ship of a captain known to take great care of his crew.

The salt beef and pork, after months at sea, stank ferociously when removed from the brine. It too was riddled with maggots— unless it had dried and hardened beyond the point where it could be reconstituted by a saltwater soaking. Even the barrels of fresh drinking water quickly became putrid or briny, hence the need for rations of beer (at the start of the voyage, before it could spoil) and later rum.[20] If Elizabeth was breastfeeding, her diet would have immediately affected the baby's health. And if the baby was weaned to solids, or was receiving a mix of solids and breast milk, the available food remained eminently unsuitable. Even an otherwise healthy baby would suffer under such conditions as well as from the continual chafing discomfort of napkins and swaddling cloths washed only in salt water. The *Neptune* was no place for a growing baby—or for a pregnant woman.

The inadequate rations were made worse by the fact that the crew, convicts and soldiers (and presumably their wives) were being short served. Trail's orders from Camden, Calvert and King were that he should provide the contractually stipulated rations, while being very careful to ensure 'there is not greater consumption than we have agreed for, including all allowance whatever'.[21] On the face of it, this seems reasonable advice. In reality, though, the captains of the three transports were free to sell any leftover rations. The more rations they withheld, the more they had to gain upon reaching their destination. The convicts slowly began to starve. Their complaints were ignored.

The soldiers complained about their rations and Lieutenant Macarthur, conscientiously enough, reported his soldiers' concerns to Captain Nepean. Elizabeth recorded the result. "'Trail does every thing to oblige me," responded Nepean "and I must give up some points to him.'"[22] The soldiers continued to receive less than their full allowance of food, and Macarthur continued to report their complaints. "'I will see into it," said Nepean'.[23] Elizabeth had every reason to believe that Nepean did indeed follow up the complaints—largely because of the 'monstrous and unprovoked insults that always issued' from Trail. The worst insult of all arrived on Saturday 30 January. After barely two weeks at sea, Trail ordered the door from the Macarthurs' cabin to the upper gallery be nailed shut.

Elizabeth and John were outraged. Such behaviour towards an officer and his wife was preposterous in the extreme. Even Trail's reason for his actions—supposedly 'to prevent Mr M from listening' to discussions in the upper cabin—was insulting.[24] Elizabeth suspected the listening suggestion to be Nepean's and was doubly hurt. The Macarthurs could now only get in and out of their cabin via the passage through the convict quarters which, just to add to the general foulness, Nepean had recently ordered be made a hospital for the sick.

John Macarthur, true to form, complained. Nepean, equally in character, did nothing while noting that 'the Master of the Ship had a right to do as he pleased'.[25] It seems Nepean had learnt something from his earlier disputes with Gilbert after all. Agent Shapcote responded to Macarthur with both admirable frankness and shameful timidity, saying 'he should not quarrel with Trail for any man'.[26] Meanwhile Elizabeth refused to use the common passage and remained confined 'within the narrow limits of a wretched cabin'.[27]

Elizabeth was pregnant and utterly miserable, surrounded by 'wretches whose dreadful imprecations and shocking discourses ever rang in my distracted ears: a sickly infant claiming constant maternal cares: my spirits failing: my health forsaking me'.[28] She was free to go up on deck at any time via the convict passage-way, but she maintained her defiant refusal to budge, under any circumstance. By this time the *Neptune* was approaching the equator and the temperature, night and day, was stifling. Outside, there was at least a chance to catch a breath of sea air, but to voluntarily remain below decks was an act of either extreme foolishness or utter heroism. Perhaps as an unmarried girl Elizabeth had been a little more carefree, but young matron Elizabeth was stalwart in her application of the rules of propriety, in maintaining her feminine honour. And perhaps she hoped to shame Nepean and Trail by her example.

John used the dark passage when called to duty, tripping

over boxes or lumber or people and 'frequently contracting heaps of the Vermin with which it was infested'.[29] Within the cabin, hourly effusions of oil of tar (a volatile, strong-smelling liquid) did little or nothing to relive the constant stench. The heat was cruel and the water ration of five quarts (five and a half litres), 'our whole allowance for every purpose', barely sufficed.[30] Elizabeth recorded that their servant, dispatched to the water barrel for the daily allowance, was constantly watched and once was stopped to have the ration examined 'lest the Seaman who had the serving [of] it (knowing our situation) should be induced by motives of humanity, to make some small addition to the scanty pittance'.[31]

Rationing water while traversing the doldrums was, in fact, a sensible and commonplace practice. Trade winds converging at the equator produce no steady surface winds—often just heated, rising air. As a result, sailing ships could be becalmed for alarmingly long periods. Whether Elizabeth's five quarts of water were for the family only, or for the servants as well, is unclear. The crew, accustomed to washing in sea water and drinking their rum ration, seem to have scorned Elizabeth's concerns. Water wasn't her only problem, though. The food rations also continued to be served up short and the family was 'insultingly told we should have less, if they thought proper'.[32]

Ten days passed before John found a way to break the impasse. Just as he came on duty, one of his sergeants made a now-familiar complaint about the short rations. This time several pounds of meat were missing. The Neptune's chief mate, overhearing the sergeant's complaint, exclaimed that the man was a damned rascal. Macarthur told the mate, in no uncertain terms, that the sergeant 'would do well to punish him for his insolence'.[33] At that, the mate turned on Macarthur, heaping him with 'every kind of abuse that can be supposed to flow from ignorance and brutality'.[34] Macarthur was livid, but honour (and the safety of all on the vessel) precluded him from immediate redress. Instead, he sent for Captain Nepean and related the incident. Nepean was unimpressed. Fed up with Macarthur's constant carping, Nepean dressed him down for interfering between the men in the first place and made it clear that he was tired of being called upon to arbitrate. When it came to remedying any wrongs offered to the men, Macarthur was on his own. John grasped at the only straw left to him and requested to swap duties with an officer from one of the other transports. Nepean was more than happy to oblige.

In her journal Elizabeth writes that Nepean's final insult combined with 'the knowledge of what we were hourly suffering & the contemplation of what we had to expect in future, determined Mr M to apply for a remove on board the *Scarborough*'.[35] Elizabeth hints at the discussion she and John must have had about their predicament. She does not say that John was determined to ask for a transfer, but implies that the facts and options were laid out for him (presumably by Elizabeth) and these pushed him to act. The reasons for her literary convolutions are found in a letter she wrote to her mother. Posted from Cape Town and written well in advance of the journal, Elizabeth artlessly writes that Trail was 'a perfect sea monster; so much so that I requested Mr Macarthur to exchange duties with one of the Officers in one of the other ships'.[36] Although the journal circumspectly attributes the decision to John, in reality the call was made by Elizabeth. The young couple was beginning to operate as a partnership.

The next calm day presented itself on 19 February and, at the searing latitude of six degrees north, the Macarthurs and their anonymous servants were rowed over to the *Scarborough*. Elizabeth wrote that baby 'Edward and I suffered greatly from the heat, but this was an inconvenience I thought lightly of—after what I had been taught to bear'.[37] Elizabeth is silent as to the sufferings of those forced to row in the heat. John Macarthur had swapped places with a Lieutenant Townson. Townson, in moving to the *Neptune*, gained his own cabin and the proximity of women. Less fortunate, perhaps, was Townson's former cabin mate Lieutenant Edward Abbott, a Canadian in his early twenties with whom the Macarthurs would now share. Poor Abbott doesn't get a mention in Elizabeth's journal.

5

The Tempestuous Southern Ocean

Our passage to the South [could] truly be called a tempestuous one.
ELIZABETH MACARTHUR'S SHIPBOARD JOURNAL, UNDATED

Elizabeth was much happier aboard the *Scarborough*. The master, John Marshall, she described as 'a plain, honest man, and disposed to make things as comfortable to me as was in his power'.[1] Marshall, like Gilbert, had commanded one of the First Fleet transports and he amused Elizabeth with his flattering accounts of the colony. He further endeared himself to her by speaking 'in the tenderest terms' of his wife and three children in England.[2] The convicts aboard the *Scarborough* were not so enamoured of the master. Only days before Elizabeth's transfer a scheme to mutiny was discovered, and the convict ringleaders were flogged and chained to the open deck. The rest of the *Scarborough* convicts were being kept in the same conditions as those aboard the *Neptune*—tightly ironed, poorly fed, inadequately exercised—and they were dying at a similar rate.

For eight weeks, the three transports—*Neptune, Scarborough* and *Surprize*—sailed down the African coast. The weather turned nasty and it was with relief that, on 14 April 1790, they anchored in False Bay, some twenty miles from Cape Town, on the southern, more protected side of the peninsula. As keen as the voyagers were for fresh food and water, it's most likely they received fresh news first.

With dismay, they learned of the wreck of HMS *Guardian*, the forty-four-gun ship laden with provisions and valuable stores for the New South Wales colony. Holed by Antarctic ice in the Southern Ocean on Christmas Eve and struggling to keep the pumps operating at capacity, the ship's captain was forced to throw overboard most of the livestock, plants and stores in order to stay afloat. Two days later the *Guardian*'s captain, Edward Riou, allowed more than sixty men, about half of those on board, to flee in the ship's boats. At that stage no one was clear as to who was abandoning whom. However a valiant (and extraordinarily lucky) Riou managed to nurse the damaged *Guardian* back to Cape Town, arriving in February 1790. Of the men in the boats only fifteen were ever seen again, rescued after nine days by a French ship.[3] The *Guardian* was beyond repair and was eventually beached and abandoned.

News just as interesting, although of less immediate concern to the Macarthurs, was the miraculous escape of Lieutenant Bligh after losing his ship, HMS *Bounty*, to Fletcher Christian's mutineers. No one could possibly then have guessed how John Macarthur would one day himself engineer another mutinous uprising against Bligh. The mutiny on the *Bounty* had occurred near Tahiti a year earlier—on 28 April 1789—and Bligh had endured forty-seven days and 3618 nautical miles in an overcrowded open boat before he was able to land at Timor, in June 1789.[4] From there it took him nine months to get back to England and report the matter to Admiralty. Bligh spent Christmas at the Cape and had left for London in January, only a few months before Elizabeth and John arrived. He left letters for Governor Phillip (who at Sydney Cove was nearest the scene of the crime) appraising him of the mutiny, and describing each of the 'pirates'. Conscientious and expert mariner that he was, Bligh's dispatches to Phillip also included detailed descriptions of the best sea roads through the Endeavour Straits to Timor—sea roads that Bligh had traversed in that leaking, open boat. *Bounty*'s Master, John Fryer, had accompanied Bligh in the open boat and was still in Cape Town with a handful of other survivors, helping Riou with the *Guardian*'s salvage operation.[5]

The Macarthurs' ship *Scarborough* and the other transports remained at False Bay for only sixteen days. The longer the fleet tarried in port, the longer the voyage overall and the more the contractors' profit dwindled. The other reason to make haste lay in the weather. Due to the delays in leaving England, the three transports now faced crossing the dangerous Southern Ocean on the brink of winter. The sooner they got going, the better.

Captain Riou, forced to pay exorbitant storage fees for what remained of HMS *Guardian*'s cargo, was keen to transfer as much of it as he could to the *Scarborough* and the other Second Fleet transports. Much had already been transferred into the *Lady Juliana* when she had anchored at the Cape in March.[6] However, the masters of the Second Fleet transports complained: the large quantity of additional stores was not covered by contract and they were not permitted to impose freight charges. Naval agent

Shapcote, as usual, sided with the masters and was adamant that their sailing date was fixed, effectively precluding the loading of stores beyond that day. Captain Riou, who had sailed as a teenage midshipman under Cook, was considered by his peers to be an outstanding seaman and he would rise to become one of Nelson's captains at the 1801 Battle of Copenhagen.[7] In a private letter dispatched during the month following the Second Fleet's departure, Riou was exasperated and scathing: 'If ever the navy make another contract like that of the last three ships they ought to be shot and as for their agent Mr Shapcote he behaved here just as foolishly as a man could well do.'[8] Riou would never encounter Shapcote again—within a few weeks of leaving the Cape colony Shapcote would die of natural causes.

Throughout their stay at the Cape, the convicts remained on board and securely ironed. Trail much later argued that 'the ship lay so near the Shore that it was necessary to take every precaution' to prevent an escape. As a result, the lower decks were not properly cleaned out. Trail and his employers would later state that the convicts' deck was 'daily scraped, swabbed or mopped, and Twice a week sprinkled with Oil of Tar or Vinegar'.[9] But by this stage the male convicts had endured six or more months below decks (the women had greater freedom of movement). The men were suffering from scurvy, covered in lice, and prone to vomiting and diarrhoea.[10] The orlop deck was far beyond being cleaned by a sprinkle of vinegar and the wave of a swab.

The surgeons on each of the three transports used their time in port to write to naval agent Shapcote. None queried the below-decks living conditions but each articulated the seriousness of the scurvy situation. 'I am sorry to inform you', wrote Surgeon Beyer of the *Scarborough*, 'that the scurvy is making a rapid progress, both amongst the soldiers and the convicts.'[11] Crucially missing from the convicts' stipulated ration was any source of vitamin C. Scurvy was the inevitable result, with symptoms manifesting within about four weeks and continuing worse. The early symptoms are flu-like and include nausea, diarrhoea, fever and painful joints and muscles. Later symptoms include swollen and abscessed gums leading to loose teeth (and foul-smelling breath), severe and easy bruising, bulging eyes, the opening of previously healed scars, bleeding into the joints and muscles and, eventually, fatal internal haemorrhages. In babies and children, scurvy stunts bone growth. Royal Navy surgeon James Lind had proved that scurvy could be treated with citrus fruit and published his findings in 1753, but his suggestions were not widely implemented until the early nineteenth century. Across the three ships, about a third of the soldiers and convicts were afflicted. At the surgeons' urging, Shapcote authorised the daily provision of fresh beef and vegetables while they lay at anchor—whether his orders were carried out is not known.

Elizabeth remained aboard *Scarborough* for the first eight days in port. In a letter sent from the Cape to her mother, her first words express her deep concerns for her 'poor little Boy…He has been very sickly throughout the Passage, & unless a very speedy change take place I am well convinced he will shortly cease to be an inhabitant of this world'.[12] Elizabeth goes on to detail Edward's size, providing further evidence of his malnourishment. 'He is not near so large as children generally are at four months old, altho' he is now upwards of twelve.' There is also a hint that Elizabeth was not finding motherhood easy. 'He is very sensible, very lively, & affords us much pleasure; but the trouble we have had with so delicate a little creature is indescribable, & I wonder my own health hath not suffered more from the attention I have been obliged to pay him.' Elizabeth then seems to think of the effect of her letter on its reader and hastens to reassure her mother that she is now very well. 'I was nearly tired with the length of the Passage before we got into Port, & stood in need of refreshments very much; but now with the benefit of fresh meat, plenty of fruits & vegetables, I am quite recovered; & assure my beloved Mother that I never was in better health, & am in very good Spirits which are only dampened by poor Edward's illness.'[13]

Elizabeth continues the letter in this happier vein, claiming to 'have but little spare time, being busy in seeing all our Linen washed & got up, & laying in stock & refreshment to take with us to Botany Bay'. Clearly Elizabeth was determined not to have to rely solely on the ship's steward for her family's rations. She did manage, though, to squeeze in a visit to the governor, where she was 'met by his Daughter, who was dressed after our mode; but as she could not speak English, nor I Dutch, we could only exchange dumb civilities'. Presumably language continued to be a problem as Elizabeth found the locals to be 'unfriendly & Rude'. She conceded, though, that the 'Dutch live very well at their own tables—I like their houses, they are spacious & airy & their Slaves keep them remarkably clean. A Man's riches are here determined by the number of his Slaves. If you go to a genteel House you will see a dozen of them attending in the Hall.' Elizabeth offers no opinion about slavery, but appears to accept it—she presents it merely as an item of interest. Public interest in Britain about the issue was growing, and abolitionist William Wilberforce's campaign had formally begun just before Elizabeth left England, but the British slave trade would not be abolished until the passing of The Slave Trade Act 1807. Elizabeth does, however, make a passing comment on the local indigenous people. 'I have not yet seen any of the original inhabitants of this Coast—the Hottentots. There are some, I am told, who reside in the Mountains; they are a harmless set of Beings & hurt no one.'[14]

Elizabeth focuses on the local plants and produce, noting that 'every shrub & flower I saw, being new, was interesting…the face of the Country is very romantic' and 'these works of nature at the foot of the mountains represent a beautiful Shrubbery, where innumerable beautiful flowers & plants delight the eye or regale the senses'. She notes that 'fruit is to be had in great abundance. The grapes are fine, beyond what I can describe to you; you have no idea to what a pitch of luxuriance they arrive. It is here the season of Autumn & apples, pears & such fruits are now just in perfection—We get Wine for about one shilling the Bottle.'[15]

The letter Elizabeth sent to her mother from Cape Town is about 1500 words long, half the length of her entire shipboard journal. It was dispatched midway through her sojourn at the Cape. In it she also records that Surgeon Beyer advised her to spend 'as much time as possible on Shore, in order to get very strong & prepared for the remainder of the voyage'. It is the closest Elizabeth comes to mentioning her pregnancy, which was by then about five or six months advanced. Heeding the surgeon's advice, Elizabeth arranged to spend her final eight days boarding with 'a genteel private family'. John remained aboard the *Scarborough*, supervising the convicts and the transfer of goods from HMS *Guardian*, and visited her daily. 'Mr Macarthur has enjoyed a remarkably good share of health, ever since we left England' wrote Elizabeth to her mother, '& I trust will continue to do so'.[16] She was, of course, tempting fate.

Elizabeth would record in her journal that a 'few days before we quitted False Bay Mr Macarthur was attack'd with a violent, & very alarming Fever; it continued to rage until every sense was lost, & every faculty but life destroyed, and my little Boy at that time was so very ill, that I could scarcely expect him to survive a day.' She received some assistance from a Captain Reid 'who commanded an Imperial East Indiaman that then lay in the Bay with us he visited Mr M. frequently, & supplied me with a few comforts that afterwards were of the greatest service'.[17] Captain Reid—who was previously unknown to Elizabeth—provides an early example of John Macarthur's ability to spontaneously make firm friends. Unfortunately, John would demonstrate the same skill at making even firmer enemies. Once the *Scarborough* was at sea again, Captain Marshall did what he could to help, but Elizabeth complains that none of the other officers made the slightest offer of assistance. The end of Elizabeth's journal, describing this last leg of her voyage, is torn but the remaining fragments and subsequent letters home give some inkling of Elizabeth's predicament.

Leaving the Cape, the *Scarborough* travelled south and east into the maw of the Southern Ocean. Ships travelling beyond the Cape of Good Hope generally maintained a latitude of about

40 degrees south, then moved gradually northwards towards India or the Spice Islands (Indonesia). Those bound for New South Wales, however, were forced further south, often as far as 50 degrees, in order to clear the southernmost tip of New Holland (Tasmania). At such latitudes, the rigging grew icy and the cold seeped into the holds and the cabins. Icebergs were another hazard, as Captain Riou of HMS *Guardian* had discovered.

The huge stretch of open ocean east of the Cape, lacking any protective landmasses, results in consistent and often gale-force westerly winds, known as the Roaring Forties. A ship could travel here for days at speeds unheard of in the northern hemisphere. And the dangerous combination of high winds and landless sea produces enormous waves that could lift a ship up high before passing ahead and leaving it to sink into the trough where the lower sails could sag in the calm, rendering it vulnerable to swamping from the next wave. Sailing in these conditions involved running straight down the face of a wave with enough speed to cross the trough and rise back up again, up into the gale and over the crest once more.

Even in fine weather the constant pitching motion of the ship in the Southern Ocean was wearying. But Elizabeth saw little if any fine weather. The *Neptune*'s log recorded that the weather was very stormy for the Second Fleet's crossing between the Cape and New South Wales.[18] Every activity and movement, however small, required enormous effort, and throughout the crossing, Elizabeth's husband and her child 'continued intermittent for a long time'. For five weeks after they left the Cape, she had 'one, & sometimes two Soldiers sit up every night', presumably to watch over and tend to John. Elizabeth snatched rest when she could by 'laying my head on a Locker' until eventually someone gave up his cabin for her use.[19] She could not retire to bed in her own cabin while a soldier was there with her husband.

Stormy weather meant no exercise for the convicts or passengers and no cooking fires—for anyone. The inadequate rations, now served cold, continued to wreak havoc among the below-decks population, with scurvy and starvation now taking an even grimmer toll. A sailor would later allege that some convicts deliberately concealed their colleagues' deaths, so that the dead man's rations could continue to be claimed by his bunk mates. The same sailor claimed that the convicts 'were reduced to such extremities that they have eaten the [oaten] poultices taken from their sores'.[20]

The convicts were now also subject to exposure and hypothermia. Despite the sealed hatches, the orlop deck was at best damp and very often waterlogged. In any wooden ship a good deal of water normally leaked through the sides, let alone that which made its way down from the upper decks. Captain William Hill, John Macarthur's fellow officer aboard the *Surprize*, claimed the vessel was unseaworthy and shipped so much water that the convicts were often waist-deep in it.[21] Weeks later at Sydney Cove, the Reverend Johnson concurred, noting that 'sometimes for days, nay, for a considerable time together, [the convicts] have been to the middle in water chained together, hand and leg, even the sick not exempted—nay, many died with the chains upon them. Promises, entreaties, were all in vain and it was not till a very few days before they made harbour that they were released out of irons.'[22]

Sydney Parkinson, one of the two official artists who some twenty years before had sailed with Cook in the *Endeavour* wrote of his own experience of the Southern Ocean. 'The sea ran mountain-high, and tossed the ship upon the waves: she rolled so much, that we could get no rest, or scarcely lie in bed and almost every moveable on board was thrown down, and rolled about from place to place. In brief, a person, who has not been in a storm at sea, cannot form an adequate idea of the situation we were in.'[23]

Elizabeth knew. It was in such a storm, in such a sea, that Elizabeth Macarthur lost her baby girl.

6

Heavenly Bodies,
Botany and Piano Lessons

Week after Week stole away;
and Month after Month with little diversity.
ELIZABETH MACARTHUR TO BRIDGET KINGDON, 7 MARCH 1791

Elizabeth's first letters home were permeated with sadness. The arrival of the Second Fleet had done little to alleviate the problems of the fledgling colony and much to make things worse. But the ships did not stay long at Sydney Cove. By late August 1790, all of the Second Fleet vessels had sailed and the empty harbour was a constant reminder of the colony's isolation. The little brig *Supply* had been sent alone to Batavia (now Jakarta) for supplies before the Second Fleet arrived. She was expected back daily and the colonists couldn't help but keep turning to look down the long harbour, checking for the distant South Head signal flag which would announce the *Supply*'s return.

Any immediate threat of starvation had been lifted by the Second Fleet's arrival, but for the next few years the colonists mostly failed in their farming efforts and relied almost entirely on imported food: salted meat pocked with mould, flour from barrels containing nests of dead rats, and rice alive with weevils. To the horror of the New South Wales Corps, Governor Phillip insisted that every person—convicts, soldiers and officers alike— receive the same weekly ration of food from the closely guarded storehouse. Until the new settlers could grow enough to feed themselves, Phillip was forced to repeatedly recalculate the weekly ration as convicts arrived or died, and visiting ships brought stores or livestock. Those with the means to do so supplemented their grim fare of flour and salted meat by hunting or fishing but game was far from plentiful and, besides, venturing beyond the campsite at Sydney Cove had become dangerous.

The original cautiously expressed gestures of friendship between the colonists and the local Eora people[1] descended, within months of the First Fleet's landing, into acts of aggression. Convicts and sometimes soldiers—in direct opposition to Governor Phillip's orders—plundered and murdered the Eora. Unsurprisingly, those people replied in kind. Since the First Fleet's arrival, well over a dozen British men had been killed or wounded by Aboriginal people.[2] The number of Eora killed by the colonists was not recorded. Phillip inflicted judicial punishment upon convicts and soldiers both, but the Aboriginal witnesses were sickened by the spectacle of flogging, rather than heartened by any display of impartial justice.[3] In 1789 smallpox had devastated the Aboriginal clans around the harbour. Scores of corpses lay where they'd fallen, along the shore, among the trees and in caves. Bennelong, Phillip's Aboriginal captive turned ally, later told him that up to half the local population was lost.[4] By mid 1790, when Elizabeth arrived, local wildlife had been over-hunted and over-fished by the inexpert colonists. Even with the Aboriginal population tragically reduced there was never going to be enough game to cater for the influx of one then two thousand extra people. Everyone was hungry. The Eora now stayed well away from Sydney Cove but they watched the Second Fleet arrive, and saw—no doubt with dismay—the population of the colonists' campsite double.

After the initial bustle of her arrival there was very little to occupy Elizabeth's mind. Daily life in a wattle and daub hut had few entertainments to offer. Infant Edward had his own nursemaid—the same never-named woman who had travelled with the family from England—and John had his military duties and obligations. Elizabeth was bored and lonely. She could not even go for a walk. The surrounding bush appeared dense and threatening to the inexperienced new arrivals and no one ventured any distance unarmed. And, of course, the settlement itself was an open-air prison. Elizabeth lived surrounded by convict men and women who might find any number of reasons, and ways, to harm an officer's wife, so she was necessarily accompanied on excursions by at least one soldier. In her first eight months in the colony, Elizabeth did not walk more than five kilometres from Sydney Cove, and that distance only twice: 'once to a farm which Capt Nepean has for his Company, to which we sent our Tea equipage & drank Tea on the turf; and once to a Hill situated between this & Botany Bay, where I could command a prospect of that famous spot'.[5]

Elizabeth 'filled up the vacuum of many a Solitary day' by reading, or by writing long letters in which she complained of having no female friends.[6] None of the other officers were accompanied by their wives. Some of the rank-and-file soldiers had their wives with them, but the class divide rendered any friendships there impossible. Even if Elizabeth was willing to bridge that gap (although nothing suggests that she was), the social habits of a lifetime—reinforced by notions of regimental propriety and proper discipline—prevented the soldiers' wives from expressing anything beyond mere civilities to the only 'lady' in the colony. Friendship with the Reverend Johnson's wife may have been possible but Elizabeth described her as 'a person in whose society I could reap neither profit or pleasure'.[7] The Johnsons were not well liked—two months after the Second Fleet arrived, the convicts were threatened with the withdrawal of rations unless they attended the Sunday church service.[8] Elizabeth's antipathy was such that she delayed little Edward's long overdue baptism for nearly another year.[9]

But Elizabeth's natural optimism soon asserted itself. Just as she had at the Cape, Elizabeth took the time to look around and appreciate the landscape. 'Every thing was new to me, every Bird, every insect, Flower, &c in short all was novelty around me, and was noticed with a degree of eager curiosity.'[10] Elizabeth was herself noticed with a degree of eager curiosity by Sydney Cove's small society of officers, who had endured more than three tedious years of one another's constant company. Among the officers at least, Elizabeth was instantly and extraordinarily popular. They fell over one another to be her friend. Here was a pretty young woman who, protected by her marriage and her child, could converse with freedom and intelligence.

Second Lieutenant Dawes, at twenty-eight only four years older than Elizabeth, was a talented polymath whose skills encompassed engineering, science, surveying and astronomy.

'He is so much engaged with the stars,' wrote Elizabeth, 'that to Mortal Eyes he is not always visible.'[11] Elizabeth attempted to learn astronomy from Dawes and he went to great efforts to make models of the solar system for her and to explain the general principles of the heavenly bodies. Elizabeth, though, soon claimed she had mistaken her abilities and brought an end to her astronomical studies, writing 'I blush at my error' to Bridget, perhaps implying that, intellectually, she simply wasn't up to it. But she may well have been blushing about other things entirely—the evening visits to Dawes' observatory opened many opportunities for others, possibly even Dawes himself, to misinterpret her educational motives. Instead Elizabeth and Dawes sensibly looked to the daytime art of botany, and Elizabeth was soon able to class and order common plants.

Surgeon George Worgan, thirty-three, had improbably managed to bring a piano with him on the First Fleet. More like harpsichords in shape, the small five-octave pianos of the late eighteenth century were enormously popular. Worgan gallantly began to tutor Mrs Macarthur, telling her she had 'done wonders in being able to play off God save the King and Footes Minuet' and that she was 'reading the Notes with great facility'.[12] Worgan went as far as to make Elizabeth a gift of the little piano upon his departure from the colony in 1791.

Thirty-two-year-old Marine Captain Watkin Tench, the famously wry and genial observer of the colony, also became Elizabeth's friend, 'indeed we are in that habit of intimacy with Captn Tench, that there are few days pass that we do not spend some part of together'.[13] Can we judge a woman by her friends? Tench and Dawes—and indeed Governor Phillip—were genuinely willing to engage with the local Aboriginal people. Dawes, described by one of his peers as 'truly religious' yet 'without any appearance of formal sanctity',[14] was a friend of English abolitionist William Wilberforce and went on to become an active participant in the anti-slavery movement. Tench in his *Complete Account of the Settlement at Port Jackson*, published in 1793, attacked the argument that the 'sufferings of the wretched Africans' in the heat of the West Indies was necessary because apparently no white man could bear to work in such a climate. He saw that the convicts could, and did.[15] Governor Phillip, during his First Fleet preparations, wrote of New South Wales that 'there shall be no slavery in a free land'.[16] But what were Elizabeth's views? While at sea, just after her transfer to the *Scarborough,* she noted in her journal that 'we passed a French Guinea Man, bound to Martinico with Slaves'.[17] But she adds nothing else, no sympathetic remarks about injustice nor any mercantile comments about the value of the ship's cargo to indicate what she thought or felt.

Whatever Elizabeth's opinions, they seem to have had no impact on her ability to attract admirers. Many of the young officers had (or professed to have) friends and connections in Devon, and all often stood to toast 'the banks of the Tamar'.[18] The older officers also curried Mrs Macarthur's favour. Captain Nepean, who at sea had gladly washed his hands of the tiresome Lieutenant Macarthur and his obstinate wife, in Sydney found it expedient to change his mind. Generously, so did Elizabeth. 'He is truly a good hearted Man,' she wrote, 'and has I believe a great friendship for Mr McArthur.'[19] Even Governor Phillip was not immune, raiding his private garden and 'sending us some little thing or other every day'.[20] The Macarthurs dined regularly at Government House and although during these times of food rationing each guest was required to bring their own bread, Macarthur family lore has it that upon Elizabeth's invitation card there was a note from the Governor himself saying there would 'always be a roll for Mrs Macarthur'.[21]

It can be difficult to be the husband of a popular woman. But if John complained, we never hear a whisper of it from the always-loyal Elizabeth. And as a man continually with an eye to his own advantage, he must have recognised that Elizabeth's popularity was of benefit to him too. In October 1790, His Majesty's Brig *Supply* returned from its dash to the East Indies for supplies. Elizabeth couldn't resist telling Bridget that a Lieutenant Ball, the *Supply*'s commander, 'very soon call'd upon us, and complemented me with many little comforts procured at Batavia, which were truly acceptable'.[22] In a letter to her mother, though, Elizabeth was more circumspect, noting that she had received from Mr Ball 'many articles at very moderate prices'.[23] Clearly Elizabeth tailored her letters home, to cater for what she believed the recipients should hear.

Lieutenant Ball had also chartered the *Waaksaamheyd* while he was in Batavia and in December the Dutch ship arrived bearing mainly rice, with a small quantity of beef, pork and flour.[24] *The Waakzaamheid* brought news of the outside world too. Elizabeth noted to Bridget that:

In the dispatches of the Dutch Schelander to Govr Phillip is mention'd something of a Spanish War, having been declared against England in May 1790. The particulars are not well explain'd, or perhaps I should say not well understood, as the Letter is written in Dutch; and no one here understands enough of the language to transcribe it correctly.[25]

In a colony established and run by His Majesty's armed forces the patchy news only served to create anxiety and frustration. Though far from the arenas of Britain's battles, 'we longed,' wrote Tench 'to contribute to her glory, and to share her triumphs'.[26] At least one battlefront was, however, right on their doorstep.

On 7 September 1790, as many as two hundred Aboriginal people gathered about twelve sea miles away at Manly beach to feast on the carcass of a whale. Among the crowd were men known to the colonists, including Bennelong. When Governor Phillip heard about it, and having not seen or been visited by his Aboriginal associates for months, he hastened down the harbour to meet with them. Leaving his crew and muskets in the boat, Phillip walked up the beach with 'his hands and arms open'.[27] Bennelong greeted Phillip warmly and the two conversed for some time. Before long though, the British noticed that armed warriors were gradually closing in around them. The Governor quietly proposed 'retiring to the boat by degrees'.[28] In the to and fro of Phillip's gradual farewell the Governor advanced, with empty hands spread, towards one of Bennelong's colleagues, a stranger to Phillip.

Elizabeth was not a witness to what happened next but she described it at length to Bridget. The stranger 'snatch'd up a spear from the ground, and poiz'd it to throw'. Phillip continued to advance but 'the native discharg'd the spear with all his force at the Govr., it enter'd above his Collar bone, and came out at his back nine inches from the entrance; taking an Oblique direction.'[29] Phillip's horrified officers managed to break off the shaft of the weapon and, in the midst of more flying spears, bundled him into the boat for the two-hour trip back to Sydney Cove. Once home, Phillip prudently delayed the extraction until he had 'caus'd some papers to be arranged—lest the consequence might prove fatal'.[30] Happily, though, the spear was found to have touched nothing vital and Phillip healed within a few weeks. Bennelong, Elizabeth explained to Bridget, 'came many times to see the Gov'. during his confinement, and expressed great sorrow, but the reason why the mischief was done could not be learnt'.[31]

The colonists tended to believe that the stranger, in their eyes an irrational savage, had simply panicked, that the whole thing was a terrible accident. But it is now thought that Phillip was subjected to a ritual spearing to settle a number of grievances, wrongs and slights accumulated against the British. Speared at virtually point-blank range, surrounded by seasoned Aboriginal warriors known for their hunting skill and accuracy, Phillip could easily have been killed if that had been the intention. But he—and only he—was wounded just once while other spears rattled harmlessly past. He was the unwitting recipient of Aboriginal justice.

After the spearing, the relationship between the two societies shifted once more. Elizabeth told Bridget that following Phillip's recovery 'the natives visit us every day, more or less; Men, Women and Children they come with great confidence, without spears or any other offensive Weapon a great many have taken up their abode entirely among us'.[32] Elizabeth was not speaking in generalities—at least some of those 'Men, Women and Children' became visitors to Elizabeth's home. One young woman, Daringa, brought her new-born baby, wrapped in soft bark, for Elizabeth to see. 'I order'd something for the poor Woman to Eat and had her taken proper care of for some little while…she has since been regular in her visits. The Child thrives remarkably well and I discover a softness and gentleness of Manners in Daringa truly interesting.'[33] Here Elizabeth reveals her practical kindness and an open attitude to the strangeness of the Aboriginal people. We also get a rare glimpse of Elizabeth ordering the anonymous household servants.

Elizabeth's kindness, though, had its limits and she maintained a clear social divide. 'We do not in general encourage them to come to our houses,' Elizabeth wrote, because 'there are some offensive circumstances, which makes their company by no means desirable.'[34] Elizabeth writes pompously that 'their Language (if it may be so call'd) is now understood' but then a paragraph or so later discusses how 'I thought their dialect pleasing; some of their names I think much so,' and she goes on to make a list.[35] She also applied her keen eye to the working habits of the women who visited, describing their fishing activities in some detail. And she was quick to note the women's subordinate role. 'The Women appear to be under very great subjection, and are employed in the most Laborious part of their Work. They fish, and also make the Lines and Hooks and indeed seem very little otherways than slaves to their husbands.'[36]

Elizabeth's tone to Bridget may have been lofty but in practice she was not quite so condescending. At the governor's table Elizabeth and John dined alongside their Aboriginal acquaintances. On one particular day they and Governor Phillip ate with

Nanbaree, an adolescent orphaned by smallpox and living with Surgeon White, and were waited upon by the boy's slightly older kinsman, Imeerawanyee. Nanbaree issued stern instructions to his kinsman about when to replace the dirty plates with clean ones, especially with a lady present. Imeerawanyee performed his role cheerfully for all the guests—except Nanbaree, who he affected to ignore. In the face of Nanbaree's embarrassed rage Imeerawanyee only laughed, while continuing to serve the others. Tench relates this story in his account of the colony. In line with the social etiquette of the day, he quite properly never mentions his friend Mrs Macarthur in the body of the work but he includes her in a footnote to his droll anecdote. Tench leaves John out of the story completely, noting only that the lady was 'Mrs McArthur, wife of an officer of the garrison'.[37]

Not all the interactions between the Eora and the colonists were so friendly. In mid-December Governor Phillip's convict gamekeeper, John McIntyre, was speared by Pemulwuy, a warrior from Botany Bay. Where the spearhead used to injure Governor Phillip was smooth and sharp, McIntyre was felled by a weapon cruelly barbed, designed to cause massive injury as it went in, and further injury and infection if it were removed. McIntyre, 'an uncommonly robust, muscular man' took weeks to die.[38] The gamekeeper was not highly regarded and many suspected he'd brought his fate upon himself, but Governor Phillip could not afford to let the matter rest.[39] The spearing situation, with some seventeen British now killed or wounded since the arrival of the First Fleet, had become untenable. He had to silence the fears and mutterings of his officers and impress upon both the convicts and the Eora people the strength of British law. Within days of

McIntyre's spearing, Phillip ordered up a punitive expedition of marines and soldiers against the clans from Botany Bay. Tench describes the expeditions (in the end there were two) at some length and his ironic tone lends an element of farce to the proceedings. No Aboriginal warriors, skilled in hunting and bushcraft, were ever going to be ambushed by fifty British redcoats smashing through the scrub. Not one Eora person was arrested or harmed. Honour appeased, and justice seen to have been done, Phillip could let the matter rest. For now.

Late in the year of 1790 John Macarthur was again 'attack'd by a severe illness', just as he had been aboard the *Scarborough* only months earlier.[40] Elizabeth gave up her botanical studies and piano lessons to nurse him. By December he was recovered, and in January the Macarthurs 'were remov'd into a more convenient House'.[41] By then, though, the heat had begun to oppress them all. Elizabeth's first summer in the colony was particularly hot. Lieutenant Dawes kept meticulous records of the temperature—up to six daily observations of temperature, barometric pressure, winds and weather[42]—and his records correspond with Elizabeth's complaints. The summer months 'have been hotter than I can describe, indeed insufferably so' wrote Elizabeth to Bridget.[43] The air shimmered with heat and the pungent scent of eucalyptus; the glare off the harbour was blinding. Usually raucous birds sat silent in the branches, beaks open, gasping. When the scorching northerly winds came, 'as if from a heated oven', Elizabeth and her family were forced to shut themselves up in their home completely.[44] If she mopped the dirt floor with water, it would usually stay hard and cool. But even after sunset the heat barely abated, leading to restless sleepless nights in the stuffy hut. The northerlies were 'generally succeeded by a Thunder Storm, so severe and awful,' wrote Elizabeth, that 'I am not yet enough used to it, to be quite unmoved, it is so different from the Thunder we have in England, I cannot help being a little Cowardly'.[45] Despite the thunderstorms, the colony had little rain and as a result 'our Gardens produce nothing, all is burnt up'.[46] Elizabeth claimed to have seen no more than a week's rain since her arrival and Tench recorded it as no more than twenty-four hours' worth.[47] The Macarthurs had yet to attempt anything in the way of farming, but Tench reported that the colony's farms 'were in wretched condition'.[48] In late February the heat was so intense that bats and birds fell dead from the sky.[49]

During this heatwave a small, familiar brig sailed up the otherwise empty harbour. It was the *Supply*, returned from Norfolk Island—a tiny but strategically positioned dot in the ocean some 1670 kilometres northeast of Sydney. Mere weeks after the arrival of the First Fleet in 1788, Phillip had dispatched a group of convicts and marines to establish an outpost there. Two years later Phillip's second-in-command, Captain Hunter, sailed to Norfolk Island in the *Sirius*, to deliver much-anticipated supplies. But Hunter wrecked the *Sirius* on a reef just off the coast of Norfolk Island and he and his crew had been stranded there ever since. In January 1791 Phillip finally sent the *Supply*, now the colony's only ship, to Norfolk Island, 'to bring hither the *Syrius* ship's Company, and learn the state of affairs at that place,' wrote Elizabeth to Bridget.[50]

When Hunter and his crew had left New South Wales a year earlier, before the arrival of the Second Fleet, the fear of starvation had been very real. But by the time of their return in early 1791, the colonists, or at least the officers, were eating more than just their weekly ration of dried meat, flour and rice from the storehouse. Elizabeth wrote to her mother about eating grapes and melons from the governor 'as fine as any I ever tasted'.[51] Apple, orange and fig trees that were planted in the very first days of the colony had begun to bear fruit too.[52] A sweet tea made from native sarsaparilla (*Smilax glyciphylla*) was considered to have many healthy properties and, according to Tench 'was drank universally'.[53] The colonists, with practice, learned to hunt kangaroos with greyhounds.[54] Sometimes the joeys discovered in a female's pouch were rescued and raised as pets.[55] Tench noted that he often ate snakes and 'always found them palatable and nutritive, though it was difficult to stew them to a tender state'.[56] Fish were never abundant, although from time to time a shoal would enter the harbour and for a few days there would be plenty.[57] Cockle Bay (now Darling Harbour) was named for good reason, the harbour supplied oysters as well, and eels were plentiful along the river that flowed past Rose Hill and into the head of the harbour. Surgeon White declared emu to taste like beef and made an 'excellent soup' from crow and cockatoo.[58] The settlement at Sydney Cove was not without livestock: pigs, goats, sheep and poultry were prized as breeding stock but many were slaughtered to assuage short-term hunger. The starvation days of the colony were past, although the food situation of the settlement was still far from secure.

Captain John Hunter joined Elizabeth's circle of friends. He also managed, during his brief visit to Sydney, to attend an Eora corroboree. Phillip went too, as did several other white men, but not Elizabeth. Hunter described as extraordinary the wide-legged dancing where the men moved 'their knees in a trembling and very surprising manner'.[59] At least some of Hunter's party gave the dance a good-natured try themselves but none could do it. When Hunter and his officers sailed in the Dutch *Waakzaamheid* for England in March, Hunter's departure 'was regretted by every one who shared the pleasure of his society'.[60] Elizabeth wrote a long letter to her friend Bridget, mainly about Norfolk Island, which speaks again to Elizabeth's loneliness and boredom. She wrote that her 'spirits are at this time low very low' because 'tomorrow we lose some valuable members of our small society, and some very good friends. In so small a Society we sensibly feel the loss of every Member more particularly those that are endear'd to us by acts of kindness and friendship.'[61] Yet Elizabeth took pains to reassure her friend that 'I never was more sincerely happy than at this time, it is true I have some wishes unaccomplished…but when I consider this is not a state of perfection, I am Abundantly Content'.[62] Another, shorter and more deliberately cheerful letter was written to her mother, but even there Elizabeth hints at her ongoing concern about infant Edward. 'He has become very amusing to me. He prattles a little, but is backward with his Tongue, as he has always been in every other respect.'

The colony was now three years old and it continued to teeter on the edge of failure. Emancipist James Ruse had been working an inland allotment called Experiment Farm near Rose Hill, and in early 1791 he declared that his crops were doing well enough to render his family self-sufficient. It was just as well because in April Phillip was forced to reduce the colonists' rations again, just when people's gardens were at their lowest ebb, exhausted by the long drought. The government's corn crop was meagre and the stores carried from Batavia with so much trouble and expense by the *Waakzaamheid* were deeply inferior. 'The rice was found to be full of weevils; the pork was ill-flavoured, rusty, and smoked; and the beef was lean, and, by being cured with spices, truly unpalatable,' reported Phillip's deputy judge advocate (and bureaucratic mainstay) David Collins.[63]

Yet again everyone's hopes were pinned on assistance from England, and the future of the settlement seemed far from sure. Elizabeth reflected this uncertainty in her letters. 'If the British Government think fit to continue the Colony...' she wrote to Bridget, and in a letter to her mother she implied that the Macarthurs' return to England would occur as soon as John gained a promotion 'in which event our thoughts will be in some measure turned again towards "old England"'. Elizabeth's logic here is far from clear but her longing for her family is obvious. 'I have yet great hopes of seeing my Grandfather once more.'[64] New South Wales, as far as the Macarthurs were concerned, was simply a career stepping stone.

In June John and Elizabeth moved to Rose Hill with the rest of Captain Nepean's Company—just in time to celebrate the King's birthday and the governor's renaming of the Rose Hill settlement as Parramatta. It was the first place to be given a name by Europeans that was based on an Aboriginal name.[65] By July David Collins reported, without any trace of irony, that in addition to the barracks and the governor's residence, the township of Parramatta boasted eight huts.[66] Although Elizabeth had long harboured a desire to visit the inland settlement, where most of the convicts were posted and where all the 'Works and Farming schemes are carried on',[67] she soon decided that the advantage lay with Sydney and that 'it will be the most desirable place for an Officer's family for years'.[68] She saw the Macarthur family's future as lying firmly beyond the confines of New South Wales. 'Parramatta may have advantages, particularly to such as wish to cultivate the Land, but officers have so little encouragement in this respect, that few will in future attempt it, as evident impediments are thrown in the way to check their undertaking it.'[69] Elizabeth was right about the impediments. Governor Phillip was legally allowed to grant land to private soldiers, and to emancipated convicts, but he had no authority to issue grants to the officers.

Elizabeth had no sooner moved to Parramatta when the Third Fleet transports began to arrive. The *Mary Ann* carried 141 female convicts, six children, and one free woman. All were healthy and spoke well of the treatment they had received. The ship also carried some clothing and a small amount of very welcome stores. *Mary Ann* sailed into the harbour alone, but her captain reported that another nine transports were following, collectively carrying almost two thousand male convicts as well as their military guards. The colonists also discovered that from now on the British government planned to dispatch two embarkations every year, sending convicts and provisions each time. And more good news was to come—in the form of rain. The drought broke, and 116 bushels of wheat were sown at Parramatta.[70] The spectre of starvation began to retreat.

No fewer than twelve ships arrived throughout that spring, including a cargo of grain from Bengal and a transport with livestock from the northwest coast of America. The settlement at Sydney Cove seemed filled with strangers. Although the livestock was welcome, the American captain was a disappointment: he carried no private letters, or a single newspaper and, 'having been but a few weeks from Greenland before he sailed for this country, he was destitute of any kind of information'.[71] In late September HMS *Gorgon* also arrived from England. Elizabeth and her friends in New South Wales had been looking out for her for more than a year. *Gorgon* carried livestock, trees, seeds and stores, including the remains of the stores from the now-abandoned *Guardian*. Of far more value to Elizabeth, though, *Gorgon* also carried a small group of officers' wives. Elizabeth finally had some ladies to talk to.

7

A Change in Fortune

...our little circle has been of late quite brilliant.

ELIZABETH MACARTHUR IN A LETTER TO ENGLAND
(EXTRACT) 18 NOVEMBER 1791

Two young women stepped ashore from the *Gorgon*'s barge: Mrs
Mary Ann Parker accompanied her husband Captain Parker,
master of HMS *Gorgon*, and Anna Josepha King accompanied
her husband, Phillip Gidley King, a naval officer. As a young
lieutenant Phillip King had arrived with the First Fleet and
was then sent straight to Norfolk Island. For two years he had
battled to establish the island settlement before Governor Phillip,
just prior to the arrival of the Second Fleet, sent him back to
England to report the colony's difficulties.

King worked fast. Arriving in England just before Christmas
1790, he saw the home secretary Lord Grenville and royal adviser
Sir Joseph Banks and discussed with both men the problems
of New South Wales. On 2 March 1791 he was promoted
to commander. On 11 March he married, and four days
later sailed with his bride in HMS *Gorgon* with Captain and

Mrs Parker. King had a commission as lieutenant-governor of Norfolk Island[1] and was stopping briefly in Sydney before travelling on to his new post. The wife of one of the agents on a convict transport also arrived in the colony with her husband and at least some of the newly arrived officers of the New South Wales Corps, including Captain Paterson, were accompanied by their wives. As Elizabeth wrote to her friends in Bridgerule, there were now 'so many ladies in the Regiment that I am not likely to feel the want of female society as I first did'.[2]

Elizabeth had been perhaps the only free person in the colony feeling that 'want of female society'. Many of the officers lived openly with convict mistresses and more than a few later happily acknowledged and cared for the subsequent children. But the convict 'wives' were not women Elizabeth could associate with. This socially awkward situation was, for Elizabeth at least, partially relieved that spring. The officers took little parties of ladies on boating excursions up and down the various inlets between Sydney Cove and Parramatta, as well as across the harbour to Manly. Elizabeth described the entertainments in a letter to Bridgerule, writing about 'taking refreshments with us, & dining out under an awning upon some pleasant point of Land, or in some of the Creeks or Coves'.[3] Elizabeth described Mrs Parker as 'a very amiable intelligent Woman',[4] and immediately warmed to Mrs King, who was also from Devon and who had lived many years in Bideford, not more than forty kilometres from Bridgerule. Mrs King was expecting her first child and perhaps Elizabeth was able to confide in her: Elizabeth was newly pregnant again too.

During his two years establishing the colony on Norfolk Island, Lieutenant King had fathered two sons with convict woman Ann Innett. The eldest boy, named Norfolk and born on 8 January 1789, was the first colonial child born on the island. King returned to the settlement at Sydney Cove from Norfolk Island a year later and it seems likely that Ann and little Norfolk travelled with him. The second boy, Sydney, was born in early 1790,[5] perhaps shortly before King sailed away in March to Batavia, then to England and marriage to the genteel Anna Josepha. But if the colony of late 1791 was agog to see the new Mrs King's reaction to her husband's earlier indiscretions, they were disappointed. The boys would be welcomed into Anna's life and home, and Elizabeth was able to write with discretion and approval that 'Her stay here being very short I saw but little of her; but I had reason to believe her possessed of a great share of good nature & frankness.'[6]

With her new circle of women friends, Elizabeth was pleased to enjoy some society events. On 25 October 1791, the thirty-first anniversary of King George III's accession to the throne, a salute of twenty-one guns was fired by the *Gorgon* and a dinner was held at Government House. The meal 'was served to upwards of fifty officers, a greater number than the colony had ever before seen assembled together'.[7] The next day the Patersons and the Kings, along with King's son Norfolk, left for Norfolk Island aboard the *Atlantic*, which was en route to Calcutta to obtain yet more stores for the New South Wales colony. Seven weeks later on Norfolk Island, in December 1791, Mrs King was safely delivered of a boy whom she named Phillip Parker King. Phillip, for his father, and Parker for Captain Parker of the *Gorgon*.[8] Baby Phillip's future son, also Phillip, would one day marry a Macarthur girl.

By the end of the year most of the Third Fleet transports had left Sydney, several trying their luck with mixed results at the whale-fisheries along the coast of New South Wales. In November the Macarthurs moved from Parramatta back to Sydney. 'We are at present here rather in an unsettled state,' wrote Elizabeth, although the change of scenery seemed to agree with little Edward, now almost three years old. 'Edward grows a strong and healthy child, & from being a great deal of trouble to me ceases almost to be any at all—he prattles every thing—& is quite Papa's Darling.'[9] Elizabeth's November letter was written just in time to be taken to England aboard the *Supply*. The little brig had been the first vessel of the First Fleet to arrive at Botany Bay. Under the command of Lieutenant Ball the *Supply* had served as the colonists' lifeline in her constant to and fro between Sydney Cove and Norfolk Island and had braved the Great Barrier Reef of northeastern Australia and the miasmas of Batavia to fetch fresh stores. 'It was impossible to view our separation with insensibility,' wrote Tench. The *Supply* 'which had so often agitated our hopes and fears, which from long acquaintance we had learned to regard as part of ourselves,'[10] was leaving for home. She carried on board a kangaroo, the first to be shipped live to England, as a present for King George III.[11]

Finally, on 18 December 1791, HMS *Gorgon* sailed too. She carried away not only Captain and Mrs Parker, but most of the marines who had come from England in the First Fleet— including Dawes and Tench. After nearly four years of service both men seemed ambivalent about the New South Wales experiment. Dawes had sought to stay on and, over the years, asked to return but was never permitted or otherwise able to do so. Tench painted a grim picture of the Sydney he was leaving: 'this place had long been considered only as a depot for stores'. The settlement 'exhibited nothing but a few old scattered huts and some sterile gardens. Cultivation of the ground was abandoned, and all our strength transferred to Rose Hill.' As a marine and an officer, Tench felt put upon. 'The barracks, so long talked of, so long promised, for the accommodation and discipline of the troops, were not even begun when I left the country.' Nor was there a new hospital. Instead 'the old one was patched up' and annexed by the field hospital originally brought from England in pieces.[12] Sydney, nevertheless, continued to be the place of the governor's formal residence, and, consequently, the headquarters of the colony.

Everyone missed the *Gorgon*. 'The cove and the settlement were now resuming that dull uniformity of uninteresting circumstances which had generally prevailed,'[13] wrote the chief bureaucrat, David Collins. With the public stores again running low, Christmas was expected to pass quietly. A divine service was performed in the open air at Sydney and at Parramatta. After almost four years of delivering sermons in the sun or wind or rain the Reverend Johnson longed for a church. 'It cannot be wondered at,' complained Johnson to Governor Phillip 'that persons, whether of higher or lower rank, come so seldom and so reluctantly to public worship. I have, not seldom, found very great inconveniences attending it myself.'[14] Someone took it upon themselves, however, to lighten the mood and on Christmas night the store was robbed of twenty-two gallons of spirits.[15]

In mid-February 1792 Major Francis Grose, the commanding officer of the New South Wales Corps and newly appointed lieutenant-governor of the colony, finally arrived, on HMS *Pitt*. Grose, then aged thirty-four, was accompanied by his wife, Frances, and their young son (also Francis), who was the same age as Edward Macarthur.[16] In stark contrast to Tench's descriptions, Grose liked what he saw. 'Instead of the rock I expected to see I find myself surrounded with gardens that flourish and produce fruit of every description. Vegetables here are in great abundance and I live in as good a house as I wish for.' Grose was allocated the farm of his predecessor, Major Ross of the marines, and considered that it produced everything his family needed. 'All that is wanting to put this colony in an independent state,' wrote Grose after just seven weeks in the colony, 'is one ship freighted with corn and black cattle. Was that but done, all difficulties would be over.'[17] But storms in April added to the difficulties, causing floods and bringing down trees and huge branches. Most of the houses were rendered damp and seeds recently sown were washed out of the ground.[18] The stores ran low and once again rations were reduced.

In early May, though, the Macarthurs had cause to celebrate. Elizabeth gave birth to a healthy baby girl. It was two years almost to the day since their first little girl had been born—and lost—at sea. This second baby girl was given a name: Elizabeth. With her arrival, the tide began to turn for the Macarthur family. Major Grose, a comfortably built man variously described as affable, indolent or downright lazy, took a shine to Lieutenant Macarthur and appointed him the regimental paymaster. The job was a juicy plum. As well as an additional £15 a month in pay, standard practice throughout the service saw a variety of kickbacks and perquisites flow John Macarthur's way.

Two more store ships arrived in June and July, bringing food, livestock, clothing and a renewed sense of optimism to the colony. The first ship, the *Atlantic*, carried news of the shipwrecked HMS *Pandora*, which had been sent from England to capture the mutinous *Bounty* crew. In August 1791 *Pandora* had struck a reef near the northern tip of the Australian mainland and, as Bligh had done only two years earlier, the survivors (eighty-nine crew and ten captured mutineers) made their way to Timor in open boats.[19] The second ship, the *Britannia* from London, brought better news. 'Some steps had been taken towards prosecuting Donald Trail, the master of the *Neptune* transport, for his treatment of the convicts.'[20]

Barrels of stores were unloaded from each ship, laboriously warehoused and, in the weeks following the ships' departures, finally opened. The colonists found themselves short-changed, with provisions well under the stated weights. And what remnants of food existed were variously putrid, rancid, or full of husks.[21] Grose, a man accustomed to eating well, took decisive action—or perhaps was persuaded to take action by John Macarthur. 'The soldiers under my command,' Grose wrote to Governor Phillip, 'have scarcely shoes to their feet and have no other comforts than the reduced and unwholesome rations served out from the stores.'[22] Grose assembled the captains of his corps to discuss what could be done to relieve the situation, and the entrepreneurial leaders of the New South Wales Corps raised over £4000 in £200 shares to charter the *Britannia*, dispatching her to the Cape to buy cattle, horses, stores and comforts.

Governor Phillip was unhappy with the arrangement. He grumbled that other ships with provisions from Europe would arrive before the *Britannia* could return.[23] He worried that the action might 'affect the interest of the East India Company by opening a door to contraband trade'.[24] He was right to worry—the East India Company held a formal and legally enforceable monopoly on all British trade in the region, although it was almost impossible to police. Phillip also wondered at the corps' intestinal fortitude, refuting the notion that 'the ration served from the public stores is unwholesome; I see it daily at my own table'.[25] Governor Phillip declined to take a share in the venture but, in the face of public support for it, did not prevent it from going ahead. The *Britannia* sailed out of Port Jackson in October 1792. By this stage Governor Phillip, aged fifty-four, had had enough. He'd been away from home for more than five years and under his leadership the colony was 'approaching that state in which I have so long and anxiously wished to see it'.[26] Although his spear wound had healed quickly, Phillip was now plagued by a pain in his side which 'hourly grew worse'.[27] It was probably kidney stones. At the end of October, Governor Phillip let it be generally known that he was resigning, and returning to England in the *Atlantic*.[28] But before he left, Lieutenant John Macarthur managed to argue with him.

It was a relatively minor altercation, the sort that had regularly erupted between Governor Phillip and the other officers since the establishment of the colony. No one at the time thought it warranted even the slightest mention in their diaries or dispatches. The quarrel didn't come to light at all until Macarthur himself recalled it (apparently word for word and with almost superhuman clarity) almost twenty years later. He had never, Macarthur said, had any difference with Governor Phillip but one.[29] Macarthur had control of the regimental store. Grose had ordered that, from the recently arrived trading ship *Royal Admiral*, a keg of spirits be purchased for each company of the New South Wales Corps, to be served as a daily ration. Some mistake was made during the unloading and one of these kegs was landed without being recorded. A disagreement ensued between the wharf constables, the company commander whose keg it was, the commissary and, eventually, John Macarthur.

Macarthur took the dispute to Governor Phillip. Phillip, harassed in the face of his imminent departure and in constant pain, flew into a rage. He censured Macarthur strongly and directed that the cask be given up to the commissary. The more Macarthur tried to present his case, the angrier Phillip became. In the end, the governor threatened the young lieutenant with arrest. That, for an imprudent Macarthur, was a bridge too far. 'Sir, you may please yourself. You are the first officer that ever threatened me with an arrest. And I give you my word of honour that if I am put in arrest, I shall require a full and sufficient explanation of the cause before I consent to sit quietly down under such a disgrace.'[30]

Such was Macarthur's account of this episode almost two decades after the alleged incident. If Macarthur's account was accurate, it is surprising that Governor Phillip failed to arrest the hot-headed young officer for insubordination. Apparently, the next day a cooler Phillip allowed the company commander who had bought the disputed keg to explain, and the cask was returned to the regimental store. But for the remaining month of Phillip's stay in the colony, John Macarthur refused all invitations to dine at Government House.[31] This can only have been a disappointment to Elizabeth, who in her loyal way would have followed her husband's lead. Perhaps Elizabeth quietly managed to bid Phillip a fond farewell before he left.

In his last days Phillip gave to each of the marines and sailors who were establishing their own smallholdings, and to each married convict couple who were doing the same, 'one ewe for the purpose of breeding; and to others he gave such female goats as could be spared'.[32] These animals represented the colony's future and had been procured and nurtured at great expense. Phillip hoped that they would be cherished accordingly. They were not. Most were eaten or sold to officers in exchange for rum. With all the honours due his rank and station, Phillip sailed on the morning of 11 December 1792. He was accompanied 'voluntarily and cheerfully' by local Eora men Bennelong and Imeerawanyee, much to the distress of their wives and kin. The latter was the same cheeky young man Tench had written about, when Imeerawanyee served Elizabeth Macarthur at Governor Phillip's table. The *Atlantic* also carried various specimens of timber, plants, animals and birds including 'four fine kangaroos and several native dogs'.[33] Only Bennelong would return. Imeerawanyee died in England and was buried there.

In the absence of a replacement governor, lieutenant-governor Grose took charge. The civil magistrates were sidelined and the justice system, always partially overseen by the military, became wholly so. For the first time a distinction was made between the rations received by the military and the allowance received by the convicts.[34] Grose also began to delegate much of the work that had previously caused Governor Phillip such 'infinite fatigue'.[35] He appointed his protégé John Macarthur to inspector of public works. John Macarthur became the man on the spot: issuing orders and attending to the various and constant requests of the emancipated settlers.[36] Entrusted with the direction of all the superintendents, storekeepers, overseers and convicts working at Parramatta and at nearby Toongabbie (a farm and convict station Phillip had established in 1791), Lieutenant John Macarthur was, at the age of twenty-six, in charge of the agricultural development of the colony. At last Elizabeth could see her husband, and therefore her family, making progress.

Throughout his time in office, Phillip had received no instructions about granting land to officers. To emancipated convicts, yes. To common marines and soldiers, yes. But the officers remained in a legal limbo. And to some extent the situation suited Phillip. If the officers were granted land, they must also be granted convicts to work it, taking much-needed men away from the clearing, construction and agricultural work of the government.[37] But on the day Grose took office he granted twenty-five acres (ten hectares) to a Lieutenant Cummings. Two weeks later the papers attesting to Grose's formal authority to grant land arrived on the *Bellona*, along with the colony's first group of free settlers. And so the land rush began. Grose allotted 'such officers as asked one hundred acres of land which, with great spirit, they began to clear at their own expense'.[38] Macarthur, of course, was one of those who asked, and Grose was happy to oblige him. Elizabeth wrote to England with joy, telling her friends and family that Major Grose 'has given us a grant of one Hundred acres of Land on the Banks of the river close to the Town of Parramatta. It is some of the best ground that has been discovered, & ten men are allowed us for the purpose of clearing & cultivating it'.[39]

Elizabeth's celebratory mood was shared by the other free men and women of the settlement, and was reflected in their cheerful reception, in March 1793, of some unexpected visitors from Spain. Two corvettes arrived, midway through a five-year circumnavigation of the globe for scientific and mapping purposes. Despite the various wars between England and Spain, the Spanish officers were received with pleasure by Grose and treated as honoured guests. In return, the visiting Spaniards set up a pavilion on the harbour foreshore, to serve chocolate and other delicacies to the ladies of Sydney.[40] But Elizabeth's riches did not end there. 'I have one more gift to speak of,' wrote Elizabeth to Bridget, 'it is a very fine Cow in Calf, of which I am very proud, & for this also we are indebted to Major Grose; & to a Family in this Country in its present situation, it is a gift beyond any value than can be placed upon it'. The changes to her family's fortune coloured everything, and Elizabeth seems to have relaxed into her role as a parent. 'Edward grows and improves beyond even our sanguine expectations; & little Elizabeth is able to walk by one hand though not ten months old.'[41] Nothing was quite so difficult any more.

8

Elizabeth Farm

Judge then my friend if I ought not to consider myself a happy woman.
ELIZABETH MACARTHUR TO BRIDGET KINGDON,
1 SEPTEMBER 1798

John, in his privileged position as inspector of public works, had chosen some of the best land in the colony for his grant. His hundred acres were adjacent to the original Experiment Farm, so the soil was already known to be fertile. A small creek, the Clay Cliff, provided fresh water. The land sloped gently to the north, down to the Parramatta River—then the main means of travelling to and from the Sydney Cove settlement.

Presumably John chose the name: Elizabeth Farm. But he could hardly have done so without Elizabeth's approval, even if she at first modestly demurred. Many settlers named their properties in memory of their English homes and villages; and landmarks and settlements were rapidly bestowed with the names of patrons (real or hoped-for) from the colonial office and Admiralty. But for the Macarthurs there was no looking back with names like Lodgeworthy or Bridgerule. Obtaining this land grant was the very reason they had endured so much, travelled so far. Naming the farm was a deliberate and public means for John to honour his wife, something he would continue to do privately in many letters in the years to come. Naming the farm may have helped to warm Elizabeth to the realisation that, with so much to do on their own granted lands, she and John would not be returning to England any time soon. And finally, the farm's name was also a subtle marker of John's special status as a married man—one in the eye for all those mistress-keeping gentlemen, John's peers and superiors, without a genteel wife of their own to similarly honour. John Macarthur was never a man to let pass an opportunity for one-upmanship.

Dated February 1793, the deed of grant ink was hardly dry before John started work. By November that same year he'd built, with all the convicts in Parramatta at his disposal, 'a most excellent brick house' for his family.[1] That was gilding the lily—what he actually built was a sturdy cottage. Twenty-one metres wide and a little over five metres deep, the single-storey home had four rooms, a central hall, cellars and adjoining servants' quarters, kitchen, scullery, laundry, bakehouse. The house was, perhaps deliberately, slightly larger than the house Governor Phillip had built at nearby Rose Hill. The steeply pitched roof was shingled, but at first there were no eaves or any shady overhang. At some point after the family's first summer at Elizabeth Farm, an innovation called a verandah—new to the colony and eagerly embraced by the Macarthurs—was added to the front and sides of the house, with some sections enclosed to create additional rooms. This house was to serve Elizabeth and her family for the next thirty years.

Set on a small rise, the flat, symmetrical façade of Elizabeth's home faced north, and looked across the Clay Cliff Creek and over the Macarthurs' land to the Parramatta River, less than a kilometre away. The position of the house was second to none. Visitors approached from in front and below, crossing the creek before travelling up the driveway to the northwest corner of the house. The Macarthurs were safe from floods and afforded a pleasant outlook. The regimental barracks were no more than a brisk five minute walk to the northwest, the fledgling township just beyond. The governor's Parramatta house, often used as second seat of government, was another ten minutes further west—hardly worth harnessing a horse for.

John, with his military expertise, may also have considered defence in choosing the site. It was hard to cross the creek and approach the house without being seen, and the slope of the land gave any defenders of the house an immediate advantage. Convicts were a potential threat, even though most of the household staff was drawn from convict ranks. But the convicts were dangerous—if they were dangerous—in predictable ways. Nothing a few soldiers couldn't sort out quickly, without troubling the ladies. The real danger lay with the colonists' inability to understand the Aboriginal people.

Parramatta, or Burramatta, means 'where the eels lie down' or perhaps 'place of the eels'. Elizabeth thought it meant 'head of a river'.[2] The Burramattagal were the people of the Parramatta area—the suffix 'gal' denoting 'people of' and a linguistic convention widely used by the Aboriginal peoples of the Sydney basin. The Burramattagal carefully managed and maintained the land, as did Aboriginal peoples throughout the Australian continent.

The colonists could only think of the landscape in terms of what they knew, and Elizabeth's description of it, in a letter to Bridget, is typical. 'The greater part of the country is like an English Park, & the trees give to it the appearance of a Wilderness or shrubbery, commonly attached to the habitations of people of fortune.'[3] However, the park-like landscapes described over and over by various colonists weren't natural at all. The newcomers completely failed to understand that the Australian landscape was every bit as managed, via deliberate seeding and fire-stick farming as the parklands of the English gentry. The landscape encountered by those of the First Fleet in 1788 was the result of generation upon generation of systematic work to create the ideal living and breeding conditions for every component of the food chain.[4] There was no wilderness.[5] The result in Parramatta was plentiful wildlife and plant foods throughout the year, with Clay Cliff Creek as the Burramattagal's primary source of fresh water—at least until the colonists came.

A fundamental difference in seeing the world lay between the Europeans and the Aboriginal locals. The Europeans saw the carefully managed landscape of New South Wales as virgin bush and grasslands, untended and therefore not valued and saw Aboriginal people as shiftless wanderers who failed to lay claim to the land by working it. Yet the Aboriginal people weren't nomads at all, but in the course of the year simply moved about within their own region to follow the seasonal harvest. In the same way, the Europeans almost completely failed to grasp the Aboriginal people's relationship to the land, or to understand the locals' deeply and daily lived experience of spirituality and family relationships.

Men and women from both groups did attempt to reach an understanding, even to become friends. Eora man Bennelong famously had befriended Governor Phillip and, with his colleague Imeerawanyee, sailed to England. Gentle Daringa had brought her newborn baby to show Elizabeth. And Elizabeth's friend and teacher Lieutenant Dawes befriended teenager Patyegarang and attempted to learn her language.[6] At first the Eora were remarkably forbearing towards their boorish and greedy white guests but as the colonists encroached ever further upon their lands, produce and families, it became clear that these were guests who never intended to leave, and conflict became inevitable. Aboriginal men, women and children were, alone or in groups, in cold blood or in retribution, raped, tortured and killed. Aboriginal women and children were kidnapped. Family groups, excluded from their lands by the new colonial farmers, starved. Aboriginal people with an entrenched tradition of sharing resources were accused of theft when the white settlers refused to share theirs. The local people resorted to the tactics of guerrilla warfare and reprisal. The battlelines, though, were never clear.

The various nations of Aboriginal peoples did not join together to fight against all the white invaders. There was no agreed line of battle, in the European sense. In those early days when the settlement was scarcely more than a small town, each clash was the talk of the colony, and Elizabeth could not help but be aware of the stories, of the increasing fear and tensions. Yet she never writes about it. Her letters focus on what she thinks her readers want to hear. In that, she was like the soldier who writes jolly letters home without ever mentioning the war.

In May 1792, a convict digging wells along the road to

Parramatta was killed. He had thirty spear wounds, his head was cut open and most of his teeth were knocked out.[7] In December 1793, mere weeks after Elizabeth and her family had moved to Elizabeth Farm, a large group of Aboriginal men attacked settlers returning to Parramatta, stealing their provisions before fleeing back into the bush. Even at the time, though, many believed that most of the attacks were the result of the settlers' own acts of violence. In October 1794 settlers along the Hawkesbury seized an Aboriginal boy, who they claimed to be a spy. They tied him up, dragged him through a fire and threw him into the river, where they shot and killed him.[8] In 1799 a colonist kidnapped an Eora woman. He and another colonist were subsequently killed by an Eora man while they sat around a fire one night. In a ghastly chain of retaliation five colonists grabbed three Eora youths who were working on a nearby farm. One teenager managed to flee, jumping into a river and swimming to safety despite his bound hands, but then the colonists turned to the other two boys, aged twelve and fifteen, and killed them with a sword. The five white men were tried and convicted of murder but the court was 'unable to decide on the sentence, and they went unpunished'.[9] And back and forth it went with attacks and counter-attacks.

The Macarthur family were a perfect example of the dissonant relationship between the Aboriginal and European peoples. John and Elizabeth believed the land was there for the taking. They had no sense of their own ignorance of Aboriginal law, land management and custom. Yet John and Elizabeth were not unkind. With Governor Phillip, they had dined with Aboriginal men at Government House and would continue to do so in their own home. Son William would later recall that, as far back as he could remember, Aboriginal people used to 'come about our house at Parramatta, generally a few families only, but occasionally in large parties'.[10] William also recalled a scene, probably in 1817–18, where two local men emerged from the surrounding bush, seeking John Macarthur. John was dining at the time, so the two men were seated with him and given wine—later, one of the men made an eloquent speech complimenting the master of the house. Corroborees of more than a hundred people were held on Macarthur properties into the 1850s.[11]

The Macarthurs moved into their new home in time for Edward, now almost five, and little Elizabeth, eighteen months, to celebrate Christmas 1793 at Elizabeth Farm. Elizabeth and John were in their late twenties, full of hopes and prepared to work hard. They had further cause to celebrate: Elizabeth was pregnant again. Baby John was born in May 1794 and over the next six years Mrs Macarthur 'was happily brought to bed' four more times.[12] In general there was a gap of eighteen to twenty-four months (or longer) between each of Elizabeth's children. This may have been due to the contraceptive effects of breastfeeding, but was more likely the result of deliberate abstinence. Contemporary opinion considered sex during lactation extremely undesirable. It was thought to affect the quality of the milk and was considered too tiring for a woman already reduced by the demands of nursing.[13]

Elizabeth established her home with the help of convict staff. Officers with land grants were each allocated a certain number of convicts: at this time it was ten men for the fields and three for the house. But some officers were able to finagle more free convict workers than others, and it was a constant source of dissatisfaction and at times open warfare between the officers of the New South Wales Corps. By 1795 the Macarthurs employed up to forty people, depending on the season. 'Eight are employed as stock keepers,' wrote Elizabeth to her friends in England, 'in the garden, stables and house; and five more, besides women servants; these we both feed and clothe, or, at least, we furnish them with the means of providing clothes for themselves. We have but two men fed at the expense of the Crown, altho' there are persons who contrive to get twenty or more, which the governor does not or will not notice.'[14]

Skilled or experienced emancipists or ticket-of-leave men often knew their own value in a colony where skilled workers were scarce, and they set their daily fees accordingly. And convicts still serving their time were permitted to work for pay in the afternoons, once their daily supervised labours were complete. Elizabeth considered their price enormous, 'seldom less than 4s or 5s a day'. The Macarthurs had so many convicts working for them it was 'necessary to keep on hand large supplies of such articles as are most needed by these people, for shops there are none'.[15] A large number of pigs were fattened and killed to keep everyone fed. Elizabeth doesn't say so, but it was likely that the cost of those necessary articles (brought into the colony by the officers), and possibly the cost of the food, was docked from the weekly wages.

Just as they were among the ladies of England, discussions about the servant problem were commonplace. Elizabeth was accompanied from England by Edward's never-named nursemaid who was still with the family in 1791 but then vanishes without a trace. She may have died, or married, or served the Macarthurs into her dotage. In these early years though, before free settlers began to arrive in any sort of numbers, Elizabeth's servants were convicts or the children of convicts, drawn from London poverty (and likely unskilled) or rural poverty (with possibly some skills). Any exceptions to this rule were, to speculate, the widows of common soldiers. So Elizabeth, the farmer's daughter brought up to run a country house but with little experience of being in charge, now had to train and manage a household of unskilled—and perhaps unwilling—staff. With small children and while pregnant. Her husband, meanwhile, had a day job which entailed overseeing all the inland settlements as 'autocrat and adviser for several hundred souls, mostly small farmers'.[16]

Many convicts were transported to New South Wales for crimes committed to assuage their poverty, but certainly not all. Each convict, each living breathing thinking person that staggered onto the shore at Sydney Cove after months at sea, had a separate story of their own. However, the typical female convict was unmarried, in her twenties and could probably read but not write, except perhaps for her own name. She was most likely English, from the slums of London or another port city, and she had most likely been convicted of robbery and transported for seven years. Her chances of ever returning home were negligible. A man could work in return for passage home but a woman had to save enough to pay for her own berth, or find a protector who would let her share his. The convict women, as a group, were routinely described as prostitutes—or damned whores. This doesn't mean that they were all sex workers, in the modern sense, although many of them were. In the language of the day, it meant that they were unmarried women who had had sex. It made no difference if they had been raped, or sold, or obliged to co-habit with one man to escape the predations of all the others. On the ship out they were subject to the molestations of the sailors, soldiers and officers. When the women's ships arrived the men of the colony (officers and administrators first, then the marines or soldiers, then the male convicts in positions of relative privilege, then the rest) were each allowed to select one newly arrived woman 'at his pleasure, not only as servants but as avowed objects of intercourse...rendering the whole colony little better than an extensive brothel'.[17] With far more men in the colony than women, even walking in daylight was a hazardous venture. A kind protector, a de facto husband, was often the least worst option.

In total, some 87,500 convicts were transported to the colony of New South Wales but only just over 10 per cent of them were women.[18] The minority status of convict women contributed to their exclusion from the history books, but the problem may have been exacerbated by the sense that the women were considered morally tainted. A man could, at least to some extent, leave his convict past behind, but it was far more difficult for women to do the same. John would happily do business with emancipists, the ex-convicts who flourished in the new colony, and Elizabeth quite literally rubbed shoulders with convicts in the kitchen and the pantry. But convict women were, by definition, fallen women who could never, ever have any social interaction with a woman like Elizabeth Macarthur. Given that many of John's brother officers had convict mistresses of their own, awkward encounters could only have been inevitable.

New South Wales offered commercial opportunities unavailable to the working poor of England. Some convicts made a go of it and prospered. Others continued to reoffend for the rest of their lives. Some returned to England as soon as they could, others never returned to the old country again. And some of them, fortunate ones hand-picked by John Macarthur, came to work at Elizabeth Farm. In the employ of the Macarthurs, convict workers ate better than ever they had back in England. Life as a servant in an officer's household meant hard work but was a far cry from a cold and hungry life in a reeking slum. Anyone willing and able to work was in demand, and for once their background did not, could not, count against them.

And there was a great deal of work to be done. The fine cow Elizabeth so gratefully received from Major Grose required the building of a dairy, to store the precious milk in the forms of butter, cheese and cream. The kitchens, pantries and sculleries, built separate from the house so as to minimise the risk of fire, had to serve the needs of the family as well as all the workers. Snug in winter but a summer inferno, the fires in the hearth and the ovens were stoked all day for cooking and heating. No simple jug of warm water could exist without chopping wood, starting a fire with tinder and flint, and putting a pot on to heat. The kitchens were also factories, preserving and storing the produce of the gardens, vineyard, orchards and fields to ensure seasonal gluts could be eaten later in the year. By the middle of 1794 John Macarthur could boast to his shopkeeping brother back in Plymouth about a bounty that even he had to admit was 'scarcely credible'.

Almost half the farm, which John had increased through

additional grants and purchases to 250 acres (100 hectares), was under cultivation. 'Of this year's produce I have sold £400 worth & I have now remaining in my Granaries upwards of 1800 Bushels of Corn. I have at this moment 20 acres of very fine wheat growing—& 80 Acres prepared for Indian Corn and Potatoes.'[19] John listed his livestock too: a horse (a stallion), two mares, two cows, one hundred and thirty goats and upwards of one hundred hogs. 'Poultry of all kinds I have in the greatest abundance,' he wrote, although Elizabeth probably had the management of them. Meat raised on the farm was supplemented with game. 'With the assistance of one Man & half a dozen greyhounds, which I keep,' continued John, 'my table is constantly supplied with Wild Ducks or Kangaroos.' On average the dogs killed two or three kangaroos a week, and dozens of ducks.[20] All of it had to be plucked or skinned, gutted, and cleaned before being butchered and cooked or salted and stored for later.

Elizabeth, the amateur botanist who so carefully described the gardens of Cape Town to her mother, would have overseen the layout of the new gardens at Elizabeth Farm, a bountiful mix of the productive (just over a hectare of vines, fruit trees and vegetables in squared off allotments to the east of the house, down beside the creek) and the ornamental (closer to the house).[21] In the evenings, or when she had a moment to sit, there was still no opportunity for rest. Elizabeth would have been unusual if she didn't make clothes for herself and the family. The diary of Mary Braidwood Mowle, a woman who settled with her husband in the Canberra district in the 1850s, records almost every day the unremarked phrase 'worked'; by which she meant making and altering clothes.[22]

Elizabeth was not too busy, though, to visit friends now that she had some women of her own age and class to mix with and a drawing room in which to receive them. Years later, Elizabeth, in a letter to a grown-up Edward, drolly apologised for not writing sooner. Instead of hiding away at the writing desk, 'I kept myself disengaged to talk, which occasionally you know Edward I am very fond of'.[23] But just as in any modern expatriate community, lasting friendships were made difficult by the constant comings and goings, as officers and high-ranking civilians were routinely transferred and reassigned to other settlements and countries.

The Reverend and Mrs Marsden arrived in early 1794, cradling a baby girl who was born at sea nine days earlier during a gale blowing strong enough to split the mainsail. The child was no sooner born than the cabin was swamped by a cold wave, drenching mother, infant and all the linen.[24] When Betsy Marsden first arrived she sent a letter home saying there were 'several ladies' so at least she had 'some respectable society'. Before the year was out the Marsdens took up a large land grant at the Field of Mars, just across the Parramatta River from Elizabeth Farm. Elizabeth warmed to Betsy and it seems the feeling was mutual. Elizabeth Macarthur was Mrs Marsden's 'one companion at Parramatta…a very pleasant agreeable lady, mother of three fine children'.[25] But John Macarthur and Samuel Marsden would very soon fall out, professionally and personally, and it became difficult for their wives to visit each other.

Senior among the ladies of the colony when the Marsdens arrived was Major Grose's wife Frances. Next in the hierarchy was Captain Paterson's wife, Elizabeth. Plump, 'pleasant and obliging,'[26] Elizabeth Paterson was also described by one of the marines as 'a good, cosy, Scotch lass, and fit for a soldier's wife'.[27] Mrs Paterson had been one of those enjoying the boating picnics on the harbour with Elizabeth, before she and her husband left with Lieutenant King and his wife for Norfolk Island. The Patersons returned to New South Wales in early 1793; Major and Mrs Grose departed the colony in 1794 and Captain Paterson became acting lieutenant-governor. Elizabeth's friend Elizabeth Paterson was, for a little while, the colony's first lady. The new governor, John Hunter, was expected daily although as it happened he didn't arrive for nearly another year. This was the same John Hunter that Elizabeth had met and liked during her early days in Sydney, who had lost the *Sirius* on the reef at Norfolk Island in 1790. Hunter was exonerated during the subsequent court martial and he returned to New South Wales in September 1795. As things turned out, Captain Hunter might have been better off staying away.

9

Babies, Bluster and Boasting

He is an indulgent Father—beloved as a Master, & universally respected for the integrity of his Character.

ELIZABETH MACARTHUR TO BRIDGET KINGDON,
1 SEPTEMBER 1798

Elizabeth may have excused herself from attending the ceremonies to welcome her old friend Governor Hunter, because within weeks of his arrival her three fine children became four, with the birth of Mary Isabella in October 1795. Less than two years later, a fifth child, James, was born. Elizabeth then had five children under the age of eight. Caring for the children, the household and at least some aspects of the farm, she certainly had no time for piano lessons or botany any more. Meanwhile John was also working hard, in his unpaid role as inspector of public works, and Governor Hunter's first impressions of the colony and of John Macarthur were favourable. That didn't last.

With Hunter's appointment the governorship was back in naval hands and a halcyon period ended for the New South Wales Corps. Lieutenant-Governors Grose and Paterson were both army men; they served beside John Macarthur. It is difficult to overestimate their *esprit de corps*, their sense of brotherhood. If life under Grose and then Paterson was kind to the Macarthurs, it was no coincidence—officers looked out for one another. The population of New South Wales when Hunter arrived was only 3211 and convicts made up 59 per cent. Almost all the rest were military and administrative personnel or prisoners who had served their time.[1] Elizabeth's small circle of female friends were the wives of the officers, the clergy or the civilian administrators. There were only a dozen or so free settlers, and the settlement was confined to a small region close to the coast, with its economic centre at Parramatta.

Toy-town political games leading to intense rivalries and bitterness were inevitable in a claustrophobic settlement full of alpha males and unclear chains of command. Surgeon Harris (who had seconded John in his duel on the wharves at Plymouth) had, in April 1793, purchased Experiment Farm from emancipist James Ruse and was the Macarthurs' nearest neighbour. But he and John were no longer friends. 'Captain Nepean is quite in the dumps, and my friend Mac being more so, by God I am perfectly happy,' he wrote.[2] The ranking wives of the colony could not avoid becoming embroiled. As their husbands fell in and out of alliances they could either follow suit by cutting off the relevant wife in a social sense, or else continue to pay and receive visits while feigning a brittle ignorance of the men's disputes. Similarly, the genteel wives of the colony were not immune to rivalries and resentments of their own. John and Elizabeth Macarthur were very much in the centre of these seething social maelstroms.

When Hunter was last in the colony, during Phillip's time as governor, most work had been concentrated on the public farms and on the construction of roads and buildings. By late 1795, though, privately held farms far exceeded in area those belonging to the government. Although the colony was not yet self-sufficient, the officers and small farmers produced much of the grain supply and owned most of the livestock. So many convicts were employed privately that few were left for public works, even though the male convicts were required to work their 'government hours' in the morning, for which they received no remuneration. But in the afternoons they were free to work their own holdings, or to undertake paid work for others. Rum had become the currency of choice for the convicts and they often refused to work outside government hours for anything else. This suited the officers, given that they were the colony's chief importers of liquor. Throughout his governorship, Hunter attempted to regulate the importation of spirits but the task was beyond him. The whole trade was controlled, in practice, by those very officers who most profited by it. Under these circumstances, even a wise man would have to tread carefully. Hunter, experienced in the ways of the sea rather than politics, began to step on some toes.

Hunter, deliberately or not, began to undermine Macarthur's authority, and in February 1796 Macarthur submitted his resignation as inspector of public works, although he continued his work as a commissioned officer. Perhaps Elizabeth hoped he might now spend a little more time focusing on the needs of Elizabeth Farm, rather than leaving it all largely to her. Instead John used his spare time to stir up the hornets' nest that was the New South Wales administration. While he commanded the respect of the troops, and had the loyalty of his brother officers, few of the civilian officials were on friendly terms with John Macarthur, with one writing to call John a 'base rascal and an atrocious liar and a villain'.[3] While Hunter had initially been pleased with Macarthur's efforts, many in the colony were delighted to see him step down. Hunter accepted Macarthur's resignation 'without reluctance'[4] and within days appointed to the inspectorate position the man perhaps least qualified for the role: Richard Atkins.

Atkins was about fifty years old, tall and handsome with an easy and engaging manner. He was also habitually drunk, frequently unclean and notorious for frauds and unpaid debts. His family were, and had been for hundreds of years, closely associated with royalty—a fact to which Atkins regularly alluded: he was the third son of a baronet; his elder brother was a general and a baronet; his second brother was also a baronet and, crucially for Hunter's future career in the Royal Navy, an admiral. Atkins was, in other words, unassailable. Yet John Macarthur was determined to take him on.

In mid-1796 Macarthur and Atkins started arguing about turnips.[5] Atkins alleged that soldiers were stealing from the governor's garden. Macarthur, writing in response to Atkins, sought the names of the offenders. John, usually a very careful correspondent, entirely failed to include the appellation of *Esquire*. Atkins protested strongly at the snub, and while still refusing to yield the names of the thieves, took further offence at John implying that by keeping the names to himself he might be involved in fraud. Macarthur called in Governor Hunter and although the soldiers were eventually tried (and both found not guilty), the argument escalated. Atkins' allegations, and the subsequent trial, were widely discussed and roundly condemned by the soldiers and officers of the New South Wales Corps. Parramatta and Sydney Town buzzed with talk about it. As far as the private soldiers were concerned, Captain Macarthur was their staunch defender. Elizabeth, living as she did so near the barracks at Parramatta, must have been aware of the spat, but we cannot know the extent to which she and John discussed the particulars. However throughout her life Elizabeth exhibited steadfast loyalty to John and—publicly at least—always took her husband's side.

Not content to let the matter rest, John wrote to Governor Hunter, vowing to 'prove that Mr Atkins is a public cheater, living in the most boundless dissipation'. John lacked the self-control to leave it there. 'In Mr Atkins public and official capacity drunkenness and indecency are almost inseparable from him.' Then came the clinching argument: John could prove that recently 'he was exposing himself at an early hour of the morning in the public streets in the most disgracing state of intoxication'.[6] This put Governor Hunter in rather an awkward position. However, a string of partisan and malleable witnesses was found to testify to Atkins' sobriety and strength of character, and Atkins was triumphantly cleared of all charges—charges that Macarthur had in fact yet to formulate and bring before the governor.

Atkins couldn't resist sending Captain Macarthur a gloating letter. He sidestepped the accusations of fraud and vice and instead focused on what he knew would have the greatest impact:

class. 'Your original meanness and despicable littleness pervades
your every action. It shows the cloven foot. Return to your
original nothing; we know what you have been and what you
are now...You have passed the Rubicon of dishonour...you
are a leper in reputation...you ought to be driven from society
lest you be infectious.'[7] John decided to sue for libel. Hunter
refused to allow it. Then, further infuriating Macarthur, he
appointed Atkins as judge-advocate, effectively the chief justice
for the colony. John Macarthur took what he saw as his only
remaining course of action, a gamble that put his entire career
at stake. He went over Governor Hunter's head, and yet again
John's hair-trigger sense of honour drove him to put his family's
future at risk.

He wrote to the colonial secretary, then the duke of Portland,
enclosing copies of his unsatisfactory exchanges with Government
House and, in a further effort to undermine Hunter, outlining a
plan he had put to the governor earlier in the year about farmers
feeding their own convict workers. Unsurprisingly, the view of
English officialdom was that private farmers should themselves
feed and clothe their convict labourers. Equally unsurprising, the
view of New South Wales farmers was that the free labour was
vital to their fledgling endeavours. John Macarthur, though, saw
a way through and explained his views in his career-risking letter
to the colonial office. In his opinion 'officers and persons holding
farms ought, in return for the very liberal indulgences granted
to them, to maintain their servants in bread, by which means
Government wou'd be relieved from the expense of purchasing
grain for the greater part of the colony'.[8] John and Elizabeth,
by feeding and maintaining nearly all of their servants, were

therefore leading by example. The reality was not so simple. The government in England was keen to see the public farms in New South Wales thrive in order to reduce the costs of buying or importing the food necessary to feed the convicts. The private farmers, though, made their money by selling produce to the commissary—if the commissary gained all its requirements from the public farms, the private farmers would have no market. Governor Hunter was caught in the middle.

Macarthur also wrote to the British commander-in-chief, via his old friend and supporter Major Grose. There was no skulking involved, no subterfuge. Macarthur clearly informed Hunter of his letter-writing plans. Hunter, understandably disgruntled, sent the colonial secretary a letter of his own outlining how difficult things were, which in many ways directly contradicted his earlier glowing dispatches. Then both men had to metaphorically sit back, waiting on the interminable mail to discover which way their gambling chips would fall. It would be nearly a year before they knew. We can only speculate about the extent to which Elizabeth was aware of John's letters, and whether she influenced how they were worded. A decade of marriage, with rarely a night spent apart, had seen them work successfully together, both committed to securing financial stability for their growing family. So while John was arguing with Atkins and Hunter, Elizabeth was concentrating on the needs of her children.

She was thinking hard about the future of their oldest son, Edward. There was nowhere in New South Wales to educate the children adequately and, even if there were, Elizabeth felt 'it would be unjust towards them to confine them to so narrow a society. My desire is that they may see a little more of the world, & better learn to appreciate this retirement.'[9] Like many immigrants before and since, John and Elizabeth had painted for their children a glowing picture of England as home. Elizabeth, writing to Bridget Kingdon in Bridgerule, acknowledged that she and John had over-egged the pudding somewhat, noting that the children considered England as no less than 'a seat of happiness and delight' that contained 'all that can be gratifying to their senses' and where 'of course they are there to possess all they desire'. [10] Elizabeth recognised that her children needed to experience England for themselves but she did hope that some of them would then choose to make Parramatta their home. So little Edward Macarthur, aged eight, was sent to school in England. He travelled in the care of Captain Hogan, aboard the *Marquis Cornwallis,*[11] and had for company Lieutenant King's illegitimate son Norfolk King, also eight, who until then had been living with his father and stepmother on Norfolk Island.[12] To Elizabeth's dismay Edward 'almost quitted me without a tear'.[13] But as if losing Edward wasn't enough, Elizabeth and John subsequently endured another, more searing bereavement.

'I have had the misfortune to lose a sweet boy of eleven months old,' wrote Elizabeth to her old friend Bridget about baby James, 'who died very suddenly by an illness occasioned by teething.'[14] Just as for the baby girl who died at sea, a single sentence written months later encapsulates all Elizabeth's sorrow. Her claim that James's death was caused by teething may well have been correct. A common treatment at the time was to use a razor or sharp knife to cut the baby's gums and ease the passage of an erupting tooth. But any infection, whether caused by such an intervention or not, was potentially fatal. A baby who woke healthy and strong in the morning could, with a sudden spike of fever, be gone by nightfall.

Elizabeth didn't dwell on her grief and the tone of her letter shifts almost immediately. 'The other three Elizabeth, John and Mary are well. I have lately been made very happy learning the safe arrival of Edward in England.'[15] Bridget told Elizabeth in her next letter that Edward was having the time of his life. Upon arriving in England, he spent a happy week at Bridgerule, chasing after hares with the Reverend Kingdon and returning to the vicarage covered with dirt.[16] All was not sadness for Elizabeth, despite her loss. In December 1798, she safely delivered a healthy baby boy; in a bittersweet gesture she called him James. He grew to be, according to the newspaper of the day, a 'fair-minded, courteous gentleman',[17] and from the surviving correspondence it is obvious he always remained very close to his mother. This James lived out his full allotment of three score years and ten.

When the second James was born, the Macarthurs had been living at Elizabeth Farm for five years. They had made remarkable progress. Their holding now encompassed more than 400 hectares and was bordered on three sides by rivers or streams. More than forty hectares was cultivated with wheat; the Macarthurs had been first in the colony to use a horse- or oxen-drawn plough, rather than having the soil manually turned with a hoe. Elizabeth and John employed (on a seasonal basis) up to fifty people with all, excepting two convicts still kept by the Crown, fed and clothed by the Macarthurs, who fattened and killed hogs, and kept large stores of supplies for the purpose.

'You will wonder,' wrote Elizabeth to Bridget, 'how a return is made for the daily expense...we incur.' [18]

Elizabeth wasn't inclined to let Bridget wonder for very long. With an astute grasp of the commercial realities of the fledgling New South Wales economy, Elizabeth explained in some detail how it worked. If the lesson had ended there, Bridget might have considered herself well-informed, but Elizabeth, in the same letter, couldn't help exclaiming about the high prices of livestock, before detailing exactly what those high prices were and enumerating the ridiculously high-priced beasts she and John owned. From the single cow that Grose had given to Elizabeth, their herd now numbered some fifty head. The Macarthurs were also, according to Elizabeth, running almost a thousand sheep.

At this stage John and Elizabeth were beginning to select rams for fleece rather than for meat and John had purchased from Lieutenant Waterhouse three of the famous 'Spanish breed', forbears of the modern merino. In 1796 Waterhouse, sent to the Cape by Governor Hunter to buy food for the colony, had privately procured a small flock of so-called Spanish sheep from a Dutch widow. Waterhouse ran out of fodder on the return trip and only five rams and seven or eight ewes survived. Macarthur took three, with others disbursed to Hunter's nephew Captain Kent, Reverend Marsden and a Mr Laycock. Waterhouse kept a couple for himself. At up to £16 for each sheep, Waterhouse (the true initiator of Australia's fine wool industry) made a tidy sum from animals that were most likely half-breeds, at best.[19]

In the late 1700s the Macarthurs were not the largest

wool-growers in the colony, with sheep just one of their several agricultural and entrepreneurial ventures. Like sensible business people everywhere, the Macarthurs always sought to diversify. Elizabeth wrote to Bridget of their flowering orchard, which now included almond, apricot, pear and apple trees. John was a keen rider, and horses were yet another of the Macarthurs' pursuits. In 1798 the Macarthurs kept a dozen horses, which they used, according to Elizabeth, 'both for pleasure and profit— they run alternately in the Chaise or Cart'.[20] Horses were extremely valuable and there were fewer than one hundred in the colony in total, with eighteen government-owned and the rest owned by the officers. The shortage pushed up the prices, as Elizabeth explained to Bridget, a 'good horse is worth £140 to £150. Be it ever so bad it never sells for less than £100'.[21] The private importation of horses and other livestock—from the Cape, India and the American colonies—flew in the face of the British East India Company's monopoly on trade so the practice largely went unrecorded. Even Collins, an administrator who was a stickler for detail and a dogged recorder of incoming goods, could mysteriously fail to notice each half tonne of horseflesh being unloaded at Circular Quay.[22]

Elizabeth could ride too. The Reverend Marsden boasted about his own wife's riding prowess, noting that Betsy 'rides a good deal for amusement and exercise on horse back, being a good horsewoman—she will ride to Sydney and return the same day'.[23] No such comment exists about Elizabeth but, even if she didn't ride with her friend for pleasure, she could certainly do so as required. Around this time Elizabeth made a journey to the Hawkesbury, on horseback, and stayed for three days. The road from Parramatta stretched about twenty miles in a direct line through wooded country. She enjoyed a day sightseeing on the river and could happily have spent more time there, 'but we were not without apprehensions of being interrupted by the Natives, as about that time they were very troublesome, & had killed many white people on the banks of the river'.[24] Elizabeth's wariness was warranted—despite the relative tranquillity of Elizabeth Farm, and her family's benign relationships with the Aboriginal people of that region, battles at the frontier of white occupation continued unabated. Elizabeth also enjoyed trips to Sydney, particularly as the twenty-two kilometre carriage road between Parramatta and Sydney was already a very good one. John was sometimes required to attend to his duties at headquarters, rather than at the Parramatta Barracks, and Elizabeth told Bridget that 'Myself or one or more of the children occasionally accompany him. As the distance is convenient—our stay is prolonged as business or pleasure require, or we return the same day, but as our family is large we do not choose to be long absent from home together.'[25]

Ten years after a pregnant Elizabeth had, in the eyes of her village, married unwisely, she was finally able to imply *I told you so*. She wrote to Bridget:

> …how bountifully Providence has dealt with us. At this time I can truly say no two people on earth can be happier than we are. In Mr Macarthur's society I experience the tenderest affection of a Husband who is instructive & cheerful as a companion. He is an indulgent Father—beloved as a Master, & universally respected for the integrity of his Character. Judge then my friend if I ought not to consider myself a happy woman.[26]

It's hard to believe that Elizabeth was so naïve, or so ill-informed, as to truly believe that there was universal respect within the colony for the integrity of John's character. A more self-confident woman might have left it there. But Elizabeth, right at the end of the letter, couldn't resist one more dig:

> How is it my dearest friend that you are still single—Are you difficult to please—or has the War left you so few Bachelors from amongst whom to choose. But suffer me to offer you a piece of advice—abate a few of your scruples & marry.[27]

Elizabeth's letter was dated 1 September 1798, and probably written while a ship waited in the harbour to take it straight 'home'. Bridget Kingdon's reply, although remarkably restrained, has all the vividness of an immediate response. In a telling illustration of the slowness of the mail to a remote destination like Bridgerule, Bridget's reply was dated 15 September 1799.[28]

Bridget spent a long paragraph pointing out how close she and Elizabeth had once been and sincerely hoping that nothing would ever intervene to lessen their regard for one another. Bridget admitted that she was indeed an old maid—she was thirty-two—and perhaps the subject of ridicule 'though I think undeservedly, at least the ridiculers should first point out what these unfortunate females are to do who have not an offer from a person they can approve'. She wondered what Elizabeth would have her do? 'Not surely be so eccentric as to reverse the matter, and make an offer (if you would) I have not the courage, nor vanity enough to pursue the scheme.' Money was the key, thought Bridget, 'but having neither youth wealth or beauty to recommend me, I shall endeavour to make myself contented with the state I am in'. Bridget was cross enough to allow a little sarcasm to creep in: 'You have my grateful thanks however for your kind advice,' then immediately softened it: 'Though it is not granted me to follow it.'

Perhaps at this point Bridget drew breath. Her heart must have been a large and kind one for the very next paragraph is full of congratulations for Elizabeth's good fortune in finding such an excellent husband. 'God grant your present happiness may be continued to you.' [29] Her kindness continues as she finishes the letter with details of young Edward, who Bridget described as a charming boy, enjoying his visit with the Kingdons. Perhaps her letter took a year to reach Parramatta, perhaps it took two. Regardless, soon after it had arrived in Elizabeth's hands, everything had changed for Bridget.

On 1 March 1802 she stood before her father, the Reverend Kingdon, inside the church after which she was named and was married to John Braddon. Bridget had finally received an offer from a person she could accept. Sadly, just six months later, on 31 August 1802, the Reverend Kingdon again presided over a ceremony for his daughter—this time it was her funeral. No cause of death is recorded but perhaps it was pregnancy-related.

After Bridget's death Elizabeth Macarthur continued to write to and receive letters from Bridgerule, but now she was corresponding with her goddaughter, Bridget's youngest sibling, Eliza. Is it telling that none of Elizabeth's surviving letters to Bridgerule mention her husband again, or at least not in anything more than a passing line? Perhaps Elizabeth found it increasingly difficult to demonstrate the colony's universal respect, as she had earlier put it, for the integrity of John's character. Certainly, Governor Hunter could not attest to it. He was still waiting to see the results of John's letter.

10

Pistols at Twenty Paces

*It is useless, my good friend, to add fuel to the fire
that has been blazing too long already.*

ELIZABETH MACARTHUR TO CAPTAIN PIPER,
'THURSDAY AFTERNOON' C. 1801

The duke of Portland's response to John Macarthur's letter
arrived in 1798, nearly a year after John had sent it, and it was
not, as far as Hunter was concerned, the least bit heartening.
His Grace was so sure of Hunter's 'penetration and judgment'
as to have no doubt that he would surely avail himself 'of every
suggestion contained in Captain Macarthur's letter.'[1]

Later letters chastised Hunter further, and continued to harp
on the subject of costs, trading monopolies and rum. Anonymous
sources made allegations of gross profiteering and trading in
liquor by the officers. This much was old news. Of particular
concern to the duke, though, were new allegations that 'this sort
of traffic is not confined to the officers, but is carried on in the
Government House'. Hunter was not implicated directly, but
his staff was. By April 1800 it was all over for Hunter. Phillip
Gidley King, who had sailed on the First Fleet as a lieutenant,

subordinate to Hunter, was back in the colony with his wife—
Elizabeth's friend Anna Josepha—and carrying Hunter's sternly
worded recall to England.

Elizabeth's coterie was brilliant again. Mrs Paterson and
her newly promoted husband had returned with the Kings, and
now the Macarthurs often stayed with the Patersons in Sydney.
Embarrassingly, King was not only a messenger but also Hunter's
replacement and Hunter treated him with a cold indifference
that soon descended into overt hostility. John Macarthur's sense
of his own importance and influence, always strong, was firmly
bolstered by this political coup but, always mercurial, he did
not spend long basking in the glow of his victory over Hunter.
Enough was enough, it seems, and it was time to return to
England.

In a move that shocked the colony John Macarthur put
Elizabeth Farm up for sale: lock, stock and barrel. Macarthur
offered the farm to the only purchaser who could afford it—
the crown. He set the price at £4000, which included all the
livestock, buildings and more than 500 hectares of land (of
which 160 were cleared). Newly appointed Governor King
thought buying it would be a good idea but needed to wait for
permission from the colonial office. The duke of Portland, in
his eventual reply, vetoed the purchase of Elizabeth Farm and,
highly disapprovingly, agreed only that King could buy the
cattle and the sheep. Ignoring every positive thing that had been
written about Captain Macarthur's farming efforts since 1793,
Portland could 'by no means account for his being a farmer to
the extent he appears to be,' because he already had a job, as
a serving regimental officer.[2] It seems not to have occurred to

the duke that the extent of the Macarthurs' farming activities may have been just as much the result of Elizabeth's efforts as of John's.

It is entirely possible that Elizabeth was unaware, at least initially, of John's offer to sell the farm. She certainly had enough on her plate at home. Young Edward had left for school in England but Elizabeth was, in 1800, caring for four children—Elizabeth (aged eight), John (six), Mary (five) and James (two)—and she was pregnant with another (William, who would be born on 15 December, the same birthdate as his living brother James). Or perhaps Elizabeth was aware, and had had enough of New South Wales, too, and fully supported the sale. Ideally she and John could sell up, with enough profit to move back to a comfortable life in England, and raise their children in proximity to family and friends. Either way the reasons for deciding to sell remain obscure. But by 1801, before Governor King had received the duke of Portland's reply, the Macarthurs had decided not to sell after all. There are no records explaining the change of heart, but it is hard to believe that Elizabeth's views weren't being expressed, perhaps vehemently so, when she learned of the intended sale.

As if Elizabeth didn't already have enough to worry about, in June 1801, when baby William was only six months old, John Macarthur was involved in yet another fracas. A visiting naval lieutenant, Marshall, allegedly stole from the effects of a young man who had been lost overboard. Captain Macarthur, acting commandant of the troops at the time, investigated the claims, and Marshall eventually confessed. Governor King issued Marshall with a severe reprimand and booked him an ignominious passage home. Marshall focused his embarrassed rage entirely on John Macarthur, accosting him in the parade ground, the hub of Sydney Town. After a brief exchange of insults, John Macarthur challenged Marshall to a duel.

This time it is certain that Elizabeth had no idea. The combatants were both in Sydney, well over an hour's ride from Parramatta, but although they were scheduled to meet later that same afternoon, technical points of honour meant the duel did not take place. Feverish negotiations continued all afternoon but an appropriately senior second for Marshall could not be found or agreed on. Marshall turned up anyway and was incensed when Captain Macarthur and his second, Captain Abbott, did not. Marshall had all night to stew on it. The following day just before noon, again at the parade ground, a furious and shouting Marshall struck Abbott on the shoulder with a bludgeon before looking set to use it on John Macarthur's head. John drew his sword and threatened to run the young naval lieutenant through. Marshall lowered his own crude weapon, and was taken to the guard house.[3]

Did John Macarthur manage to keep this escapade from his wife? In the small world of New South Wales society, it seems unlikely. Just as she had in the wake of John's first duel, on the wharves of Plymouth over a decade before, Elizabeth once again faced losing her husband—and her family's financial future—as a direct result of his impulsive behaviour. At the subsequent trial Marshall escaped the noose, although his naval career was over. On the charge of attacking Abbott, Marshall was fined £50 and ordered to be gaoled for twelve months, in England. Given that Macarthur had received no actual blow, Marshall's attack on him was referred to London.

The court was presided over by Atkins, but otherwise made up of officers from the New South Wales Corps and a solitary naval lieutenant. Not one to take life's blows quietly, Marshall strongly protested that the military make-up of the bench rendered it impossibly biased against him. Governor King, a navy man, prevaricated and called on Judge-Advocate Atkins to reconvene the court, but the officers of the corps were incensed: King's request constituted an insult of the highest order. How dare the governor imply that the military men did not act impartially? Macarthur threatened to write to the authorities in England and any friendly goodwill between the King and the Macarthur families evaporated. Almost a decade later King would write that there was no society where the clashing of duty and interest between the governor and the governed was more violent than in New South Wales, and more particularly so if the governor did his duty.[4]

No matter what Elizabeth thought of her husband's views, her hard-won friendships with Anna King and Elizabeth Paterson were affected by them. Among the ladies' friends was a young Lieutenant Matthew Flinders, who had, in 1798–99, circumnavigated Van Diemen's Land and proved it to be an island. He then sailed back to England, married, and in 1802 was again in New South Wales. He wrote regretfully to his wife in England about how much she might have enjoyed Sydney, if only he'd been allowed to bring her. Flinders was friends with all the ladies in Elizabeth's circle but clearly had his favourites. 'Two better or more agreeable women than Mrs King and Mrs Paterson are not easily found; these would have been thy choicest friends,' he wrote to his wife, although he also noted that the other ladies, including Elizabeth Macarthur, would be perfectly fine as 'visiting acquaintances' and, he conceded, 'very agreeable for short periods'.[5]

As it happened, Elizabeth Paterson and Anna King were close friends. A decade earlier the Patersons and the Kings spent fifteen months living on Norfolk Island. Together Mrs Paterson and Mrs King were instrumental in establishing Sydney's first home for orphans, and the children of 'undesirable' parents. One or both of the ladies visited every day to 'ensure the cleanliness, the instruction and the good quality of the food', and visitors were impressed by their 'solicitude and touching care'.[6] Elizabeth was never involved with the orphanage and perhaps this further accelerated her family's falling out with the Kings. Elizabeth Macarthur was not the sort of woman, nor did she have the time, to indulge in the public performance of good works, particularly when friends closer to home needed her more. In August 1801 Elizabeth's friend and neighbour Betsy Marsden had a terrible accident. Not twenty metres from the Marsden farm gate her carriage overturned, spilling out a pregnant Betsy and her three-year-old son, Charles, who died in his mother's arms. Two months later Betsy gave birth to another boy, John, but this didn't cure her heartbreak and depression, and she didn't write to friends in England for more than a year.

Betsy Marsden wasn't alone in her grief. Almost all of Elizabeth's friends had lost, or would lose, a child. Mrs King's daughter Utricia, the third of her five children, was about two when she died in 1797.[7] And now the King's older children, Phillip and Maria, rather than returning to Sydney with their parents, remained in England, safe from colonial mishaps. Louisa Abbott's third child, Harriet, daughter of John Macarthur's friend and colleague Captain Edward Abbott, died aged about two.[8] Elizabeth Paterson had no children, or at least none that survived long enough to be recorded, and it would be a rare woman who didn't grieve for what she couldn't have. And a rare woman too who, like Elizabeth Macarthur, didn't share her friends' hurts and sorrows.

But Elizabeth's friendship woes continued apace. After falling out with Anna King, it was almost inevitable that Elizabeth's friendship with Elizabeth Paterson would not endure. During the Marshall affair, John's commanding officer, William Paterson, at first provided his full support. (Paterson was in fact one of the five who had passed judgment on Marshall and he joined Macarthur in writing to the authorities at home to complain about Governor King.) But John pushed the friendship too far when he tried to induce Paterson to end his social relationship with the governor. King and Paterson were both protégés of the redoubtable Sir Joseph Banks, and they shared a keen interest in the natural sciences. But even without King and Paterson's shared interests, John should also have known that the relationship between Paterson's wife and King's made any rift impossible

Then somehow, amidst all the bickering, Colonel Paterson came to believe that a private friendly letter, written by his wife to Elizabeth Macarthur, had been made public by John, who 'in communicating its contents, misconstrued it'.[9] If only we knew what the letter said! The offence caused was enough to have Paterson challenge John Macarthur to a duel. It was an extraordinary move for a colonel to make against his second-in-command,

and hardly conducive to regimental discipline. Surely for any other offence Paterson could, or should, have invoked military regulations and reprimanded or punished Macarthur accordingly. Paterson's challenge was issued on 10 September 1801, for a rendezvous the following day, but rain prevented the contest for another four days. Again, it is unlikely that either wife was told of, or knew of, her husband's impending folly, although the letter must also have been a source of friction between them. For the women though, their only recourse was to cut each other dead socially, rather than to shoot each other dead literally. In the event, it was Anna King who proved herself to be quite the social duellist.

On 13 September 1801, the day before the duel eventually took place, Elizabeth Macarthur received a shocking social slight. Governor and Mrs King sent out invitations to celebrate the anniversary of King George III's coronation to every officer of the NSW Corps—except to John and Elizabeth Macarthur. In a demonstration of solidarity, Macarthur's closest allies, known usually to be the most peaceable of men, declined their own invitations: Captain Abbott (who had known the Macarthurs since he shared a cabin with them on the *Scarborough*); Ensign Minchin (whose descendants would make sparkling wine at Minchinbury, the family estate); and brothers Captain John Piper (who would become a good friend to Elizabeth and who named his Sydney property Point Piper) and Ensign Hugh Piper.

The following day, at one in the afternoon, William Paterson and John Macarthur met near Parramatta. Surgeon Harris, who had acted as John Macarthur's second ten years before at the Plymouth wharves oversaw the proceedings. It wasn't the first duel to be fought in the colony and it was far from the last, but it turned out to be one of the most unusual: against the odds, Macarthur hit his target. Paterson took a ball through his right shoulder and fell. Macarthur stood his ground while Paterson was assisted, waiting for Paterson to shoot in return, as was the protocol, but was soon informed that he should leave. Macarthur subsequently sent a note saying that he would be ready for Captain Paterson at any time. Paterson's second interpreted the note to be 'exulting in victory', infuriating Macarthur, who never spoke to the man again.[10]

Governor King arrived in Parramatta that same afternoon, unaware of the incident, and found himself in the midst of a public furore. Perhaps John Macarthur, on arrival at home, found himself in the midst of a private one. Surely Elizabeth was fed up with John's foolish and dangerous bravado. Paterson received medical care, and although for the first few days his situation was touch and go, he recovered. Macarthur and the two seconds were placed under 'close arrest', an arrangement which in practice meant the men merely stayed within the confines of their properties. Although Paterson had clearly erred in calling out his subordinate officer, King glossed over this and laid most of the blame, and all of his fury, squarely on Macarthur.

If John was berated at home by his wife, his subsequent correspondence shows nothing of it and instead shimmers with all the gleeful happiness of a man intent on needling his enemies. John was a man riding high on adrenalin and audacity and nothing anyone said could bring him back to earth. At first King threatened to send Macarthur to Norfolk Island; Macarthur, all innocent good faith, enquired whether his proposed exile was 'intended as a punishment for some supposed offence, or whether it is considered as in the ordinary course of duty?'[11] If it was a punishment, John demanded a copy of the charge and permission to answer it immediately before a general court martial. If it was the latter then John was forced, with all due respect, to point out to His Excellency that actually it was Captain Abbott's duty, as Macarthur's junior, to go to Norfolk Island. Here, for once, John's impeccable logic saved Elizabeth from exile to the tiny Pacific island.

King could legally only keep Macarthur, and the seconds, under close arrest for eight days. So, in lieu of confining him to the common gaol, King offered bail if Macarthur would be bound under civil law to keep the peace. Macarthur was affronted by the implication that he intended to break the peace and yet again made a stand. He declined to come out of close arrest, but said that in the interests of the service he was willing to perform his duties if it remained understood that he was still under arrest. Further, John again demanded to be brought before a court martial so that:

> I may have an opportunity of clearly proving that I have betrayed no private correspondence, no private conversations, that I have displayed no exultation over a wounded opponent, or in any way behaved unlike a gentleman, but that, on the contrary, I am the person who has been betrayed, who has been exulted over and who has been treated with the basest ingratitude and the blackest treachery.[12]

Governor King, besieged by the many who wished Macarthur ill and completely fed up himself, decided to grant John's request.

King ordered him to stand trial—in England.

If the decision seemed extreme to the colonists, it did not to those in England to whom King had been sending his formal dispatches, which were full of his frustrations with John Macarthur and the rest of the New South Wales Corps. Indeed, King was almost hysterical in his hatred of John Macarthur—though within a year he would confess that he pitied and esteemed Elizabeth.[13] In these sentiments he was not alone. The senior men of the colony invariably liked Elizabeth Macarthur, even as she fell in and out of their wives' good graces. While John was written about by many as a devious villain, it is impossible to find even the merest hint of dislike for Elizabeth.

Elizabeth, however, had many reasons not to love Governor King. How hurtful that a former friend would deliberately send her husband into exile. By ordering John Macarthur to England for trial, King rid himself of a constant irritant and freed himself from any claims of an unfair judicial process. The only thing souring his plans was John himself, who, while waiting for an appropriate ship to England, remained in high spirits. John purchased 1200 sheep and a farm at Toongabbie from Colonel Foveaux, who was posted to Norfolk Island (where he proved himself a sadist of the highest order). Some have suggested that Macarthur bought Foveaux's sheep just to vex King, who was on the verge of buying them for the colony. John dashed off genial farewell notes to his friends, and enhanced his popularity with his soldiers by treating each of them to a pound each of meat and wheat, and a gill of spirits to wash it down.

While John was saying his jolly farewells, Elizabeth was worrying about the details. She had mere weeks to prepare the household and enterprises for John's absence. At the same time, everything had to be prepared in haste for the voyage: clothes, food, travelling trunks and baggage. There was linen to be washed and mended, before being carefully folded and packed away. And there were dozens of decisions to be made about the farms (including the new one just purchased), the finances and, most important of all, the children. Should the older ones stay home with their mother, or travel with their father?

England had been at war with France and her allies, off and on, for nearly a decade so the usual dangers of a sea voyage were exacerbated by the possibility of an encounter with an enemy warship. Elizabeth had long been a soldier's wife, but she'd never before sent her husband, let alone her children, off towards a conflict. A mere two months after his duel with Paterson, on 15 November 1801, John sailed for England, leaving Elizabeth to manage without him. No one was quite sure when, or if, he would come home. With John so buoyant and all the children's spirits to be kept up, if Elizabeth wept she did so in private.

11

Managing Alone

The management of our concerns gets troublesome
to me in the extreme and I am perpetually annoyed
by some vexation or other.

ELIZABETH MACARTHUR TO CAPTAIN PIPER, 15 APRIL 1804

As John's ship sailed down the harbour and out of sight Elizabeth stood at the water's edge with Mary (aged six), James (almost three) and William (not quite one). Elizabeth farewelled not only her husband, but two more of her children. Although it may well have broken her heart, Elizabeth had agreed to send her eldest daughter Elizabeth (nine) and her second son John (seven) to England with their father. With typical bravura John managed to turn his own banishment into a grand tour for his children. In England, young Eliza would remain with her father, but John was to join his brother Edward at the Grove Hall Academy.

The result was that every one of those feverishly busy last few weeks had also to be savoured—Elizabeth knew it would be at least a year before husband John and her daughter would return, and many more years before her son could. Sadly, though, young John would grow to manhood and die in England without ever returning to New South Wales. Although he and his mother regularly wrote to one another, Elizabeth never saw him again. The unhappy drive back home to Parramatta—the family could hardly stay in Sydney with the Kings or the Patersons now—gave Elizabeth plenty of time to contemplate her responsibilities. Elizabeth Farm she knew well, but the newly acquired Seven Hills farm at Toongabbie was an unwelcome burden.

Why didn't Elizabeth go with John and the children to England? Having seen one too many toddlers die recently, was she scared to sail with the little ones, or was it simply too expensive to take the whole family? John could live alone in England more frugally and in less style than he could in all conscience keep his wife. And money was, and always would be, key to Macarthur motivations. Buying the Seven Hills property depleted their credit and cash reserves, so having a competent manager to maintain and rebuild their finances was vital. While the Macarthurs would in later years employ a farm manager for their outlying properties, at this stage skilled and, more to the point, trustworthy labour was hard to come by. Elizabeth, whether she liked it or not, was best placed for the job.

Her situation was unusual, but only among women of her social standing. In the British Empire of 1801 ideas of a woman's place were underpinned by legal, political and social practices that subordinated women, but these were pragmatically combined with the recognition of women's economic worth in family enterprises. No one blinked at the draper's daughter helping in the shop, the printer's widow carrying on his business, the publican's wife serving at the bar. Sometimes the publican was herself a woman—by 1815, of the ninety-six licences issued in the Sydney area to sell alcohol, twelve were held by women.[1] Still more women, no doubt, made a living selling alcohol without a licence. It was certainly true that in New South Wales Elizabeth Macarthur was not the only woman running a farm, although she was perhaps the most genteel.

By 1800 about twenty women held land in their own name. Some lived in town while men worked it for them; some owned the land but ceded control of it to their husbands or partners. But a few managed their land themselves. Midwife Margaret Catchpole lived alone on her fifteen acres (six hectares) where she raised goats, pigs and sheep. Eleanor Fraser, a widow with two small boys, was granted forty acres (sixteen hectares) at Concord. She subsequently cohabited with a soldier who had land of his own but they seemed to have kept their farming interests separate. In 1797 Jane Poole was granted 160 acres (sixty-five hectares) on the Hawkesbury River 'as a provision for herself and her family' when her soldier partner died, leaving her to care for the children of their de facto marriage.[2] First Fleet convict Esther Abrahams went on to manage Annandale, the farm she shared with her de facto husband, Major George Johnston, when he was transferred to Norfolk Island in 1796[3] and she continued to run the farm when George went back to England, under arrest for illegal trading in spirits. Under her management it became a thriving estate that included a fine brick home.

So Elizabeth had female peers, but none who was her social equal, none who managed such large holdings, and most likely none who had her eye for breeding quality livestock. Elizabeth wrote, with a breeder's sensibility, about her favourite mare, Kitty, to her friend Captain Piper. 'I took a particular survey of

Kitty and her foal yesterday. The mare looks well & has much improved within this week...The young one does not promise to be large but in action much resembles her Grandmama.[4] As well as the horses, Elizabeth oversaw the farms' extensive production of fruit and grains; a large vegetable garden and poultry yard; goats; hogs; and a herd of cattle, some for meat, others to provide milk for the dairy. And, of course, she also managed the sheep.

In 1801 nearly all of the colony's sheep farmers were breeding for meat rather than wool. The return for meat was immediate and nearly four times that of wool,[5] and the colony provided a ready, albeit small, market. The Macarthurs, though, had begun to take a longer view. They concentrated on using their so-called Spanish rams to improve the quality of a flock consisting mainly of hairy Bengal, Irish and Californian sheep imported from India and the Cape. More by chance than design, the offspring of those particular hairy sheep and the Spanish rams were versatile animals that coped well with the dry, Australian conditions. In the years to come they would be bred to create the redoubtable Australian merino.

In October 1800, not long before John Macarthur left for England, Governor King had dispatched samples of eight fleeces to England to be examined by Sir Joseph Banks' wool experts. Included in the sample were two fleeces from Elizabeth Farm. 'Nearly as good as the King's Spanish Wool at Oatlands', noted Banks' wool classer, 'and an excellent quality; worth 5/- per pound; and could the colony produce such kinds of wools it would be a great addition to our manufactury in England'.[6] John was not, of course, aware of that remark when he left Sydney, but it did mean that on his arrival in England he had the ear of industry players.

Elizabeth settled into a farmer's routine of early mornings and long days, the tasks dictated by the seasons. She had a team of workers, of course, but managing people was hard work in itself, and Elizabeth never had as many workers as she needed. With John's purchase of Foveaux's holdings at Toongabbie the Macarthurs became the colony's largest sheep producers. By mid-1802 their flock numbered 2750 and, claimed John in England, by the end of the year it had increased to more than 3000.[7] The sheep grazed on unfenced grassland with shepherds employed to keep them from straying, and to keep them from harm and theft. Shepherding was a difficult task for a farm manager to oversee effectively. Several shepherds were killed by Aboriginal people (including two who worked for Elizabeth), some absconded, and some drank themselves to the point of being useless. Elizabeth had sixteen assigned convicts when John left, but needed more. So did everyone else. Wars in Europe meant convicts tended to be pressed into (that is, forced to serve in) the armed forces rather than be sent at great expense to New South Wales. The colony certainly felt the lack. And while John was away the Macarthur sheep numbers grew too large to maintain—Elizabeth was forced to cull the flock.[8]

Elizabeth confessed, again to her friend Captain Piper, that she was prey to anxiety and 'much uncertainty'. 'The management of our concerns gets troublesome to me in the extreme and I am perpetually annoyed by some vexation or other…God grant me Health and patience, for indeed my good friend, I have need of *both* to keep my mind in tolerable frame.'[9]

In 1803 Matthew Flinders, who had recently completed his circumnavigation of the continent, was once more in Sydney and Elizabeth sought his advice on how to enforce payment for £500, relating to the sale of some cattle. Although many women ran successful businesses, when those women had to deal with people—men—outside the family, problems often arose. Elizabeth's labouring employees, suppliers, bankers, agents were all men, with certain expectations of appropriate feminine behaviour, leaving her at a distinct disadvantage over any outstanding payments.[10] In his letter of reply Flinders, clearly all at sea when it came to matters of agricultural commerce, referred to the *Encyclopedia Britannica*.

'Under the head "Sale" of the *Encyclopedia Britannica*,' wrote Flinders to Elizabeth 'it appears that "if" the buyer proves insolvent before delivery, the seller is not bound to deliver the "goods without payment or security".'[11] Flinders' advice was not helpful, amounting to little more than a reiteration of Elizabeth's problem. All Elizabeth's contracts were in her husband's name and, with his continued absence, they may have been legally unenforceable. Elizabeth faced other difficulties in business too, and she felt she was given poor terms when procuring a supply of goods for her stockmen. 'I have every reason to suppose that the most unfair advantage has been taken of me, without my having the means of redress. Had I known the man before I should have taken clear precautions.'[12] It is unlikely, though, that Elizabeth allowed herself to be played for a fool a second time and, in time, any trader would have cause to regret having offended the Macarthurs.

In a flurry of letter writing undertaken before he left Sydney for England, Flinders also wrote to Mrs Kent, who had just arrived back in Sydney after an absence of two years. Eliza Kent was married to former Governor Hunter's nephew and was a member of Elizabeth's social circle. Flinders' words provide an insight into the ongoing ill-feeling among the ladies of the colony. He mentions the welcome assistance he received from Governor King and his:

> ...kind friend Mrs King; and it is a cause of much uneasiness to me that Colonel & Mrs Paterson should be upon terms of disagreement with them. There is now Mrs King, Mrs Paterson and Mrs McArthur for all of whom I have the greatest regard, who can scarcely speak to each other; it is really a miserable thing to split a small society into such small parts: why do you ladies meddle with politics? But I do not mean you.[13]

Flinders was right. The ladies of the colony really did form only a very small society. Betsy Marsden, though, was grateful to see the numbers growing. In 1802 she could claim that of 'our society of married ladies...we have now twenty'.[14]

Although it was easier for Elizabeth to socialise with her women friends now that John was away and not arguing with their husbands, her relationship with Elizabeth Paterson and Anna King remained cool. Closer to hand was Betsy Marsden, who needed friends more than ever. The Reverend Marsden was busy overseeing the building of Parramatta's first church, St John's, which was consecrated at the Easter of 1803, an event to which the ladies of the colony turned up in force.[15] That achievement should have marked a happy year for the Marsdens but in August that year the family was struck by tragedy once again. Little John Marsden, the baby born two months after his mother and brother were flung from the carriage in August two years earlier, died from a scalding accident in his mother's kitchen. Betsy never regained her equilibrium. From then on she considered August a fearful month, and could hardly bear to let her children out of her sight.[16]

Elizabeth also had plenty of male friends to turn to. With the barracks at Parramatta only five minutes from Elizabeth Farm, she could rely on the help and support of John's fellow officers and his loyal subordinates. Captain Edward Abbott remained a stalwart friend, and his visits are mentioned in Elizabeth's letters. Elizabeth cultivated friendships in the navy too, and Flinders and other officers from visiting ships regularly stayed at Elizabeth Farm.

Captain Nicholas Baudin, commander of the famed French scientific expedition, and his officers were welcomed as guests by Elizabeth, when their ships stopped briefly at Sydney in late 1802. The French spent their time socialising with the English officers and their ladies, and, like the Spanish before them, secretly compiling intelligence reports for their government back home. Elizabeth made enough of an impression that seventeen years later when one of Baudin's officers, now Captain de Freycinet, returned in his own ship to Sydney, his stowaway wife, Rose, happily stayed two days at Elizabeth Farm.[17]

The problem with having friends in the armed forces, though, was that Elizabeth was forever saying goodbye. In 1803 Matthew Flinders wrote to her from Sydney, expressing his joy at finally being able to sail for England and back to his beloved wife. 'Adieu my dear Madam—I am going home with the promise of being attended by fortunes smiles, and with the delightful prospect of enfolding one to whom my return will be a return of happiness.' Flinders didn't have time to visit Elizabeth again. 'It would be much pleasure to me to have waited upon you at Parramatta, but my business will not allow me to bestow two days upon personal gratifications.' Flinders was happy, though, to run any errands for Elizabeth in town and he doesn't forget the cares of his friend. 'For you, my dear friend I leave you with anxious suspense, and borne down with the cares attendant upon the interests of a large family, the oppressive weight of which your single shoulders are at present left to bear.' Flinders' letter alludes to Elizabeth's strong religious conviction: 'May that Almighty Power whom you reverence and adore impart such fortitude to your mind and health to your person as will enable you to discharge your various duties with the satisfaction that attends upon having done every thing well.'[18] By the year's end Flinders would be imprisoned by the French on Mauritius. He wouldn't reach England for more than six years. Matthew Flinders died in 1814, the day after the publication of his magnum opus *A Voyage to Terra Australis*.[19]

Overall, though, Elizabeth does not seem to have had the time or the inclination to hover over her friends. A typical day would see the family rise early, eat breakfast at about seven before following their own pursuits until mid-afternoon.[20] Elizabeth might ride out to oversee work on the farm and check her livestock, or she might spend a day in the kitchens, ensuring produce was properly prepared and preserved. There were tradesmen to meet, servants to direct and, always, the children. With John away there was only Elizabeth to teach them their letters and numbers, their bible, and their manners.

As an elderly man, Elizabeth's youngest son William reminisced about his childhood to his niece. He did not recall having had any toys except a wheelbarrow. 'I remember once taking a long walk with our house maid [and siblings] dear James & Mary & returning home with this wheel barrow wreathed with Clematis. Suddenly the barrow broke—my grief was intense—the others were older & did not care so much.'[21] William could not have been more than four years old when this incident occurred. Perhaps he consoled himself with the other 'toy' the children played with, a 'cannon, with which we would fire royal salutes on High Days and holidays'. They were most likely pretending but with the garrison so close, and with so many soldier friends, anything might be possible.

William also claimed that, until the age of seven, he never had more than two garments—presumably a shirt and pants—and as a result suffered some bitterly cold winter evenings. This is the sort of childhood memory that mothers of those now grown-up children hear with incredulity, and often quickly refute. In this case we only have William's word for it, but clearly, although Elizabeth loved her children, she did not indulge them. William did, however, remember the moment he discovered he could read. He had picked up a book and:

> ...there was a poem about a rose in it. It suddenly flashed upon me what it meant and I read it off. My sister Elizabeth has told me I read quite fluently at the time of her return to the Colony when I must have been about four years old.[22]

It says something about Elizabeth's household that there was a book of poetry lying around for a bright child to pick up.

The main meal of the day was eaten in the mid-afternoon while there was still light to see by. The family could eat by the light of their whale-oil lamps, of course, but for the servants preparing and clearing up after a meal was much easier done by daylight. After dinner, although perhaps not every evening, Elizabeth as the head of the family may well have read a short sermon to the assembled household, while the small children fidgeted. Elizabeth may not have lavished her children with doting attention, but nor was she a strict disciplinarian. She generally enjoyed the children's company and in many of her later letters she and her sons use the word 'merry' to describe family gatherings at the table.

Elizabeth and her children were also welcomed at her friends' tables, and it was in such a situation—dining with friends—that on Sunday 4 March 1804 they were caught in an ill-fated uprising of Irish convicts. Many of the Irish convicts at this time were political prisoners, transported for their role (or supposed role) in the 1798 rebellion of the United Irish. The rebellion sought to take advantage of Britain's war against the newly conceived French Republic and was timed in the hope of coinciding with a French invasion of Ireland. By the end of the year the rebellion had been crushed, with large numbers of casualties on both sides. More than 300 men were sentenced to death, and between 1800 and 1802 about 500 Irish men and women were transported for political crimes.[23] Convinced of the injustice of their imprisonment in New South Wales, several hundred Irish and English convicts employed on the government farm at Castle

Hill, near Parramatta, raided nearby settlements for weapons. Their cry, as it was in Ireland, was 'Death or Liberty!' But they were poorly organised and ill-equipped, with little thought given to what might happen next—some convicts seemed to believe they might be able to negotiate a ship to take them home.[24]

That very March evening, some seven months after little John Marsden died, Mrs Marsden was coping well enough to have her friend and neighbour Elizabeth Macarthur over for supper. Elizabeth was accompanied by her daughter Mary, then aged eight, and her son James, aged five. William Macarthur, aged three, was being looked after at home. In a letter to her friend Captain Piper six weeks later, Elizabeth vividly describes the scene in Betsy's parlour:

> ...we were sitting at supper [when] Old Joice burst into the parlour Pale & in violent agitation. 'Sir says he looking wildly at Mr Marsden 'come with me'—'and you too madam' looking at me. Then half shutting the door he told us that the Croppies had risen, that they were at my Seven Hills Farm & that numbers were approaching Parramatta. Mrs Marsden, myself & our children repaired to the Barracks.[25]

Elizabeth can certainly tell a story. That half-shut door is a descriptive triumph, in its implication that Old Joice didn't want the other servants to hear. 'Croppies' is Joice's word—throughout the letter Elizabeth usually refers to the mutinous convicts as Irishmen or rebels.

At the barracks, only minutes from the Marsden home, the women learnt that Castle Hill was in turmoil. Elizabeth could see the flames. The Irishmen, reported to number 300, 'were expected every minute to enter the town'.[26] Elizabeth's friends at the barracks suggested 'as many ladies as chose should go to Sydney' but Elizabeth could go nowhere without her son William. It was 11 pm before the boy was collected and Elizabeth, Mrs Marsden, Mrs Abbott and a Mrs Williamson departed down the Parramatta River with all their children by the light of a half-moon. They were accompanied by the Reverend Marsden (who carried a request from Captain Abbott at Parramatta for more ammunition) and presumably by the boat's crew. By this time the Irish rebels were on the outskirts of Parramatta and, according to Elizabeth, were 'making hideous shouts'.[27]

The river at Parramatta is relatively narrow, no more than fifty metres across. These days the banks are lined with impenetrable mangroves but contemporaneous paintings depict an open, grassy landscape along the river, with the occasional enormous eucalypt leaning over the water—perfect cover for a sniper. Not until nearly a kilometre or so downstream, past the easternmost border of Elizabeth Farm at Duck Creek, does the river widen, allowing nervous voyagers to steer a course safely out of musket range. At least, at the tail end of the summer, the weather was mild. The journey down the river and into the Port Jackson harbour took four interminable hours. They arrived at Sydney Cove at about 3 am, to a scene of lantern-lit activity and bustle, centring on HMS *Calcutta*, which was anchored close to shore. Elizabeth wrote:

> The Town was all in arms. The Marines from the *Calcutta* disembarked & a great number of the Sailors armed. The *Calcutta* was beautifully lighted up. Most of the officers were on there & kindly received us, poor

fugitives, at the Wharf. We had determined to take up our abode at Mrs Marsden's House excusing only Mrs Williamson who went to Mrs Campbell's. To this House we & our little frightened sleepy tribe were escorted & civilities were poured in upon us from every quarter.[28]

Elizabeth's account is a polished anecdote, told and retold to her Sydney friends until all the fear and confusion had been edited out. It reads like a jolly midnight adventure—which it was only in hindsight. The convict rebels were quickly overcome by a detachment of soldiers led by Major George Johnston, recently back from England. He reported that over a dozen Irishmen were killed, and more were wounded. Johnston's list of weapons taken from the rebels provides an insight into the Irishmen's chances of success: 'twenty-six muskets, one fowling piece, four bayonets on poles, one pitchfork, one pistol, eight reaping hooks, two swords'.[29]

Elizabeth's adventure provided the perfect excuse for at least a partial thawing of her icy relationships and in her letter she makes special note of it. 'Mrs King's behaviour to us was most attentive and kind during our stay at Sydney as was also Colonel & Mrs Paterson's & most of the other inhabitants.'[30] Later that year Elizabeth would willingly dine with a party of women friends, including Anna King, Eliza Kent and Betsy Marsden, who met for a meal (without their husbands) in Sydney.[31] After escaping the uprising, Elizabeth and her children and the Marsdens remained in Sydney for several days, until 'the govt appraised us that we might return in safety to our Habitations'.[32] It was only once she was again at home that Elizabeth discovered the very real danger she and her family had faced.

The rebels had planned to light two fires in Parramatta during the course of their attack: one in the town, and the other at Elizabeth Farm, encompassing the house or at least some of the outbuildings. As was afterwards confessed, and as Elizabeth described to Captain Piper, the fire at Elizabeth Farm was designed 'to catch the attention of the Soldiery'. Elizabeth's 'lonely situation & the attachment the soldiers had to my family would induce them upon seeing the fire to repair initially to my relief' leaving the barracks an easier target. 'Thank God,' wrote Elizabeth, 'all was happily prevented.'[33]

The convict rebels were entirely right in assuming that the military would have rushed to Elizabeth's aid. Less than a year later, in January 1805, one of her outbuildings caught fire and, according to a small article at the back of the four-page *Sydney Gazette*, the soldiers on duty in Parramatta were able to save the day.

> Yesterday, between the hours of twelve and one at noon, a fire broke out on the farm of Mrs M'Arthur, at Parramatta, by which a detached kitchen was in a short time destroyed. From the direction of the wind the flame several times reached the dwelling house but was happily extinguished every time with scarce perceptible damage by the military detachment on duty at Parramatta, whose active excursions prevailed in subduing the fire and limiting its ravage to the former building which was however totally consumed.[34]

It is interesting that the newspaper describes the farm as belonging to Mrs Macarthur. In effect it did—John had been absent for more than three years at this stage and the strain was beginning to tell on Elizabeth. She had neither the workers nor, it seems, the inclination to begin rebuilding the kitchen wing and the replacement would not be finished for four years.[35]

Around this time, during the summer of 1804-05, Elizabeth Farm was the scene of another distressing and sad event. Little William would remember it for the rest of his life. In his adult reminiscences, he mentions nothing of his late night flight down the river, or the kitchen fire. But he writes at some length about the local Aboriginal people who were regular visitors at Elizabeth Farm.[36] It was not unusual for the colonists to encourage friendly Aboriginal people to camp on their land, 'to keep [away] strange blacks who might otherwise make dangerous incursions'.[37] The Aboriginal visitors to Elizabeth Farm included two friends, who were known as Harry and Bill. Related to each other and inseparable companions, both became attached to a particular young woman. She favoured Harry, however, and Bill, in his jealousy, speared Harry one night while he slept. Harry was badly wounded but he recovered; Bill fled to avoid the retributive justice of his clan and was not heard of for several months—until he turned up with a favour for Elizabeth.

'It happened,' wrote William, 'that a favourite cow of ours (cows in those days were things of great price) had been for some time missing—and Bill found her in the neighbourhood of the South Creek.' Bill knew the cow had been anxiously sought after so, still hoping to elude his clan, he came in secretly during the night to speak with 'the Missis', to tell Elizabeth the welcome news that her cow was safe. Elizabeth, even if roused from sleep, was no doubt pleased to hear it, but Bill had risked too much by bearing the message. 'His affectionate nature cost him his life,' remembered William. Bill's people found him and compelled him to a trial by ordeal: he was to have spears thrown at him by the men of his clan—including his old friend Harry. Bill chose the site, some bare clean land a few hundred yards from the house at Elizabeth Farm, and William was a wide-eyed witness to the ritual. 'He had many opponents and was at length mortally wounded by a spear thrown by Gogie, a native belonging to the Cowpasture tribe. Harry I believe, threw spears more for form's sake.'[38]

Bill was taken into one of Elizabeth's outbuildings and carefully tended by his clan until his death a few days later. Elizabeth visited every day, and her presence was greatly appreciated. William remembered that on his last day Bill said, 'Goodbye Missis, I shall never see you again.' At his own request, Bill was buried within view of the front of the Macarthurs' home, with his face turned towards the house. Harry was devastated. For a long time he 'shunned the neighbourhood and I believe to the hour of his death, never ventured near Bill's grave'.[39] It is possible that Gogie made an error, deliberate or otherwise, in fatally spearing Bill. Gogie was not from Parramatta, and may not have been clear as to the intended outcome of the ritual. If so, it was perhaps not coincidental that Gogie was himself attacked with spears a short time later, in March 1805, by Bennelong and Nanberry, men well known to the Sydney colonists.[40] A month after Gogie was attacked, two of Elizabeth's stockmen, working only thirty kilometres or so from Elizabeth Farm, were killed—reportedly by Aboriginal people.[41] A party led by former soldier Obadiah Ikins shot an Aboriginal man, Tallonn, in retribution and apparently 'killed many others' but Ikins was never charged or tried.[42] There is nothing to suggest Ikins was acting on Elizabeth's behalf and with the murderous skirmishes and vigilantism of the frontier wars now so close to home, in May 1805 Elizabeth fled Parramatta for the safest place in the colony—Government House in Sydney.

In John's absence and with the passing of time, many of the rifts in Elizabeth's social circle had been mended. Elizabeth Paterson had recently joined her husband in Van Diemen's Land, where he was establishing a new settlement on the northern coast and subsequently the relationship between Anna King and Elizabeth Macarthur seems to have rekindled. Anna, aged forty, gave birth to a daughter in February 1805, eight years after the birth of her previous child. In these circumstances Elizabeth's support and friendship would have been very welcome. In fact, Elizabeth, along with at least two of her children, stayed with the Kings at Government House for more than five weeks.[43]

Perhaps Elizabeth stayed to help while the new baby settled in. Or perhaps Elizabeth was aware that Government House was by far the best vantage point for checking the flag at South Head, the signal that a ship had been sighted. Elizabeth knew that her husband was sailing home—he was due any day. Was it mere coincidence that Governor King had recently ordered a new and taller signal staff to be erected in place of the old one?[44] During the first week of June 1805 the signal was indeed made at the South Head. Elizabeth's long wait was over.

12

The King's Merinos

Peace has succeeded ungovernable rage, and those who were before ready to annihilate each other are now as friendly in appearances as if their whole lives had been spent in the constant interchange of kind offices.
JOHN MACARTHUR TO A FRIEND IN THE COLONIAL OFFICE,
20 JULY 1805

The reunion on shore was a scene of merry chaos. Elizabeth and John, together again at last, were swept up in a whirl of introductions, unloading and high spirits. Elizabeth could finally embrace her eldest daughter who, having just turned thirteen, was very nearly a young lady. She was accompanied by a governess. Miss Penelope Lucas, aged thirty-nine, had sailed out to New South Wales to further the education of Miss Macarthur and her sister, nine-year-old Miss Mary.

John brought welcome news of their sons: Edward was almost finished at school and would sail home the following year; and John, the second son and quite the prodigy, was thriving in the academic environment of Grove Hall. Some of his mathematics workbooks remain among the Macarthur papers—perhaps his proud father brought them home to show Elizabeth.

John Macarthur, having left the colony in 1801 under the

cloud of a pending court martial, returned triumphant in a ship he part-owned, unsubtly named the *Argo*. Its figurehead was, equally unsubtly, a golden fleece. John Macarthur had brought out with him on the *Argo* two wool sorters, some skilled tradesmen and their families, a gardener and a number of servants.[1] He had also brought seedlings, plants and seeds he had collected in the course of his travels. These included several olive trees from which John, always with an eye to diversifying his income sources, planned to produce and sell oil. One of those olive trees may well be the ancient one that still grows in the garden of Elizabeth Farm.

John introduced Elizabeth to two young gentlemen: his seventeen-year-old nephew Hannibal Macarthur and twenty-year-old Walter Davidson, nephew of Sir Walter Farquhar, who was physician to the Prince of Wales. The sixth child of fourteen, and the eldest son of John's older brother, Hannibal was keen to make his way in the world—using the networks of kin to give a young man experience in another household and enterprise was a common way to round out a young man's education.[2] Walter Davidson was part of John's latest set of entrepreneurial plans. En route to England in 1801, John stopped at the Spice Islands (modern-day Indonesia), befriended a young man and played a small role in assisting his career. The young man went on to become the governor of Penang and Mauritius and his father, Sir Walter Farquhar, was suitably impressed and grateful. Upon John's eventual arrival in London Sir Walter welcomed him and his children into his home and family. His ongoing friendship would prove invaluable to John Macarthur.

While Elizabeth no doubt talked ten to the dozen with

her daughter, John proudly oversaw the unloading of a cargo both precious and rare: five Spanish rams and one ewe, sourced directly from the royal flocks at Kew. The true Spanish merino in the eighteenth and nineteenth centuries was the result of hundreds of years of careful breeding and market control. The dry, harsh climate of Spain (and earlier, of North Africa) had led to the selection of an animal able to thrive in those conditions but not in wet and cold England. Much smaller than a modern Australian merino, a fully grown ram then weighed as little as forty-five kilograms and produced a fleece of up to two kilograms. By way of contrast, a twenty-first-century Peppin merino ram can produce up to eighteen kilograms of wool per year.[3] But the Spanish merino's wool, even then, was the finest in the world and the Spanish were careful to guard it. Since the medieval period, Spain had prohibited the export of its sheep and as a result had created the greatest textile monopoly ever seen in world trade.[4]

Over time, though, Spain's monopoly became unenforceable and throughout the eighteenth century, merinos were smuggled out by entrepreneurs or presented as gifts by monarchs seeking political favours. By the end of the eighteenth century, Britain was desperate to secure a wool supply for the country's booming textile manufacturing sector, particularly with the ongoing demand for military uniforms in this period of perpetual wars. Unfortunately though, much of the famous English broadcloth was woven from Spanish wool. Enemy wool. So the promise of wool from the colonies was an opportunity keenly eyed by the manufacturers, despite the extra costs of transport.[5]

Joseph Banks had been given some merinos in 1785 and 1788, by his scientific peers in France. Then, via an elaborate smuggling operation across the Portuguese border undertaken on behalf of King George III, Banks obtained fourteen Spanish rams and seventy-three ewes, all destined for the king's Kew estate.[6] By August 1804, under Banks' careful supervision, the king's flock had grown to the point where a public sale of surplus sheep was held.[7] This was where John Macarthur stepped in—and up.

John's trial for shooting Colonel Paterson had come to nothing, though all the parties, including Governor King, were censured. This affected King's career but not Macarthur's, and John seized the opportunity while in England to sell his military commission. Macarthur did not originally sail to England with a view to selling his fleeces, but he took advantage of the circumstances when approached by manufacturers keen for a new, secure source of wool. He happily promised them the world. In July 1803, he published *Statement of the Improvement and Progress of the Breed of Fine Woolled Sheep in New South Wales*, in which he claimed that within twenty years New South Wales would replace Spain as England's source of fine wool. By the time he left England, John was, according to himself, virtually the sole facilitator and instigator of wool production in the colony, with the initiatives of any other men (or women) conveniently overlooked. Joseph Banks dismissed Macarthur's published statement as 'mere theoretical Speculation', and in 1804 he tried to dissuade John Macarthur from purchasing any sheep at the king's auction, publicly pointing out that exporting the animals was illegal.[8] Yet John Macarthur was the biggest buyer at the sale, spending £150 to buy himself seven rams and three ewes.

In typical fashion, John had acted first and sorted out the details later. In the following months he obtained from Lord Camden, secretary of state for war and colonies, nothing less than the keys to the kingdom: a treasury warrant permitting export of his latest ovine purchases.[9] Gaining access through his new friend Sir Walter Farquhar, John convinced the government that New South Wales could become a crucial source of prime fleece and that he, John Macarthur, was the man to lead the way. So it was that many months and a lengthy sea voyage later, John presented Elizabeth with half a dozen precious sheep as she stood on the shores of Sydney Cove. The sheep, however, were not John's best surprise.

He carefully unfolded a letter and showed it to Elizabeth: it was from Lord Camden to Governor King granting John Macarthur 5000 acres (2000 hectares) of the best land yet discovered by the colonists, with the promise of 5000 more.[10] It was by far the largest grant ever made in the colony[11] and its prime location in the Cow Pastures region was no lucky coincidence—John had written in 1803 to his former colleague Lieutenant Waterhouse, the man who had imported the first merinos to Sydney, asking how his sheep had fared in that area. Waterhouse replied very much in the affirmative[12] and John obviously pressed his claims to Lord Camden all the more firmly. Under the terms of the grant, the Macarthurs were to be allocated no fewer than thirty convicts, who they were to feed and keep at their own expense, thus saving the government the cost of their keep, an innovation long pushed for by John. Walter Davidson, Sir Walter Farquhar's nephew, was also to have a grant of 2000 acres (800 hectares), adjacent to the Macarthurs' new estate.[13]

Lord Camden noted the 'pains which had been taken by John Macarthur Esquire in increasing and improving the breed of sheep in New South Wales', and pointedly warned Governor King that 'His Majesty's Government takes a particular interest in forwarding the objects of this letter. I am therefore persuaded you will do everything in your power to promote its success…'[14]

King took the hint. 'Such a communication was not to be disregarded by me,' wrote King in a private letter to Joseph Banks, and indeed it was not—the Macarthurs now really did have friends in high places. King continued 'and whether right or wrong, the noble advisor's motives were of so honourable and public-spirited a nature, that I offered McA my hand who gratefully received it.'[15] Despite their previous enmity, Governor King and John Macarthur managed to bury the hatchet, if only in a shallow grave. And John, having won the day, was prepared to be magnanimous in victory. 'I am happy to say,' wrote John to Captain Piper, 'that not a trace of former misunderstanding is now discoverable. Indeed, the Governor is uncommonly kind and obliging.'[16] John Macarthur was not immune to the irony of his new-found armistice with the governor. In a letter to one of his new friends in England, the under-secretary of the colonial office, John wrote that Camden's letter 'operated like a necromantick spell, and lulled every angry passion to sleep'.[17]

So, by the time Elizabeth met him on shore back in Sydney, John had gained an important friend, avoided sanction for duelling with his commanding officer, sold his military commission, convinced the British government that the future of New South Wales rested with him, and wangled the purchase of the rare and prized Spanish merinos. There is luck here, certainly, but also a canny ability to spot an opportunity and to capitalise upon it. The *Argo* was unloaded and refitted to commence whaling in the South Seas. Even now the Macarthurs were careful to spread their risk, and procure income from multiple sources.

After the reunion and introductions, John and Elizabeth Macarthur, Hannibal and Walter, and all their new retainers drove the last weary miles to Parramatta. They arrived home late, long after little William was in bed. William, as an old man, explained to his niece that his usual bedfellow was his sister Mary but on this night his returning eldest sister Elizabeth slipped in beside him. The sleepy boy woke in confusion, thinking Mary was home, and Elizabeth comforted him with kisses and kind words. William was astonished—that was not like Mary at all. Elizabeth kept speaking but William remained confused. 'The voice is the voice of Mary,' four-year-old William observed at the time, 'but the tallness is not the tallness of Mary.' Presumably William solved the mystery by morning but by then another problem had presented itself to him. A tall man much marked by smallpox had arrived in the house and he was told this unfamiliar man was his father. William was not impressed. 'You are so ugly,' he said to John. 'I don't like you.' Happily, John must have persevered to win his son over because during the course of the day William was able to tell him 'I like you better now'.[18]

If John was bemused by his youngest son, he was dismayed to find that his colonial sheep were not plentiful as he had expected. In this his naked ambition is obvious: by 1805 there were some 20,000 sheep in the colony, of which almost a quarter belonged to John and Elizabeth.[19] John may well have asked some pointed questions, but Elizabeth soon set him straight: without enough working men and shepherds to take care of the flocks, she had been forced to cull.[20] John complained to Governor King about the lack of convict labour, and King almost immediately doubled the number assigned to the Macarthur estates, meeting Camden's request. Those extra workers Elizabeth had needed so badly were signed over to her husband as easy as kiss my hand. Though happy to receive them, it would only be human for Elizabeth to have felt a little sour about it all.

John now began negotiating the location of his new 2000-hectare land grant. Although King was bound to ratify it, the governor delayed as long as he could. The government had more than a thousand head of cattle grazing in the desirable Cow Pastures region, and King feared Macarthur would find some clever way to take possession of them. It is easy to imagine that King's cattle problem could have been simply solved by relocating the livestock. But without fenced paddocks, there was little to stop the cattle making their way back to the prime grazing land. King asked Macarthur to look for land elsewhere.

John for once did as he was asked. He rode over much of the country to the southwest of the Sydney settlement but apparently could find no pasture that was not too wet for sheep. The Cow Pastures area remained ideal, and Macarthur's determination to acquire the land was relentless. If Elizabeth played a role in the negotiations, it was only as a publicly silent, supportive partner. By October, King finally allowed John to take the land. Shortly afterwards John Macarthur proposed to catch and tame the government's surplus bulls—if only he could have the labour of twenty men (victualled at the crown's expense) and if he could keep one-third of the captured bulls for himself. King managed to hold his temper and politely declined.[21]

In December 1805, the Macarthurs paused in their expansionary activities to welcome some unusual visitors. Maori chief Te Pahi and his four sons were visiting Sydney from New Zealand and staying with the Kings at Government House for three months. The visitors travelled upriver to Parramatta, where the *Sydney Gazette* reported they were 'very hospitably received' by the Macarthurs. Chief Te Pahi and his sons were particularly impressed to see the processes of cloth and wool manufacture at the female factory in Parramatta. Elizabeth was well accustomed to hosting guests and although she'd never dined with tattooed Maori warriors before, she likely took it all in her stride. The chief and his sons, diplomatic visitors in a strange land, were hardly going to pose more of social challenge than a celebratory meal at the barracks' mess, full of drunken officers. The New Zealanders stayed with the Macarthurs for 'three days in a manner highly gratifying', before returning to stay with the Kings.[22]

Born and raised beside the docks at Plymouth, John was exposed from an early age to sailors, travellers and ideas from all parts of the globe. But it speaks well of Elizabeth, given her comparatively sheltered upbringing in Bridgerule, that she too was willing to engage with a wide variety of people. Since the arrival of the First Fleet nearly eighteen years earlier, the colony had been home to individuals from around the globe. Elizabeth's household reflected the cultural diversity of Sydney Town. There is a rumour, for example, that the first Chinese man to live in New South Wales was engaged as a gardener by the Macarthurs.[23] As well, a Tahitian youth known as Jem lived with the Macarthurs for some time, and often visited the Reverend Marsden's house. Marsden was, a decade or so later, astonished to come across Jem in New Zealand, married to a Maori chief's daughter.[24] In 1806 the Macarthurs, who were Anglicans, engaged a Royalist French Catholic tutor for William and James: Gabriel-Louis-Marie Huon, the Chevalier de Kerillieu. Huon de Kerillieu was, until this appointment, a mere private in the New South Wales Corps but he was a regular visitor to Government House and some claimed he was a member of the French royal family.[25] For the next three years Huon de Kerillieu instilled in the youngest Macarthur boys the basis of a classical education, a firm understanding of the French language and a life-long respect for the Catholic faith.[26] The Macarthur girls remained under the tutelage of their governess, Penelope Lucas. Their education focused on the biblical, rather than the classical, but in later life the girls were described as 'well educated' and 'kind'.[27] The Macarthurs, like many other settler families, apparently also took an Aboriginal teen, called Tjedboro, into their household. Elizabeth's youngest son William would write about him, many years later. Tjedboro's presence in the Macarthur household is remarkable mainly because of the boy's father: Pemulwuy.

Pemulwuy was an Aboriginal warrior and cleverman, a Bediagal man from the Botany Bay area.[28] It was he who had fatally speared Governor Phillip's gamekeeper, McIntyre. From 1792 Pemulwuy led intermittent raids on settlers at Prospect, Toongabbie, Georges River, Parramatta, Brickfield Hill and the Hawkesbury River. Civilian administrator David Collins thought him 'a most active enemy to the settlers, plundering them of their property, and endangering their personal safety'.[29] In 1797 Pemulwuy organised a force of more than a hundred warriors and raided farms in the Parramatta district.[30] There is no record of Elizabeth Farm being directly attacked. Pemulwuy was shot in 1802 and Governor King—who supposedly held Pemulwuy in some esteem—sent his pickled head to Joseph Banks in England.[31] It seems that Pemulwuy simply began dispensing justice according to Aboriginal law. Governor Arthur Phillip, and his predecessors, were also implementing justice, according to British law. [32] The intersection between belief systems was an unbridgeable cataract, with the waters further muddied by those from both sides who disobeyed their own laws. It is also possible Pemulwuy was a father-figure to Tjedboro, rather than his actual father.

But fatherless or not, Tjedboro (or Tedbury, as he was also called) caused some trouble; the records contain hints of raided farms. According the *Sydney Gazette* of 4 August 1805, Tjedboro was locked up in gaol and given his liberty only after his Aboriginal friends pleaded for his release and vouched for his future good behaviour. It seems that soon after this, John Macarthur took Tjedboro 'in hand to reclaim him'. Elizabeth yet again welcomed a stranger into her home and treated the youth with kindness—perhaps she believed the charges against him to be false or perhaps, with four boys of her own, she simply found it easy to take in one more. Tjedboro was, initially, 'quite happy and docile', but the novelty of living with the Macarthur family soon palled and within a few weeks he 'took to the woods' and was not seen for several months.[33]

Tjedboro did come back to Elizabeth Farm for visits, coming and going as he pleased. He was taught to call John 'Master' although, as William happily admits, Tjedboro never participated in any activities which the family might have called work. 'He used to say he should "like to be as white man" that is civilized that he might be a gentleman; but then the idea of being controlled he could not endure.' With the two eldest Macarthur sons away in England, Tjedboro (with Elizabeth's tacit approval) seems to have taken the role of an older brother, with William noting he 'has often chidden and restrained me in some of my boyish pranks'. However, the ugly assumptions of race were never far from the surface. William goes on to write: 'No being could be more devotedly attached to another than this poor savage was to us.'[34] William was right about Tjedboro's loyalty—in 1808, during the immediate aftermath of the rebellion against Bligh, Tjedboro arrived one evening at Elizabeth Farm armed to the teeth and prepared, he said, to spear the governor in order to protect John. Tjedboro's services were not, as it happened, required, and 'he was given a meal, shown a corner to sleep and advised to go home in the morning with thanks for his goodwill'.[35] Two years later Tjedboro was shot and killed by white settlers.[36]

On 16 January 1806—the day of nephew Hannibal Macarthur's eighteenth birthday—the Macarthurs were finally granted their land along the Nepean River at Cow Pastures. King made certain stipulations limiting the length of river frontage for the grant but John slipped around these by taking his land in two parts, with Walter Davidson's grant in between.[37] It was, according to one historian, 'a fine piece of geometric jobbery'.[38]

From the very beginning Walter Davidson gave John the free use of his property, receiving from the Macarthurs an agreed share of the estates' earnings. Decades later, after Davidson had long left the colony, the Macarthurs bought him out.[39]

If January was a time of celebration for the Macarthurs, it was tempered by the foul weather of February and March. A wet summer resulted in terrible flooding and in late March 1806 the Hawkesbury River burst its banks. Families were rescued from rooftops and rafts of floating debris. Trees and animals were washed away. Elizabeth and her family were safe: the Hawkesbury flows along a convoluted path well to the north and east of Parramatta. The settlements along the river were largely populated by convicts, ex-convicts and small-scale farmers growing hogs, wheat and corn and producing sly grog. The floods destroyed the farms and reduced farm families to sodden poverty. Over 85,000 bushels of grain and 4000 head of stock, mostly pigs, were lost leaving little seed for new crops and soon rendering the whole colony desperately short of bread, meat and home-brewed alcohol.[40] The Parramatta River did not flood, and the officer farmers along its banks were soon benefitting from soaring grain and livestock prices. In a letter to Captain Piper, John Macarthur described the floods as 'a calamity that threatens the very existence of the colony' and he and Elizabeth feared that many families would be ruined.[41] He blamed Governor King for lacking the foresight to secure the colony's grain supplies. The Hawkesbury settlers blamed, and envied, the wealthy farmers who profited from their misfortune. It certainly wasn't the first time the officers had done so.

In the first years of the colony the regimental officers regularly purchased the whole cargo of visiting ships, to prevent the ships' captains from profiteering. Unfortunately, the officers quickly turned to profiteering themselves, keeping the best of the cargo and selling the rest. Any emancipist who complained faced retribution from the troops. In time, some of the officers also drew goods from the public stores, and sold those for a private profit too. The officers also initially obtained a monopoly over the sale of all imported spirits. They did not usually sell the spirits themselves, but used agents to sell the liquor on their behalf. In the absence of hard currency, by 1795 rum became the standard unit of exchange. Even labour could only be purchased with sprits. It was a practice that resulted in immense profits flowing to the officers of the New South Wales Corps. Although there is no direct evidence to involve Captain John Macarthur, the circumstantial evidence is clear.[42] Elizabeth apparently turned a blind eye, but, to be fair, the dubious entrepreneurial activities of the officers in New South Wales were commonplace in English colonies around the world. Elizabeth is not likely to have tried to dissuade her husband from taking part, given the very real benefits that flowed to her family. The profiteering continued for several years, although the officers' initial very lucrative trade diminished as other entrepreneurial folk invited themselves to the party.

Now, with the floods ensuring that the colony was once again at the edge of ruin, the emancipists and small-scale farmers were beginning to speak up and complain. Governor King, who like his predecessor Hunter had failed to halt the illegal rum trade or to substantially reduce the colony's expenses, was recalled to England. The arrival of the new governor, Captain William

Bligh, was daily expected. Bligh was well known as an excellent sailor and navigator. But he seems to have been one of those men who found technical skills easy and the effective management of people very hard. And this was the man appointed to oversee a colony which, in the aftermath of the floods, seethed with rancour and heat.

John's safe return to New South Wales had relieved an anxious Elizabeth of many of her cares. Maybe she even relaxed, for a time, enjoying the company of her daughters and their new governess. But John was a man who could not step back from an argument, who thrived on controversy and debate. If Elizabeth could not prevent him starting a fight, she certainly couldn't stop him from finishing it. The relationship between the poorer settlers, most of them ex-convicts, and the New South Wales Corps was never going to be cordial. The gaoled cannot love his gaoler. Tensions had simmered between the two groups for a long time and looked set to boil over. The *Bounty* was Bligh's first mutiny, but it would not be his last. There was trouble to come—and Elizabeth's husband would be at the heart of it.

13

Malignant Falsehoods

*[Bligh] has already shown the inhabitants of Sydney that he is violent,
rash, tyrannical. No very pleasing prospect at the beginning of his reign.*

ELIZABETH MACARTHUR TO ELIZA KINGDON, 29 JANUARY 1807

In early August 1806, William Bligh arrived in New South Wales
aboard the *Porpoise*. Also on board was Edward Macarthur,
the eldest of Elizabeth's sons, having finished his schooling in
England. John Macarthur may have hoped his son used the
opportunity to forge a diplomatic alliance with the new governor
but no such relationship had developed. With Bligh came news
of the outside world or, more particularly, of the English world.
To many it was much the same thing. Elizabeth, along with the
rest of the colony, learnt of the glorious death of Lord Nelson.
Ten months previously, in October 1805, he had destroyed
the French and Spanish fleets, but was killed in action. 'These
particulars we have' the *Sydney Gazette* noted 'collected from the
various details given in the London papers; and are therefore
to be depended on.'[1]

William Bligh was officially sworn in on 13 August

1806—John Macarthur's birthday. The ladies weren't present at the official ceremonies, but Elizabeth's social circle was joined by Bligh's daughter, Mrs Mary Putland. Mary's husband served both as Bligh's aide-de-camp and one of *Porpoise's* officers. The men of the Sydney Loyal Association (a volunteer militia company) and the New South Wales Corps all turned out and Bligh was presented with an address of welcome, signed by Johnston for the military, Atkins for the civil authorities and by John Macarthur for the free inhabitants.[2] However the majority of free inhabitants, those emancipists from the flooded Hawkesbury, were horrified to be represented by Macarthur.

They promptly wrote to the new governor, pointing out that John Macarthur had taken a liberty they bitterly resented; he was not their representative; and if they had deputed anyone John Macarthur was the last man to be chosen as they considered him 'an unfit person to step forward' and attributed 'the rise in the price of mutton to his with-holding the large flock of wethers he now has to make such price as he may choose to demand'.[3] It is unlikely that Bligh took much notice of their complaint. He and former governor King swiftly made a series of land grants to each other, all illegal, but by the standards of the day not unusual. One of the properties, granted to Mrs King, was given the name 'Thanks'.[4]

It was surely a happy time for Elizabeth Macarthur, with five of her six children back under her own roof (son John remained at school in England). It wasn't a large roof however, and it now had to accommodate John's nephew Hannibal and family friend Walter Davidson, as well as the seven Macarthurs. The cottage at Elizabeth Farm had grown very little, if at all, from the four humble rooms first erected in 1793, and the expanded family made for a lively household. It was a time for readjustment and compromise. Elizabeth was no longer in charge, and while she might have been grateful to hand over the worries, it was perhaps difficult to submit gracefully to the authority of her husband. The added presence of Hannibal and now Edward did little to make things easier.

Edward Macarthur didn't warm to farming life and he was not as 'strong in constitution' as his mother could wish.[5] His father attempted to teach him about running the farm but—according to William, many years later—young Edward was often heard to remark upon how 'distasteful' he found it all.

It is unlikely he said so within his father's hearing. John was, after all, a former army officer and 'the tones of command' came naturally to him.[6] As an adult Edward would write letters to his father that verged on the obsequious. Even when John Macarthur was an old man, unwell and in his bed, William only disagreed with him 'as much as I dared.'[7] James Macarthur found his father a delightful companion, albeit only when he was 'in his happier moods'.[8] Yet the boys' love and respect for their father also shines very clearly. Edward would soon, for example, write a letter in which he hoped that his father would 'enjoy health and happiness with every other blessing which ought to befall so good a Father.'[9] This was Elizabeth's gift to her children, to be the peacekeeper and mediator who, to the extent possible, ensured the household remained harmonious. The children revered and feared their father, but they were able to take the love and consistency of their mother for granted.

At first the Macarthurs welcomed the new governor and his

daughter. In October 1806, Bligh toured Parramatta and the Cow Pastures district. In honour of the visit the Macarthurs threw a 'splendid entertainment' for a 'large party of Officers and Ladies'.[10] John broached the subject of government support for a fine wool industry and further Macarthur land grants on the Cow Pastures lands, but Bligh was having none of it. The friendly visitor rapidly turned nasty. 'What have I to do with your sheep, sir?' shouted Bligh. 'What have I to do with your cattle? Are you to have such flocks of sheep and herds of cattle as no man ever heard of before? No, sir, I have heard your concerns, sir. You have got five thousand acres of land, sir, in the finest situation in the country but by God you shan't keep it!'[11] This is John Macarthur's account. Bligh, questioned later, had no memory of it. But clearly he had said something to put the Macarthurs offside. Within two months Elizabeth was writing home to England about Bligh, saying he 'has already shown the inhabitants of Sydney that he is violent, rash, tyrannical. No very pleasing prospect at the beginning of his reign.'[12] She recognised that Bligh would be an obstacle to her ambitions for the family, and she was right. As Bligh wrote in his letters, he considered that with the colony's food shortages, the immediate advantages of growing cattle for meat far outweighed any future benefits of growing sheep for wool. He was certainly not inclined to offer government assistance to build the Macarthur empire. In fact, he brought about several changes which angered the officer class.

Almost immediately, Bligh regulated the importation of wine and spirits, bringing it back into government administration and so out of private hands. He required that all transactions in the colony were made in hard currency and he strictly controlled the allocation of Crown land, food and livestock. He put limits on the use of convict labour by settlers. No one was to be arrested without a warrant, and suspects could no longer be tortured in order to obtain a confession. The poor were fed from government stores and smaller farmers were supported and encouraged. One of those farmers was Scotsman John Turnbull. So grateful was he to Governor Bligh that he gave his newborn son the middle name of Bligh. Every eldest son has since also carried that name, including Australia's twenty-ninth prime minister, Malcolm Bligh Turnbull. The officer class found themselves embarrassed, frustrated and incriminated at every turn.[13]

And yet the Macarthurs and Bligh maintained a cordial relationship, at least on the face of it. John regularly dined at Government House, and Bligh was apologetic that there was no spare bed at his Sydney house to accommodate Macarthur family members when they visited town.[14] Perhaps, then, Bligh was invited to the party held by John and Elizabeth a week or so before Christmas 1806. According to a somewhat overwrought piece in the *Sydney Gazette*:

> A select party of ladies and gentleman, twenty-one in number exclusive of attendants, made an aquatic excursion from Parramatta to Captain McArthur's estate in Cockle Bay, being highly favoured by the uninterrupted serenity of a salubrious atmosphere and after examining with inexpressible satisfaction the picturesque beauties which that romantic scene afforded, a handsome collation ushered in the evening's festivity beneath the shelter of a spreading fig tree, whose waving foliage whispered to refreshing breezes.[15]

At this party the Macarthur's new estate was officially named Pyrmont; the native beauty of the place was duly admired; and at five in the afternoon the company took their leave, being 'much gratified with the rational festivities of the day'.

In February 1807 the Kings finally left the colony and, on the same ship, so did the Reverend and Betsy Marsden. The Marsdens were planning to sort out some family business in England before returning once more, but Betsy privately hoped they might never come back. Her husband had other ideas and his baggage contained samples of his own Merino-cross wool. In England he had the wool spun, woven and made into a suit which he wore when he was presented to King George III. The king was so impressed that he asked for a suit of his own and, after the gift was duly made up and delivered, he presented Reverend Marsden with a ram and four ewes from his Spanish flock. The Marsdens returned to Sydney with the sheep in 1810 and for a brief period surpassed even the Macarthurs in fine wool production.

Elizabeth likely attended the farewell dinner party held aboard the *Buffalo* the night before the Kings and Marsdens sailed, and the next day John and Edward Macarthur were among those on small craft accompanying the ship through the heads of Sydney Harbour and out into the ocean beyond. Perhaps Elizabeth was there too. As a squall approached, the boats retreated and Mrs King wrote later in her diary that she felt the parting very much.[16] Elizabeth, too, farewelled several friends all at once. No wonder then, that in a letter to her goddaughter in Bridgerule she wrote that 'I have great hopes of again being permitted to see "Old England". Mr Macarthur has promised I shall go in a year or two, whether he can or cannot accompany me.'[17] John is painted as the decision-maker here, albeit a decision-maker at pains to please his wife, but Elizabeth is also providing excuses for failing to return to Bridgerule. If the decision were her husband's, she could not be held responsible for the subsequent disappointment of her family and friends. But now and into the future Elizabeth was more than capable of making and contributing to important decisions, and it seems likely she had more say in the matter than she was prepared to state in writing.

Just a few months later, though, all thoughts of travel were forgotten. In May 1807 the Macarthurs' eldest daughter, Elizabeth, just turned fifteen, fell gravely ill.[18] Letters imply that she lost the use of her legs, which suggests polio and if the disease followed its typical progress, young Elizabeth would first have suffered fever, pain and vomiting. Elizabeth was by now intimately familiar with the sick room. Her first experience of nursing may have occurred aboard the *Scarborough* when John and baby Edward were so unwell but, as mother to eight children so far, it certainly would not have been her last. At the beginning of her daughter's illness, Elizabeth may not have been particularly concerned. Cool flannels and tepid baths for the fever, and perhaps some tisanes prescribed by the doctor.

But the next stages of polio were far more terrifying—increasingly severe muscle aches, loose and floppy limbs often worse on one side of the body.[19] It was any mother's idea of hell, but at least Elizabeth had some support. Penelope Lucas, the nominal governess and Elizabeth's friend, was there to help, and daughter Mary, now going on twelve, was old enough to assist too. But there was little anyone could do except to keep young Elizabeth comfortable and coax her to drink and eat. Months passed, and Elizabeth watched her daughter fail to improve. She also watched her husband's behaviour grow increasingly erratic.

John channelled his nervous energies into initiating or contesting an escalating series of civil suits and litigation. In one instance he tried to enforce payment of a promissory note where the value was set in bushels of grain. The note had been written before the Hawkesbury floods caused grain prices to skyrocket and the debtor was unwilling to now pay what amounted to ten times more than the original note was worth. Macarthur sued, lost in the lower court and took it to Bligh in the court of appeal. In July 1807 Bligh ruled firmly against John, further salting the wound by awarding the original debtor £5 in costs. In October there was more trouble when Bligh insisted that a copper boiler—part of an alcohol still that had never been assembled—be seized from John Macarthur, without a warrant. Macarthur was furious at Bligh's appropriation of his private property and contested the seizure. This case was decided in Macarthur's favour. By now Macarthur and Bligh had more or less declared war.

Governor Bligh, meanwhile, determined to lay the foundations of a proper city at Sydney Cove and proceeded to regularise the township's haphazard leasehold arrangements. However his implementation of the new policies was cackhanded and impolitic. Most Sydney dwellings sat on Crown land. Officers and civil servants held fourteen-year leases but few of the lower orders had any sort of formal arrangements. Most people simply presumed they owned the land on which their modest homes stood. So they were shocked when Bligh decreed that all buildings on informally occupied allotments had to be pulled down. Convict chain gangs began to demolish buildings on Crown land, and the Sydney community was appalled. Formal lease-holders were also affected. John Macarthur had a vacant acre block in Sydney, which under the new regime was deemed to belong to the new St Phillips Church. Other targeted lease-holders included John's comrades and brothers-in-arms. Bligh was attempting to reinstate Governor Phillip's original agrarian vision (that all the land surrounding Sydney Cove remain Crown land) without seeming to realise that even Phillip himself had abandoned it. [20]

Throughout the conflict, peacemaker Elizabeth continued to keep up appearances. She visited the governor at his Parramatta residence and apologised for her husband's absence, saying he was unwell and in bed. Bligh immediately offered to visit John, although whether the visit was planned in a spirit of kindness or vindictiveness, it is hard to say. The following day Bligh arrived at Elizabeth Farm, just in time to meet John riding in from the paddocks. The governor expressed surprise at John's recovery. Perhaps in receipt of some meaningful looks from Elizabeth, John parried lamely, explaining that it was his first outing since his illness. Governor Bligh was unimpressed and his relationship with John soured even further.

Bligh's threat to demolish houses was triggering great concern. When the chief commissary clerk went to the governor in person in order to save his house, Bligh met him on the doorstep of Government House and shouted at him. The clerk pleaded that the house was worth £600 and that under English law he was entitled to possession. At this point Bligh really did lose his temper. 'Damn your laws of England! Don't talk to me of your laws of England! I will make the laws of this Colony and every wretch of you, son of a bitch, shall be governed by them; or there—' Bligh pointed towards the gaol— 'there shall be your habitation.' The clerk bowed, wished Bligh good day and departed. He went to his immediate supervisors with the warning that the people of Sydney were in great fright, worried that their home would be next to go, and that unless steps were taken to conciliate them 'a revolution, in my opinion, would shortly happen'.[21] Significantly, at least half of the rank and file members of the New South Wales Corps held property of their own, many of them on land Bligh claimed was reserved by the government. Sergeant-Major Thomas Whittle was one, and he later alleged that Bligh told him 'I will have the house down again by 10 o'clock and you shall neither take bricks, nor anything else away, but it shall be mine, house, and ground, and all'.[22] Inevitably, tensions rose and Whittle's friends and colleagues in uniform began to mutter among themselves.

Meanwhile, John Macarthur was in court again. Several convicts had escaped the colony in ships part-owned by the Macarthurs. Three had left mid-year in the *Argo* and later in the year another fled to Tahiti in the *Parramatta*. Such escapes were common as many sailing masters failed to resist the temptation of an extra crewman, particularly one accompanied by a juicy bribe. But the ships' owners were liable to pay a bond to the naval officer (effectively a fine) worth almost as much as the ship itself. And when the naval officer placed armed constables on board the *Parramatta* to prevent any of its cargo from being landed, John and his co-owner lodged an appeal in the court presided over by Governor Bligh. Macarthur, in a move of dubious legality, sacked the *Parramatta*'s captain and crew, noting that the naval officer had effectively repossessed the ship and in consequence he, John, had abandoned it.[23] As far as he was concerned, the crew were now in the naval officer's hands and he would not submit 'to the expense of paying and victualling of the officers and crew of a vessel over which [he] had no control'.[24]

Judge-Advocate Atkins wrote formally to John Macarthur, requesting his 'attendance at Sydney to-morrow morning, at 10 o'clock to show cause for such [of] your conduct'.[25] The letter was delivered to Elizabeth Farm by Francis Oakes, the head constable at Parramatta. John sent Oakes back with a carefully worded response, declining Atkin's request and referring him to the naval officer. The next evening, 15 December 1807, a nervous Oakes returned to Elizabeth Farm with a warrant for the arrest of John Macarthur. Oakes arrived at about 11 pm, and the family were preparing for bed, but John invited him into the parlour, mixed him a glass of grog and sat him down while he read the warrant. Oakes was right to be nervous and would later testify that John reacted 'very violently'.[26] No one in the house was sleeping now. A furious John ordered his nephew Hannibal to make a copy of the warrant. Son Edward was sent to fetch Lieutenant Bayley, who lived close by. All the while John continued to rant at Oakes. Eventually he collected himself enough to write a note, the contents of which he surely discussed with Elizabeth as he wrote, and which Oakes was to take back to Atkins.

> Mr Oakes, you will inform the persons who sent you here
> with the warrant you have now shewn me, and given me

a copy of, that I never will submit to the horrid tyranny that is attempted until I am forced; that I consider it with scorn and contempt, as I do the person who have directed it to be executed.[27]

A weary (albeit possibly relieved) Oakes was then dispatched on a midnight ride back to Sydney.

Elizabeth knew better than to try to dissuade her husband from sending the inflammatory message, but she, as ever, did what she could to minimise the damage. Oakes had not gone far before he was waylaid in the moonlight by Edward Macarthur, who quietly asked that Oakes hand back the note. Oakes refused. That note was his reason, or excuse, for failing to bring John Macarthur into custody and he needed to keep it. Oakes continued his journey back to Sydney. Edward, at almost nineteen, was very unlikely to have been a willing instigator of this course of action. Like all the Macarthur boys, he worshipped his father but never stood up to him. Hannibal, only a year older than Edward, was equally unlikely to be the mastermind. Perhaps the bold suggestion came from Lieutenant Bayley, but he would have been a brave man indeed to thwart John Macarthur in such a way. No. The most likely source is Elizabeth Macarthur, once more trying to mitigate her husband's wilder misjudgments. But we have to imagine it: a hushed yet heated conversation with Edward to send him flying out after Oakes and then a vain attempt to placate and soothe John, who soon saddled up and rode down to Sydney anyway, not far behind Oakes. By midmorning John was arrested, bailed for £1000 by his friends in town and preparing to face the magistrates who in their wisdom had decided that 'Mr Macarthur stands committed for criminal court'.[28] His trial, however, was delayed for more than a month.

No one could envy Elizabeth Macarthur. Her daughter was still bedridden and the consensus was that the girl stood little or no chance of recovery. Her husband was set to stand trial for charges unspecified. The seizure of the *Parramatta* had lost the family potential profits of thousands of pounds, and Bligh's regulation of the rum trade had likely lost them thousands more. Their leasehold in Sydney looked like being revoked without compensation. And now, at the age of forty-one, Elizabeth made the bittersweet discovery that she was pregnant again. It was seven years since her last child, William, was born and this new baby was due in the middle of 1808. Elizabeth did what she always did in the face of the seemingly impossible: she carried on.

In early January 1808 Elizabeth moved into the Sydney home of her friends Captain and Mrs Abbott, ostensibly to provide her invalid daughter with a change of air but probably also to keep a close eye on John. The Abbotts remained at their Parramatta residence. Throughout January, Macarthur and Bligh locked horns over the disputed Sydney leasehold. It had been granted by former Governor King in a very hasty manner, alleged Bligh, signed as the ship Bligh originally arrived on was sighted and backdated to 1 January 1806. Bligh was silent, however, about the 600 acre (240 hectare) grant made over by King at the same time to his daughter.[29] No one had clean hands. Bligh ordered John not to build anything on his leasehold until he, Bligh, had received instructions from England. Furthermore Bligh stated that he would 'not receive any letters on the subject'.[30] John responded by engaging a team of off-duty soldiers to build a fence around the land in question. Bligh sent armed constables to pull it down again. The whole township was watching, agog, and Elizabeth was watching too, more discreetly but possibly with greater concern. But there was more to come. The criminal court would assemble on 25 January to try John Macarthur, although on precisely what charges nobody seemed to know.

During the days before the trial, a flurry of letters passed between John and the relevant officials, as John tried to determine his alleged crimes. Their answers seemed to encompass almost everything: the importation of illegal stills; libellous words aimed at bringing the governor into the disrespect, hatred and contempt of the people; causing the crew of the *Parramatta* to come on shore in an illegal manner; and disobeying Atkins' warrant. It was rapidly becoming clear to everyone that whatever the legal niceties, Governor Bligh was determined to make an example of John Macarthur.

The evening before the trial, on Sunday 24 January, was a night of celebration. It was twenty years since the founding of the colony and Major Johnston, the Corps' commander in Sydney and himself a First Fleet arrival, had been granted the governor's permission to mark the occasion. The meal was an all-male affair, something for which Elizabeth was most likely grateful. The regimental fife band played and the wine flowed freely; by the end of the night the men were dancing drunkenly with one another. All of the officers currently in Sydney attended, although the corps' commanding officer Lieutenant-Governor Colonel Paterson was absent, overseeing the new settlements in Van Diemen's Land. Several civilians were also in attendance, including the men who had stood bail for John Macarthur together with other men who would sit in judgment upon him the next day. Edward and Hannibal Macarthur were also there—no doubt pleased to be counted among the ranks of men—but John Macarthur was not. He spent the evening listening to the music wafting from the barracks and walking back and forth 'in the most conspicuous part of the town where I must have been seen by hundreds and particularly by every person at Government House'.[31] He was rehearsing his speeches for the next day's trial. If Elizabeth knew what he planned to say, she might have worried even more.

When the court sat at 10 am the scene was more circus then circumspect. Men had ridden for miles to see the show. The courtroom was full to bursting and those who could not find a space inside gathered nearby. Elizabeth was probably not there. She was needed at home, and the courtroom was no place for a lady. Perhaps Edward and Hannibal ran back and forth to provide her with updates or perhaps she remained on tenterhooks until her prayers were answered and her husband walked in the door that afternoon.

John was able to tell her that he had made the speech of his life, decrying Judge-Advocate Atkins' ability to sit in judgment on him given Atkins' (and by implication Bligh's) prejudice against him. John's speech spared nothing in the detail and the many onlookers were variously shocked and hugely entertained by what he had to say about Atkins' 'malignant falsehoods', his 'vindictive malice', and his 'false imprisonment of me'. At the end of it Atkins shouted, 'I will commit you to gaol, sir!', only to have Kemp, his fellow judge shout back, 'You commit, sir! No sir, I will commit *you*!'

The court adjourned in uproar, and Atkins fled to confer with the governor. The other five judges (all officers of the corps) sent a letter to Bligh asking him to replace Atkins. By late afternoon, hot and exhausted, the judicial officers from the New South Wales Corps remanded Macarthur on bail and everyone retired for dinner.[32]

That evening could not have been a peaceful one for the Macarthurs. John, buoyed by his day in court, and agitated about what might come next, was hardly likely to be restful company. Elizabeth could do her best to soothe and cajole him but John's mind was a whirlwind of accusations, resentments and plans. The next morning he was once more arrested by two of Bligh's constables and, in full view of the town, marched into gaol. The officers who had remanded him the day before were charged, by Atkins, with crimes amounting to treason. The streets of Sydney were swarming with people 'murmuring and loudly complaining'.[33]

Major Johnston, his arm injured on the night of the barracks dinner in a drunken accident, reluctantly arrived in Sydney and went straight to the barracks. There he found 'all the civil and military officers collected, and the most respectable inhabitants in conversation with them'. Johnston's advisors beseeched him 'to adopt decisive measures for the safety of the inhabitants and to dispel the great alarm'. It was generally understood that the officers who served on the bench of the criminal court were to be thrown in gaol and it 'was expected, after such a measure, nothing could limit the excess of the Governor's cruelties'.[34] The seething tensions of the colony boiled over into mutiny—the governor had to be stopped.

Elizabeth Macarthur

John Macarthur

Lodgeworthy, the house in Devon where Elizabeth was born in 1766

Edward

John

Elizabeth's children

William

Elizabeth*

Mary*

*Each of these portraits could be either Elizabeth or Mary.

James

James's wife, Emily

Hannibal Macarthur, John's nephew,
and his wife, Anna Maria (right)

Elizabeth's
friends

Anna Josepha King, wife of
Governor Philip Gidley King

Elizabeth Paterson,
wife of Lieutenant-Governor William Paterson

Elizabeth Macquarie,
wife of Governor
Lachlan Macquarie

Betsy Marsden, wife of
Reverend Samuel Marsden

DA~RING~HA,
Colebee's Wife.

In Engraving, the lights must be broke down to a sombrous tint.

Daringa, a regular visitor to
Elizabeth Farm, who brought
her new baby to show Elizabeth

Elizabeth Macarthur, aged seventy-nine

OPPOSITE TOP: The house at Elizabeth Farm today

OPPOSITE BOTTOM: Clovelly at Watsons Bay.
Elizabeth died here in 1850.

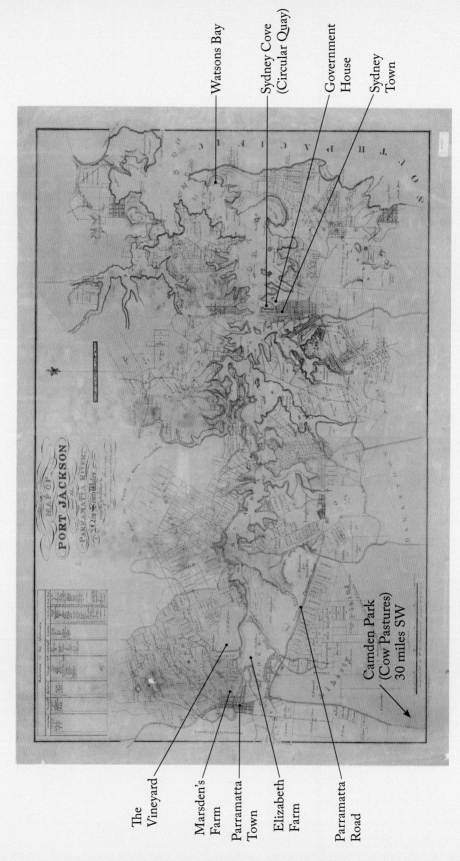

Watsons Bay

Sydney Cove
(Circular Quay)

Government
House

Sydney
Town

The
Vineyard

Marsden's
Farm

Parramatta
Town

Elizabeth
Farm

Parramatta
Road

Camden Park
(Cow Pastures)
30 miles SW

Map of Port Jackson and the Parramatta River, New South Wales, c. 1850

Johnston's first act was to order the drums beat to quarters, calling in the soldiers. His second was to have Macarthur released from gaol. John travelled straight to the barracks and added his own voice to that of Johnston's advisors. Years later, when testifying about that day, Johnston was careful to claim responsibility for his subsequent actions. 'If I did not put the Governor in arrest, an insurrection and massacre would ensue, and the blood of the inhabitants would be upon me. This representation, made by all persons present, before Macarthur came, alone influenced my conduct.' At about 5 pm in the afternoon Johnston, at the head of the New South Wales Corps and with a following of civilian administrators, respectable citizens (including John Macarthur) and various onlookers, set out for Government House to arrest Governor Bligh.

14

Rebellion and Consequences

...the excessive despotism of the ruling power called aloud for a reform,
but it never entered my head to imagine that the inhabitants would so
effectively rouse themselves from the despairing lethargy they
had fallen into, as to adopt so spirited a measure.

ELIZABETH MACARTHUR TO CAPTAIN PIPER, 5 FEBRUARY 1808

By the time Elizabeth knew what was going on it was all over.
A bloodless coup, a successful overthrow and all players in bed
before midnight. As darkness fell John returned to the Abbot's
Sydney residence a free man once more, to tell Elizabeth how
he marched with three hundred soldiers and officers up the
hill to Government House, flags flying and the band playing
'The British Grenadiers'.[1] Bligh had tried to escape but after
several hours was discovered, arrested and deposed. Major
Johnston was declared acting governor. Elizabeth, always a
clear-eyed pragmatist, could hardly fail to see the enormity of
what they'd done. What she couldn't see—what no one could
have predicted—were the consequences.

The day following the coup was a busy one for the rebel
officers. They formed committees to interview, or interrogate,
key officials; took up the business of government; and developed

a case to justify the overthrow. The implications of their mutiny were just beginning to register. Captain Abbott rushed down to Sydney from Parramatta. And John was there in the background: provoking, suggesting, reacting and inciting. It was a busy day for the soldiery too. Privates who a day earlier had stood sentry duty in order to guard Governor Bligh now stood at the same posts in order to imprison him. Other soldiers, following the lead of their warrant officers, spent the day preparing for celebrations. Wood was stacked for bonfires, wine and brandy was unloaded from a visiting American brig to be freely distributed, and the householders of Sydney were encouraged to illuminate their street-facing windows with pro-rebel artistic displays and slogans. Those who declined received threats and smashed windows.[2]

At sunset the people of Sydney lit the bonfires, roasted meat and burned effigies of Bligh. The streets were filled with men, women and children. Soldiers and sailors, shopkeepers and convicts, housemaids and prostitutes—all strolling around in the hot night, eating, drinking and viewing the decorated windows. The officers, too, enjoyed the spectacle. Major Johnston and Captain Abbott led an informal party up to Church Hill, the site of the largest bonfire and in so doing gave the celebrations their tacit approval. Johnston and Abbott were followed by John and Elizabeth Macarthur, arm in arm, and William Minchin with his wife Ann. Several other officers accompanied them. But Johnston's de facto wife, former convict Esther Abrahams, stayed at home at Annandale, and Abbott's wife Louisa remained in Parramatta. Elizabeth, always loyal, agreed with her husband about the monstrousness of Bligh, and years later would express sympathy for the descendants of the *Bounty* mutineers, who later that year were discovered living in isolation on Pitcairn Island. 'I feel more than common interest in these people—considering Bligh's Tyranny as the cause of their very being—or at least of their being in such a situation.'[3]

But John's preoccupation with the overthrow of Bligh marked something of a turning point in the Macarthurs' marriage. The timing of the rebellion could not have been worse. Elizabeth was facing childbirth again, and this time without the vigour of youth. Her daughter Elizabeth was still very ill. The thousands of new acres at Cow Pastures needed thousands of hours of work to establish the necessary infrastructure. And the streets of Sydney were now uneasy and more unsafe than ever. Elizabeth needed John. The family needed John. Yet there he was in Sydney playing honour games again, deadly games that put his life, and therefore the future of his family, at risk.

Perhaps Elizabeth saw the pattern more clearly now. Perhaps she recalled those awful months aboard the *Neptune,* wallowing in English waters before they set sail for New South Wales. She had been pregnant then too, and with sickly infant Edward and the fear of the unknown before them, she can only have felt an immense pressure. At that time John's anxiety had expressed itself in the duel with the *Neptune*'s captain. This time, John had turned on Bligh and embroiled himself in a political farrago. Maybe it had been a gradual realisation, or maybe a flash of insight, but Elizabeth began to spend less time in John's company and more time relying on the only person with the necessary strength of will to safeguard her family's future: herself.

Within days of the overthrow of Bligh, Elizabeth, now five months pregnant, left John to it. She returned with her daughter to the relative safety of Elizabeth Farm. She was accompanied on the journey home by Captain Abbott who, although initially supportive of the rebellion, had rapidly come to believe that it was more a grab for power and retribution than anything honourable. Abbott advised Johnston to call Colonel Paterson back from Van Diemen's Land, and then to travel to England with Bligh to account for his conduct. Doing so would show that Johnston had not deposed Bligh simply to obtain command.[4] Johnston failed to heed Abbott's advice, and put off contacting Paterson for as long as he could.

Back in Parramatta, Elizabeth settled her daughter and then immediately wrote to her friends and family in Bridgerule. Mutiny, treason, overthrow. Whichever way she looked at it her husband was up to his neck in trouble—a neck that was suddenly very vulnerable to a noose via an English court of justice. Elizabeth needed to ensure that her English connections were on side. It was crucial that they heard about the rebellion from her, preferably before they read about it in the London papers. Elizabeth sent the letters to John in Sydney (so he could dispatch them to England), who replied to 'My Dearest Love' that they were 'admirably written'. In the covering note, Elizabeth evidently complained of a severe headache, and of having to retire to a darkened room. This is the first, but not the last, mention of what sounds like migraine, perhaps the result of the stress she was under. John's response was typically unhelpful. 'Take care of yourself and be cheerful. Your headache will go off then.'[5]

A euphoric John remained in Sydney and within a week of Bligh's overthrow he wrote to Elizabeth: 'I have been deeply engaged all this day in contending for the liberties of this unhappy colony, and I am happy to say I have succeeded beyond what I expected.'[6] He had been working hard, writing almost every letter, proclamation and notice of appointment that went out under Johnston's name. According to John 'the Tyrant is now no doubt gnashing his teeth with vexation at his overthrow'.[7] In reality the Tyrant was working equally hard to spoil things for the military, not least by refusing to sail for London. Bligh was to remain in Sydney, living comfortably but under arrest, for another year.

John and his rebel colleagues, keen to ensure their activities displayed a veneer of lawfulness, returned to court, this time in a trial engineered to 'prove' Macarthur's innocence. Macarthur's trial that immediately preceded Bligh's overthrow had never been resolved. Elizabeth only learnt of the new trial second-hand. She wrote to Captain Piper, who was still on Norfolk Island. 'The Criminal Court is now sitting and he is before it as a prisoner, but I trust it will be for <u>no serious offences</u>.'[8] The courts were the only forum available to the colonists to air grievances, resolve disputes or, indeed, to try criminal acts. The tiny pool of magistrates, almost all officers of the New South Wales Corps or Royal Navy, meant that conflicts of interest were inevitable. As well, few, if any, of the justices, including Judge-Advocate Atkins, had any formal legal training. The results were predictably shambolic, and Macarthur's latest five-day trial was no different.

Rather than address the confused and various list of the original charges, Macarthur used the opportunity to interrogate witness after witness about Governor Bligh's plans, actions and intentions. As Bligh himself noted afterwards, 'They were trying the Governor, and that Macarthur, instead of being prisoner at the bar, directed the prosecution.'[9] Even Captain Abbott considered it a shameful, mock trial and believed that others also thought so.[10] Macarthur was acquitted, and was carried through the streets by cheering soldiers. No doubt Elizabeth heard about that at second-hand too.

Not everyone was cheering, though. On Monday 8 February John Macarthur was invited to a public meeting. It was every bit as staged as the trial but this time the script was written by those who wanted Macarthur gone. At the meeting it was proposed that a sword be purchased and presented to Major Johnston, and a silver dinner plate be given to the six officers who had supported him, by way of thanks for the overthrow of Governor Bligh. The motion carried. It was also proposed that an address of thanks be given to Macarthur 'as having been chiefly instrumental in bringing about the happy change'.[11] Again, the motion was carried, this time with sly smiles. Here were the inhabitants of Sydney clearly apportioning blame, setting it out in writing for the powers in London. But Sydney was not done with Macarthur yet. It was also proposed that a subscription be raised to send Macarthur to London as a delegate of the colonists, where he could spell out in detail their many grievances. Yet again, motion carried—this time with a roar of approval. If Macarthur was taken by surprise, he was careful not to show it. Instead he made an eloquent speech in praise of the idea, deprecating his own ability to fulfil it, and vowing to devote himself to the service of his fellow citizens. He would immediately settle his affairs in the colony and proceed to England.

Actually, Macarthur went straight from the meeting to see

Major Johnston. There was no chance that he would be beaten at his own game. Within days Johnston issued a general order: 'John Macarthur, Esq, is appointed a Magistrate and Secretary to the Colony.'[12] In effect, and drawing no wage, John was appointed as the most senior civil administrator. Johnston, having found the pressure of governing to be well-nigh intolerable, withdrew to his Annandale farm and placed Macarthur in charge. Presumably to Elizabeth's great relief, there was no further mention of the delegation to London.

In the following months John was frantically busy. He reassigned 300 convict workers, taking them away from public works and allocating them to the farming properties of his allies. This action was justified, he argued, as an act of economy. Those men no longer needed to be fed and clothed by the government. John's allies also benefited from additional land grants as Macarthur, in Johnston's name, allocated some 5660 acres (2300 hectares) of Crown land. He sold off much of the government cattle herd to the officers and soldiers, accepting IOUs that would never be paid. Bligh's regulations against the importation of spirits were reversed and the cartel of officers again monopolised the sale of imported goods, purchasing ships' cargoes in their entirety. Small farmers were once more forced to sell their grain to the government, to be paid only in wine and spirits.

John's high was followed, perhaps predictably, by a crashing low. The rebellion had not resolved any of the infighting among the officers. No one believed for a minute that the rebellion had been Johnston's idea, and now, as the dust settled, John Macarthur was felt to have badly over-reached. Many if not all of his former allies fell away. Abbott had removed himself from the scene, and Johnston, too, tried to distance himself. The Hawkesbury settlers, who had never liked Macarthur, were still actively trying to bring him down. In May John wrote despairingly to his friend Captain Piper about his former allies' multiple attempts to dislodge him from his position of power. His daughter Elizabeth, John told Piper, 'still continues in a most melancholy state, with little or no chance of recovery', and her pregnant mother was 'by no means well'.[13] John failed entirely to mention a further blow: his eldest son Edward had decided that farming was not for him and was returning to England to join the army. Elizabeth was forced to farewell her son once more, and in April 1808 Edward sailed, in a Macarthur ship called the *Dart*. Edward carried Johnston's dispatches to the Colonial and War Offices.[14] It was exciting for a young man to be a player in affairs of state. But Elizabeth would not see him again for sixteen long years, not until he returned to the colony in 1824.

Elizabeth gave birth to Emmeline Emily in early June 1808 and, now with a newborn as well as an invalid, her focus was necessarily and wholly domestic. Her husband's attention remained, however, in the public sphere. Major Johnston, despite taking upon himself the title of acting governor, was not the highest ranked military officer in the colony. That honour fell to the actual Lieutenant-Governor, Colonel Paterson—the man shot by John Macarthur in their duel of 1801. Paterson was still based in northern Van Diemen's Land, where he was unsuccessfully attempting to establish an outpost, while (with rather more success) drinking himself to destruction. Paterson had been informed of the overthrow but was disinclined to sail to Sydney to sort things out. It was suggested around town that John Macarthur's young friend Walter Davidson had quietly travelled to Van Diemen's Land to dissuade Paterson from making the trip.

The next most senior officer after Paterson was Lieutenant-Colonel Foveaux who, having taken sick leave in England, was expected back in Sydney any day. Bligh, still under house arrest, watched eagerly for Foveaux's ship in the hope that on his arrival Foveaux would reinstate him as governor. When the signal flag at South Head went up on 28 June 1808 and the *Sinclair* sailed down the harbour, the colony held its breath. As soon as *Sinclair*'s anchors hit the harbour floor, Bligh sent out three emissaries to ask Foveaux to immediately meet with him in private. But it was too late. The emissaries reached the ship only to find that John Macarthur, Major Johnston and Nicholas Bayley were already there, deep in conversation with Foveaux. Bligh's men, denied permission to come aboard, returned ignominiously to shore and within days Foveaux took over control of the colony, superseding Johnston and relieving John Macarthur of his role as colonial secretary. Foveaux continued with the rebel's regime of import monopoly, land grants and spirits as currency.

If Johnston was pleased to be rid of the cares of government, Macarthur most definitely was not. Once again he sent Walter Davidson south, this time to convince Paterson that he should return. Macarthur had decided that a weak superior officer would be easier to deal with than Foveaux, but Paterson again declined. It was nearly a year before he reluctantly agreed, and then only when Foveaux sent for him; Foveaux needed the colonel to legitimise the rebel regime. By then the rebels had worked out a plan. Poor Pat, as Paterson was widely known, would live at the governor's country residence in Parramatta where he could drink in peace as Lieutenant-Governor, while Foveaux in Sydney ran the colony. Johnston, meanwhile, would return to London with Macarthur and other witnesses to explain the situation to the government and to lay charges against Bligh. John would be sailing to London after all, and in the wake of this decision the family was left reeling.

Any hopes Elizabeth still held about returning to Bridgerule were thoroughly dashed. Once more she had to forgo a trip home and stay to take care of her daughters, as well as the farms and all the other Macarthur enterprises. Her two youngest sons were to travel to England with their father, to attend school. Her husband's nephew Hannibal was also returning to England, but he was to go by way of the Spice Islands and China, trading sandalwood for John. Once again, John's actions resulted in nothing but heartache and hard work for Elizabeth.

The Macarthurs attempted to raise some cash to fund John's trip and ran an advertisement in the *Sydney Gazette*:

> TO be disposed of by Private Contract, at Mr. M'Arthur's farm, Parramatta; SEVERAL FLOCKS of CHOICE EWES and WETHERS of the Spanish race; A number of fine Cows, Heifers, Bulls, and Oxen, of the English breed; Some valuable Brood Mares, Stallions, and Saddle Horses. The whole to be sold at low prices, for ready money only. To be also Sold, a most desirable ESTATE, containing Two Thousand Acres, situate at the Seven Hills, contiguous to the Hawkesbury Road. If it be wished by the Purchaser, security will be taken on the Estate for two-thirds of the Purchase money.[15]

The Seven Hills estate at Toongabbie was to be sold, but Elizabeth Farm and the newest lands at Cow Pastures would be kept. Perhaps the sale was also an attempt to reduce Elizabeth's coming workload, but the advertisement was largely unsuccessful. No one who could afford the Seven Hills property was interested in buying it from the tainted John Macarthur.

Even before Paterson officially assumed office, the infighting between the senior rebels could not be contained. Foveaux discovered a discrepancy in the official accounts. During Macarthur's time as secretary to the colony, some £500 worth of goods had gone missing: appropriated by Macarthur for his own use, according to Foveaux. John reacted to this public slight with deadly predictability. He challenged Foveaux to a duel. On the morning of 19 January 1809, the combatants and their seconds faced off. In an unusual move, Foveaux's second proposed that the duellists toss a coin for the right to shoot first, with the loser facing the incoming shot, defenceless. If Foveaux hoped this ploy would encourage John to back down, then he badly misjudged his man. Macarthur immediately accepted the condition, and won the toss. He 'took very deliberate aim' Foveaux's second would later report, staring down the barrel at a very wide target—Foveaux was not a thin man.[16] John fired. And missed. Foveaux insultingly refused to fire in return, instead lowering his pistol and handing it back to his second. The pair shook hands, briefly and without warmth. Whether Elizabeth knew about this duel, no one can say. If she did it was yet another worry to add to her ever-increasing inventory of cares. Foveaux was added to John's own ever-increasing list of people to whom he never spoke or wrote to again. As for the missing £500? The discrepancy was found to be real and Macarthur was obliged to repay it.

The pressure on the interim government was increased by the fact that a year after the rebellion, Bligh, like a stubborn stain, refused to budge. He and his now-widowed daughter, Mary Putland, remained holed up in Government House. When offered passage to London aboard the *Admiral Gambier*, the ship chartered by the rebel administration for Johnston and Macarthur, Bligh prevaricated. What he really wanted was to take control of HMS *Porpoise*, the naval warship anchored in Port Jackson whose captain was known to be a Bligh loyalist. Eventually an agreement was reached. Bligh solemnly swore on 'his honour as an officer and gentleman'[17] that if he could travel in the *Porpoise* he would return directly to England. In late February 1809 the *Porpoise*, with Bligh and Mary aboard, finally sailed down the harbour, while the inhabitants of Sydney variously watched on in pleasure, conjecture or dismay. Then, just inside the heads of the harbour, the *Porpoise* dropped anchor. Bligh had no intention of going anywhere.

Bligh arranged for a hand-written proclamation to be given to the master of each vessel in the harbour, announcing a state of mutiny in New South Wales and forbidding anyone from assisting the rebels to leave the colony. The proclamation listed the officers of the New South Wales Corps and named fifteen civilians including, of course, John Macarthur but also his young friend Walter Davidson. Davidson's well-placed London connections, when they found out that their young man had been named, were most affronted and Bligh would feel the ramifications for the rest of his life. The chartered ship *Admiral*

Gambier was ready to set sail, but Johnston, Macarthur and the others delayed sailing for London, unwilling to take the risk of Bligh arresting them at sea.

For nearly a month the *Porpoise* stayed there, taunting the rebel administration with Bligh's presence, before she turned and disappeared over the horizon. The *Admiral Gambier* was finally free to leave. John Macarthur, accompanied by his two youngest sons and Walter Davidson, left the colony on 29 March 1809, bound for England via Rio. Elizabeth stayed behind to manage alone once more, this time with an invalid, a baby and thirteen-year-old Mary. John expected to stay in England only for a few months,[18] but it would be more than eight years before Elizabeth saw her husband again.

15

Alone Again

May the Almighty preserve and protect my beloved wife and girls…
JOHN MACARTHUR TO ELIZABETH MACARTHUR, 30 JULY 1809

Elizabeth's first act, after John's departure, was to take the Toongabbie farm off the market. She squared up to endure yet another lengthy separation where all the responsibilities fell on her shoulders. It was heartbreaking to farewell both her youngest sons at once, but at least the boys had each other. And John? He was again sailing towards danger: towards the ongoing Napoleonic War being fiercely fought at sea just as much as on land, and towards Major Johnston's trial for treason. Johnston could well be hanged if things didn't go his way. The noose was less likely for John, as a civilian, but nothing could be certain.

After finalising her business in town, Elizabeth travelled back to Parramatta. The familiar tree-lined western road from Sydney, wide enough in most places for three carriages abreast, was kept in good condition.[1] With bridges across every stream and rivulet the journey only took an hour and a half with a well-matched pair of horses.[2] The further Elizabeth travelled from Sydney, the more fertile the soil and the more verdant the passing scenery. Elizabeth Farm was located in what had become a most desirable location. The picturesque area around Parramatta was much preferred to the mercantile Sydney Cove or the rocks, swamps and dry forests surrounding the harbour, and the region had rapidly gentrified.[3]

By 1809 the township of Parramatta consisted of about 180 houses forming a street that ran parallel to the Parramatta River. The population, including those on nearby farms, was estimated to be 1500. Along with the shops and alehouses there was a prison, a factory or 'house of industry' for female convicts, a church, and a public school for the young girls of the colony.[4] A 'brick hospital consisting of two wards' (one for men, the other for women) was, according to an 1809 report, well regulated by the principal physician and former highwayman Mr Darcy Wentworth. But within ten years the place was decried as a sinkhole of iniquity with a leaking roof, broken windows, putrid meat, and 'in the absence of a mortuary, the dead bodies had begun to be placed in the passage between the two wards'.[5] A completely rebuilt hospital would not open until 1818.

At the western end of the main street a gentle slope called Rose Hill led up to the governor's country residence and its accompanying experimental indigenous gardens, intended to supply plants for the royal gardens of Kew. The eastern end of the street culminated in brick barracks capable of housing 300 infantrymen. The paddocks of Elizabeth Farm abutted the barracks, and the homestead was only five minutes brisk walk away. Unconsciously or not, Elizabeth had very nearly replicated the site and situation of the farm where she'd been born. Just like Lodgeworthy farm in Bridgerule, the homestead at Elizabeth Farm sat on a gentle rise, overlooking the fields that reached to the river a mile or so away. The situation of the farm meant that Elizabeth and her family were never isolated. They could enjoy the social benefits of town while maintaining the privacy afforded by the hundreds of acres that Elizabeth Farm now encompassed. With the additional vast properties at Toongabbie, Cow Pastures and elsewhere, Elizabeth Farm was at this point the heart of the agricultural Macarthur enterprises. It was always Elizabeth's favourite home.

Elizabeth's neighbour Betsy Marsden wrote to an acquaintance in England about how cut off she felt from all connection with the world. 'Old England is no more than like a pleasing dream. When I think of it it appears to have no existence except in my imagination.'[6] But England was far more than a dream to Elizabeth. With all four of her sons now there or en route there, as well as her husband, it was a place very much at the forefront of her mind. Eldest son Edward, in early 1809, visited his mother's friends and relations in Bridgerule. His letters to Elizabeth, which probably arrived a few months after John's departure, are full of affectionate details and the many names of old friends wishing his mother well. They contained everything Elizabeth could wish for to take her mind from the cares of her work. She read and re-read them, especially in that first year, 1809, when heavy rains constantly threatened floods. And she kept them for the rest of her life.

Elizabeth's dear friend Bridget had died in 1802, and by the time of Edward's visit in 1809, Bridget's parents, who had stood up for Elizabeth in the face of disapproval of her marriage to John, had also died. But Bridget's younger brothers and sisters, now with families of their own, remembered Elizabeth fondly and showered Edward with friendly hospitality. Edward stayed at the vicarage where Bridget's brother was now the reverend, and where Elizabeth had spent so many happy hours with her friend. Indeed, the vicarage was inhabited by one Reverend Kingdon or another right up until the 1950s.

Edward, confined to the sofa after hurting his knee in a fall from his horse, received as his first visitor his grandmother—Elizabeth's mother. Edward told his mother that he had expected a 'decrepit old woman' but was pleasantly surprised by his grandmother's upright posture and her 'countenance bespeaking the happy contentment which dwelled within. Since you have seen her dearest Mother, time must have materially changed her, but for a woman of sixty years of age she is a prodigy.'[7] A few days later, Edward, accompanied by the reverend's wife, returned the visit. The journey to his grandmother's cottage was only a very short one but it was undertaken in the old-fashioned way still common in that area, with two people on the one horse, the woman sitting sideways behind the man riding astride. 'The old Mare was led out. I mounted before Mrs. K on the pillion behind—and thus mounted the subject of our conversation was Mrs. McArthur. Could she but see us—and the like.'[8] Edward's grandmother showed him her cottage and asked him wistfully if he thought his mother would find the bed comfortable. Over tea Edward was told all the local news and Elizabeth's half-sister Isabella Hacker dropped in to pay her respects. It is perhaps indicative of the cool relationship between the sisters that Edward wrote only a single sentence about his aunt, noting 'she has three Children, expects a fourth—and both she, and her husband are well, and doing well'.⁹

Edward enjoyed his stay with the Kingdons and their large family. 'They live hospitably but without splendour and are wise enough not to be at all corrupted by the prevailing taste of the day. Surely when you come home—you can think of spending the remainder of your days in no other part. Their ways are so consonant to your own.'¹⁰ Home—such a simple word to carry so much complex emotional weight. Even after she had lived nearly twenty years in New South Wales it was still a matter of *when* Elizabeth would come home, not *if*.

Edward's letters to his mother also provide a glimpse of Elizabeth's life in Parramatta, and everyone's fears for his sister Elizabeth, who remained gravely ill. 'Now, my dear Mother, my thoughts turn seriously towards your distant quarter. My dear Elizabeth—must I mention the name! I fear what I dare not write, poor dear Girl her last embrace made a strong impression on my mind.' Edward does not forget his other siblings: 'To my dearest Mary, my most affectionate love—& to James & little Billy the very same.' And in a final flourish of homesickness he begs to be remembered to his mother's friends. 'Remember me particularly & affectionately to Miss Lucas, and give my regards to Mrs Abbot, Mrs Minchin, &c &c &c.'

As much as Elizabeth loved receiving Edward's letters, she may have been concerned that he consistently seemed unsettled. In a letter from later in 1809, when Edward was reunited with his father and youngest brothers, he wrote, 'I am very comfortable here, and was it not for that restless, roaming disposition of mine, I should be content to remain where I am.'[11] That restless, roaming disposition would take Edward, as an officer in His Majesty's Army, across the European continent, briefly to Canada and back to France with the army of occupation. His service record was solid, if not glittering, but in time he rose through the ranks to receive a knighthood and become a lieutenant-general. He was well liked by his fellow officers, one of whom remarked 'who can help liking him, wherever he is known he becomes a Favourite'.[12]

In 1809 Elizabeth's second son, John, was still excelling in his studies at Grove Hall Academy, where the following year younger brothers James and William would begin their schooling. With all the hauteur of the older brother for his five years younger sibling, Edward wrote without irony that 'John is a very fine lad, and improves wonderfully'.[13] He also noted that John was 'almost as tall as myself, and at the same time remarkably stout'.[14] John's teachers were highly impressed with him, and John himself was keen to become a lawyer. Edward, no scholar himself, trailed around England after his new regiment which was not, in his opinion, 'considered the most crack'.[15] Later in 1809, when he was based in Hereford, the younger boys stayed with Edward while their father took care of business in London. Edward seemed to surprise himself with how much he enjoyed his brothers' company. 'I am quite a family man,' wrote Edward to his father, 'and if you were to see us our mirth would please you I am sure not a little.'[16]

Edward was careful to pass on to his mother all the little boys' best wishes for their family at home:

James and William desire their loves to Mamma and they hope that 'she is well and that Elizabeth is better' and that Mary is well, & their little Sister. Tell them, they say, we say our prayers for them when we go to bed, and drink their healths every day after dinner. They unite with me in kindest remembrances to Miss Lucas, and desire their remembrances to Lewis, & his family, and all their old friends. They do not forget Condion & his Wife, nor any of our domestics.[17]

In fact, Edward paints some delightful word pictures of his little brothers, who seemed to charm all with whom they came in contact. Thanks to the boys' French tutor in Parramatta they both spoke the language with great fluency, and while staying with Edward they continued their language, mathematics and writing studies under a variety of tutors for six hours a day:

I am sure you would be particularly delighted if you knew how diligent and good even William is. He makes the most astonishing progress...James has learned his multiplication table & in my next, I shall send a specimen of his improvement in writing. I have got a book and pencil for him and all the leisure time he has he spends in drawing.[18]

The little boys were very close to one another and would remain so for the rest of their lives.

By the time these loving letters arrived in New South Wales, Elizabeth was dealing with yet another government regime. Governor Lachlan Macquarie and his wife, Elizabeth, had sailed from England in May 1809 to replace Paterson's interim position. Edward managed to pay the Macquaries a quick visit before they left. During a stopover in Rio, Macquarie heard the news that John Macarthur and Major Johnston had just passed through on their way to London. Macquarie, carrying orders to arrest Johnston, for leading the overthrow, and Macarthur, for high treason, was pleased at the news—now he wouldn't have to deal with them on his arrival in New South Wales. Fortunately for Johnston and Macarthur, a jurisdictional technicality meant they were not arrested on arrival in London.

The Macquaries disembarked in Sydney in late December and Governor Macquarie was sworn in on 1 January 1810. Elizabeth quickly joined their social circle—to do so was both expedient and enjoyable. She soon discovered that Mrs Macquarie was a relatively new wife and that she had previously been living in Holsworthy, a mere five miles east of Bridgerule. The two women no doubt spent quite some time enjoyably discovering their mutual acquaintances. Elizabeth was also able to introduce her new friend Elizabeth Macquarie to her old friend Betsy Marsden, who had arrived back from England with her husband in February 1810.

Over the next few years the friendship between these three women was cemented by sorrow. While Elizabeth missed her husband and sons, Elizabeth Macquarie was grieving for her 'dear angelic Daughter' who had died at twelve weeks of age two years earlier.[19] Since then she had endured one miscarriage and, over the next four years, would suffer six more before successfully giving birth to a son in 1814. In 1811 Betsy Marsden suffered a stroke while giving birth to a daughter (who survived to live into old age). For the rest of her life Betsy, whose husband had previously boasted of her horse-riding prowess, was paralysed on her left side and could only leave home in a specially constructed carriage.[20] Although the Marsdens were longstanding family friends of the Blighs,[21] the esteem in which Elizabeth Macarthur was held helped her to overcome the inevitable social awkwardness occasioned by any mention of her absent husband.

In 1810, two years since the rebellion, Bligh still refused to leave for England. When the *Porpoise* had sailed from Port Jackson, it had gone only as far as Van Diemen's Land. Bligh spent a year establishing a blockade of sorts on the Derwent, harassing the people of Hobart Town and annoying its governor by stopping every vessel arriving and leaving. Dispatches were seized and supplies commandeered. Months passed with no reprieve—some wondered if Bligh was waiting for reinforcements from England to avenge his overthrow. Finally, in January 1810, he sailed back up the coast to Sydney, only to find that Macquarie was now governor. It was a crushing blow, only slightly mitigated by the news that the disgraced New South Wales Corps was being recalled to Britain to be replaced by Macquarie's 73rd Regiment. HMS *Porpoise*, with a reluctantly acquiescing Bligh aboard, would accompany HMS *Hindostan* and the storeship *Dromedary* home to England with the rank and file members of the New South Wales Corps and many of the officers, including Paterson and his wife.

In early April 1810, a month before the convoy sailed, a grand farewell ball was held aboard the *Porpoise*. It was one of many farewell dinners and entertainments held during Bligh's sojourn in Sydney, where his presence continued to be both divisive and abrasive. Although the Macquaries privately agreed that Bligh's government should never have been overthrown, they found the man himself to be very difficult. Governor Macquarie wrote to his brother that Bligh was 'a most disagreeable person to have any dealings or public business to transact with'.[22] But everyone who was anyone in Sydney was still happy to attend Bligh's ball—even Elizabeth Macarthur.

It might seem odd that Elizabeth would go, but Bligh's argument was with her husband, not with her; she was expressly invited; and all the other ladies would be there. Besides, she might find out something useful she could pass along to John. At six in the evening the guests began to assemble aboard the decorated ship and 'the atmosphere resounded with loyal airs from a large Band'.[23] The ship's huge lanterns cast a magical glow. The quarterdeck was covered with a large awning and between the gunports were sideboards groaning with wines, fruits and delicacies. At eight o'clock the dancing began, 'supported with great vivacity', until the company paused at eleven for an elegant supper. Elizabeth, always a regimental favourite, could not have lacked for dance partners. After supper the dancing continued until three in the morning, at which point the guests left the ship 'very much delighted with the hospitality of the Entertainment'.[24]

Did Bligh and Elizabeth engage in any polite chat that evening? It seems unlikely. Months later, in Rio on his way home to England, Bligh refused to dine with newly widowed Elizabeth Paterson. Her husband—shot by John Macarthur in a duel, beleaguered by the cares of governing, and a heavy drinker—died at sea off Cape Horn. Bligh's snubbing of Mrs Paterson was recorded by another officer in his diary, commenting that the incivility 'tended not a little to confirm the low estimation in which [Bligh] is already held'.[25]

In England, John Macarthur travelled to Portsmouth to meet the incoming convoy, and was told of Paterson's death. He subsequently wrote to Elizabeth to let her know, adding in a wry aside that he 'returned to town bringing under my escort Mrs Paterson, who appears grateful for this mark of attention. You know sometimes I like to return disobliging acts this way.'[26] John went on to note that Elizabeth Paterson was in good health and excellent spirits. She was indeed. In a surprise manoeuvre, Elizabeth Paterson married Major Grose in March 1814, himself a widower by then, and they took up residence in Bath. Her new husband, the former acting governor of New South Wales, died two months later and Elizabeth Grose lived on quietly in England, staying in friendly contact with the Macarthurs until her death in 1839.

Importantly, Elizabeth's presence at Bligh's farewell ball is perhaps a sign that her daughter was beginning to recover, that she no longer needed her mother in constant attendance. A further clue is a receipt still among the Macarthur family papers for a pianoforte bought at auction for £85, in 1810.[27] This was approximately four times the London price of a new square piano.[28] The Macarthur's original (and now unfashionable) table piano, which First Fleet surgeon George Worgan had presented to Elizabeth as a gift, had probably warped over time and became unplayable.[29] Yet someone—or perhaps everyone—in the house loved music enough to warrant the extravagance of a new one, and it seems young Elizabeth was well enough to enjoy the entertainment too.

Her recovery is confirmed in a letter from John to Elizabeth in May 1810. John expresses his immense gratitude to Doctor Redfern for 'discovering and applying an efficacious remedy to her extraordinary disease'.[30] But for the next year and more young Elizabeth's health was precarious enough that she spent several months living in Sydney with her mother so that she could receive treatment.[31] Although Redfern, an ex-convict, was widely held to be an excellent doctor, there was little he could prescribe that would have done more for Elizabeth than did the constant care of her mother, the household servants and the governess, Penelope Lucas.

As her daughter's health improved, Elizabeth turned her energies and focus to the farms. That is not to say, with John away, she hadn't already been working. Apart from a handful of aristocrats, Elizabeth and the other women of her era never stopped working. They worked every day of their lives and worked extraordinarily hard. The so-called 'farmer and his wife' were, in reality, both farmers and then, as now, the wife's labour inside and outside the home was crucial to the running of the farm and the economic wellbeing of the family. Elizabeth Macarthur was no exception. She was, at that time, again, merely one of a number of women who had sole responsibility for their families' farms.

In November 1810 Governor Macquarie set out on a lengthy tour of the outlying districts of Sydney. Within his diaries of the excursions, Governor Macquarie's writing style is crisp and to the point. He describes the landscape, his horses, and his servants. Mrs M, as he calls his wife, often accompanies him in the carriage or on horseback and he lovingly admires her pluck and her stamina.[32] Macquarie also describes the various farms and outposts he inspects along the way. Some of them, already overgrazed and poorly maintained, did not meet his high standards. But others clearly met with his approval, including several that were managed by women.

'We rode up the Hill to call on Mrs. Bell (the Wife of Lieut. Bell of the 102d Regt.) who resides on her Farm on the summit of this beautiful Hill,'[33] wrote the governor in his diary. And again, a week or so later, 'We found Mrs. Laycock and her two Daughters at home, in a very neat comfortable well built Farm House and well furnished; the good old Lady's Farm being also in a forward state of improvement in other respects.'[34] That women are farming does not seem in any way remarkable to Macquarie; he merely notes the names and makes some comments in the same way he does for the men's farms he visits.

One morning during Macquarie's tour of inspection, Elizabeth Macarthur arrived just as the governor and his wife were completing their camp breakfast near Elizabeth's Cow Pastures property. Elizabeth asked if she might 'ride about the Country' with the pair that day, which was 'of course readily assented to'.[35] The party set out at eleven o'clock, with a number of Aboriginal people. At the time and for many years afterwards, colonists on exploratory trips were often accompanied by one or more Aboriginal guides. The benefits for the colonists were obvious, but the guides' own reasons for helping the touring parties are more complex. They usually received some recompense, in the form of food, or goods, or a small payment, but the act of guiding also gave them a modicum of power. The guides could lead parties *to* a place but perhaps they also ensured that parties did not encroach on sacred places, family campsites, or the choicest hunting grounds. The guides were also able to listen—colonists often commented on Aboriginal people's abilities with mimicry and language—and so perhaps gathered valuable intelligence that could be relayed to their families, friends and allies.

From the top of Mount Taurus, Elizabeth and the Macquaries had a fine view of the countryside, despite the governor grumbling that Taurus was hardly high enough to deserve the name mountain. From there they rode along a ridge to Mount Hunter and were entertained by the sight of a fight between two wild bulls. By two o'clock they returned to the governor's campsite for food and a rest before setting out once again to see the farm of Walter Davidson. Davidson's property, adjacent to Macarthur lands, was stocked and managed by Elizabeth. Macquarie's description of the farm as being in 'a beautiful situation and excellent rich Land for both Tillage and Pasture' in fact summed up the whole Cow Pastures region.[36] The weary party returned to camp at five o'clock, where the Macquaries' servants had dinner waiting for them. After dinner Elizabeth left to spend the night at her Cow Pastures farm, Belgenny.[37]

The next morning the governor and Mrs Macquarie dropped in at Belgenny to see Elizabeth 'with whom we sat for a little while in a small miserable Hut'.[38] Elizabeth not only worked hard, but she worked in primitive conditions. The governor's visit was not made on the off-chance that Elizabeth would be available in the middle of a working day to sit with him. The visit was clearly pre-arranged and it speaks to Elizabeth's take-me-as-I-am attitude that she was willing to entertain her friends in what was probably a shepherd's shed. Such was the

Macarthurs' straitened financial position, any funds left over after paying for John and the boys in England had to be used wisely. Elizabeth invested in livestock rather than on improving the living quarters on outlying properties.

Elizabeth's friends were among the highest-ranking people in the colony but that was to be expected—among the small population of New South Wales she simply mixed with people of her own age, class and circumstance. But given her secluded upbringing in Bridgerule, it is also very likely that she spoke with a Devonshire accent. Any aspirations to be seen to belong to the upper classes (and Elizabeth does not seem to have harboured any) would be dashed as soon as she opened her mouth to speak. Elizabeth was not unaware of the governor's condescension. She found him the most pleasing of men 'but then he is the Governor and it is not possible to forget that he is so'. Elizabeth Macquarie, on the other hand, Elizabeth found to be 'very amiable, very benevolent, in short a very good woman'.[39]

If Elizabeth found satisfaction in her work, and solace in her friendships with other women, it was still not enough to make up for her absent husband. Elizabeth was a strong-minded woman but her natural optimism and equanimity was sorely tested in John's absence. Their love for one another, and their shared ambitions, had seen the couple successfully weather a great many storms, and, despite John's many faults, she missed him. 'I know not what to think,' she wrote to her friend Captain Piper in late 1811, 'whether my dear Mr McArthur will or will not have left England. How cruel is this perpetual state of uncertainty.'[40] Unfortunately for Elizabeth, there was a good deal more uncertainty to come.

16

Bad Debts and Sharp Words

I am perfectly aware, my beloved wife, of the difficulties you have to contend with, and fully convinced that not one woman in a thousand, (no one that I know) would have the resolution and perseverance to contend with them at all, much more to surmount them in the manner you have so happily done.

JOHN MACARTHUR TO ELIZABETH MACARTHUR, 3 AUGUST 1810

None of Elizabeth's letters to John during this his second absence in England have survived. Elizabeth, though, carefully kept the letters she received from John. And from those she learned that he was miserable in England. From his career zenith immediately after the rebellion, when he more or less ran the colony, he plummeted into a depressive nadir. In London he was a nobody with no easily discernible future, surviving on the limited funds Elizabeth could provide. He was regularly unwell, tormented with digestive complaints, debilitating gout, 'nervous affliction' and 'seized with violent spasms in my side'.[1]

His sandalwood trading enterprise, for which Hannibal had travelled to China, had amounted to nothing. A ship he part-owned was lost at sea and his sealing ventures resulted in a 'considerable loss'.[2] Several men who owed him money could not (or would not) pay. John would have liked to do a favour for

Doctor Redfern, to thank him for restoring young Elizabeth to health, but he lacked the finances to make any meaningful gesture. 'You must,' he wrote to Elizabeth, 'exert yourself to remit me all you can.'[3]

John worried, too, about his 'beloved Wife'.[4] He fretted about 'the many adverse circumstances to which you have been exposed, and the extraordinary trials that you have borne', and he was impressed and grateful that Elizabeth coped 'not only without sinking under the accumulated pressure, but with the most active fortitude and good sense'.[5] It was impossible, he wrote, for him to fully express the admiration he felt and equally impossible for him 'to repress the pride which I feel in having to boast of such a pattern for Wives and Mothers as my own'.[6] John's peers may have found him arrogant and haughty but, in London at least, he was full of self-doubt. He saw much of himself in his son Edward, in Edward's 'independence' and 'obstinacy' and John noted to Elizabeth that when he observed 'the too prominent parts of [Edward's] character which he derives from a person you well know he makes me shudder for his safety on the voyage of life'.[7] Perhaps writing these letters helped John to feel better but they cannot have given Elizabeth any peace of mind.

At one point in 1810, John seriously considered a seat in the English parliament. 'The expense will be great, but the prospect of benefit from it is still greater.'[8] This plan, like many others he hatched at around that time, came to nothing. John was despondent and his letters home were full of sorrow and complaint. He prayed for the health and happiness of his wife and daughters every day and worried that Emmeline, only a year old when he last saw her, would not know him. 'Kiss my sweet cherub Emmeline and teach her to love me,' he wrote plaintively.[9] He took some 'unexpected gratification' though, from seeing a list of naval promotions in which many officers with less seniority than Bligh were promoted above him. John took this as a sign 'that Government view his conduct as it deserves'.[10]

John, deeply anxious about the forthcoming trial, tried to curry favour with friends (and friends of friends) in high places. But until the court martial of the rebel officers was completed, John's well-placed patrons would do nothing for him. Major Abbott summed up the situation when he wrote from England to Captain Piper about their mutual acquaintance John Macarthur: 'Mack makes a very little figure in this part of the world.'[11] There was little Elizabeth could do or write, from so far away, to lift John's melancholy.

Yet the 1811 trial of the rebel officers was, in the end, an anticlimax. While it was Lieutenant-Colonel Johnston who officially stood trial as the leader of the rebellion, the focus was also on the activities of civilian John Macarthur and his nemesis Bligh. None of the three men emerged very cleanly from the treasonous mire. Bligh was in the witness stand for three and half days and managed to lose his temper several times, confirming the defence's argument that he was too easily provoked into ungentlemanly behaviour. And Macarthur himself began with his usual confidence and bluster, but soon discovered that while his dissembling, evasions and outright contradictions might have served in a colonial court, they soon dissolved in the face of fierce and intelligent cross-examination. John Macarthur was out of his depth and it showed.

Johnston was found guilty of mutiny but instead of being sentenced to a prison term, or death, he was dishonourably discharged from the army and sent on his way. His miraculously light sentence has long been considered an acknowledgment that he was never the true leader of the rebellion: John Macarthur was.

John had resigned his army commission nearly ten years earlier and, as a civilian, he could not be subject to a court martial. Nor, it was eventually determined, could be he tried in England when his alleged crimes were committed in New South Wales. Tellingly, Governor Macquarie's orders for Macarthur's arrest on charges of high treason were not revoked after Johnston's trial, so while he remained a free man in England, he was effectively and indefinitely prevented from returning to Sydney. If he did, he would be arrested the moment he disembarked. And he could not risk a trial at home where, if found guilty, he would face a gaol sentence or possibly even the noose.

So, while other rebel leaders left the army to gradually and quietly resume their lives in New South Wales, John was forced to recalibrate his future. He wondered if he and Elizabeth could make enough money from their New South Wales activities to support the whole family in England, calculating that they would need at least £1600 a year for a comfortable life.[12] John estimated there might be enough capital to establish a small estate in England. At this point he bravely wrote to Elizabeth and told her of his new plans. She would have to sail to England without him, but if she had 'the smallest dread or apprehension of coming home alone' she need only to say so, wrote John, and he would 'sacrifice every other consideration and come out for you'.[13] In this he seems to have underestimated his stoic wife. Sailing to England in the company of her daughters and trusted servants was unlikely to raise too many apprehensions for a woman who travelled and worked alone on the edge of the colonial frontier. Any dread Elizabeth may have felt was far more likely to arise from her understanding of the financial risk if they left New South Wales.

The sentiment in John's letter is quite romantic but Elizabeth's concerns were wholly pragmatic and, from John's subsequent letters, we can infer that Elizabeth's response was adamant. There would be no selling up. The family's future lay in New South Wales, not in an ignominious and impecunious return to England. The brouhaha surrounding the trial would blow over soon enough and John would surely be able to negotiate his return. Clearly Elizabeth had faith in his ability to turn the situation around, although it seems she also included some sharp words about financial speculation. Elizabeth was definitely no silent partner when it came to crucial decisions about the future of the family.

John accepted Elizabeth's decision, and subsequently thanked her for it:

> I have the greatest reason to be thankful to God, that your good sense enabled you to resist the temptation of coming to England, had it not been so—into what an Abyss of misery would you and my beloved Children have been plunged—dearest beloved Woman, how great are my obligations to you![14]

Then once again he turned his mind to the family business. His letters become full of advice and suggestions about the flocks, much of which Elizabeth could safely ignore. She was too busy getting things done.

In 1812, along with Reverend Marsden and pastoralist Alexander Riley, Elizabeth exported a commercial quantity of wool to England. It was the first time anyone in New South Wales had been able to do so. Riley, buoyed by the success of that venture, subsequently 'paid Mrs Macarthur 108 guineas…for six merino rams'.[15] John Oxley and William Lawson were inspired to buy sheep from Elizabeth too. Under her discerning eye, the Macarthurs' pioneering breeding regime, for fleece rather than for meat, was finally paying dividends. The Blaxland brothers were similarly enthusiastic about the prospects for sheep, but it had been the publicity surrounding John's 1804 purchases of rams from the King's flock at Kew that had prompted them to buy some royal rams of their own to bring with them as free settlers in 1806. In 1813 Gregory Blaxland, William Lawson and William Charles Wentworth were feted for finding a way to cross the Blue Mountains that surround the Sydney basin; they were driven to do so almost entirely by a desire to find new grazing land for their sheep.

Elizabeth received excellent prices for that first shipment of wool, in 1812, but it was otherwise a difficult year. Her letters to John were delayed, or lost, and he went without hearing from her for two whole years. He still wrote to her though, long letters full of doubts and fears. Elizabeth knew from these letters that her own had not reached him. What questions had she asked him? What advice might she have been waiting to hear? And all the while worrying about her husband and sons at a time of war. With Edward soldiering on the continent, John took an active interest in the activities of Napoleon, who he described as a 'Ruffian' and 'the great disturber of the World'.[16] In November 1812, when the outcome of the Napoleonic Wars was far from settled, even John realised that 'Never was there a more important period than the present...For my own part I cherish the most sanguine hopes that [Napoleon] can never escape out of Russia'.[17]

Meanwhile, any financial gain made by Elizabeth was lost by John. His mercantile misadventures had 'swallowed up all the money I could command, and left me considerably in debt',[18] he wrote to Elizabeth. His financial wounds were further salted when he went to some trouble, 'indeed to part with my last guinea and to depend upon my credit', to advance £400 pounds to rebel leader George Johnston so that he could afford to sail home. Elizabeth could be forgiven for exclaiming with indignation as she read this, given how hard she worked to make their businesses successful, and to keep John in funds. John went on to write that he subsequently discovered that Johnston had been advanced an additional £1200 by another New South Wales colleague and was sour. 'This is all perfectly consistent with the whole of his conduct towards me,' wrote John, as if he expected Johnston to somehow feel grateful to him for instigating a rebellion for which he, Johnston, took the fall.

But, unlike John Macarthur, in late 1812 Johnston was allowed to sail home to New South Wales, and to return to his Annandale farm. In an echo of Elizabeth's circumstances, Johnston's convict partner Esther had been ably managing the family properties—and raising their seven children—in his absence. It would be entirely understandable if Elizabeth also felt sour seeing Esther's de facto husband return so soon. A year after Johnston arrived back in the colony, in November 1814, he married Esther and legitimised their relationship. Most historians argue the marriage occurred at the urging of Governor Macquarie but I wonder if, free of the burdens of upholding regimental honour, Johnston simply and finally followed his heart.

While Elizabeth continued to wait for John's homecoming, in 1812 John's nephew Hannibal (aged twenty-four) returned to New South Wales with his bride Anna Maria King (aged nineteen). Maria, as she was usually called, was the daughter of former governor King, and John was full of praise for her. He wrote to Elizabeth of the London wedding, confident that the new bride would 'soon entitle herself to your warmest regard, since to know her was to love her'.[19] The beleaguered King had died within a year of his return to England. Since then, John Macarthur and Hannibal had visited the widowed Mrs King, who having tried, and failed, to extract a pension from the government was living in straitened circumstances.

Within days of the wedding, Hannibal and Maria set sail for New South Wales aboard the *Isabella*, overseeing a mixed cargo of retail items of Uncle John's to be sold in Sydney. This was yet another venture that did not go well, and a year later John wrote to Hannibal to say he hoped the affair would be a lesson to him. In truth, the colony was at that time enduring a commercial depression and its effects were widely felt. Hannibal was unlucky rather than incompetent, although John may have believed otherwise. To continue John's own run of bad luck, the *Isabella* was shipwrecked on her way back to England, off the

Falkland Islands, although the cargo, crew and passengers were saved.[20] Hannibal, wrote John as the newlyweds departed, was as 'blunt, honest and unsophisticated as when he left Parramatta',[21] but he sincerely hoped his presence would relieve Elizabeth from 'the necessity of attending to the laborious and more disagreeable part of an undertaking that not many men would be capable of conducting so successfully as you have done, so much to your own credit, and to the advantage of your Family'.[22]

No doubt Elizabeth warmly welcomed Hannibal and his wife in Sydney in August 1812. Apart from being pleased to see them, the extra assistance the couple could provide on the farms and in the house was much needed. Maria came equipped with her sunny disposition and a book-length letter from her godmother with enormous detail (and numerous recipes) about how best to entertain at home including menus, the placement of dishes on the table and crucial details like 'you must have 2 boats of Fish Sauce, for you have no idea how soon it is ladled away'.[23] However, Maria would have little chance to take this advice—she would give birth to eleven children over the next twenty years and, probably as a result of all those pregnancies, would be an invalid for much of her life.

By the time Hannibal and Maria arrived, Elizabeth had some interesting wedding news of her own—her fully recovered eldest daughter, Elizabeth, was to be married too. Miss Macarthur (aged twenty) had accepted Mr John Oxley (aged twenty-eight), a handsome, dark-haired naval officer and long-time family friend. Unfortunately, though, the couple had become engaged without John Macarthur's permission, and Oxley had subsequently departed for England, seeking a civilian appointment to the role of New South Wales' surveyor-general as well as John's consent. John gave it, albeit hedged with many provisos about marriage settlements. He knew Oxley was heavily in debt and while noting the young man's good nature, he doubted his financial prudence and economy. Without knowing Elizabeth's or his daughter's views on the matter, but wishing that he did, he left it all up to his wife to determine. 'In whatever way you decide upon this momentous question of the happiness of our dear Child, be satisfied my beloved wife, I shall be sure to approve your decision.'[24]

But within a year, and still without hearing from Elizabeth about whether or not the marriage had gone ahead—or was even agreeable to his daughter—John discovered the true extent of John Oxley's debts and promptly retracted his consent, forbidding the marriage. As a result, Oxley withdrew and the marriage did not go ahead. It was all very well for John to make the principled decision, but it was Elizabeth who had to break the news and then comfort her daughter in her disappointment. There is no happy ending here; daughter Elizabeth never married—she lived out her life in her parents' home. John Oxley eventually married in Sydney and had two sons. Before then he had two daughters with one woman and a third daughter by another.[25] Perhaps that news had also reached John and influenced his change of mind. Oxley served the colony in various senior positions, earning a handsome wage and accumulating land grants, but when he died in 1828 at the age of forty-two he was 'much embarrassed in his pecuniary circumstances'.[26] His one-time fiancée was, as Elizabeth noted in a letter, deeply affected by his death.[27]

In 1813 Hannibal and Maria, expecting their first child, paid

£160 for a property on the opposite bank of the Parramatta River from Elizabeth Farm. Hannibal confessed to his uncle that he was not suited to be a merchant and that farming was, anyway, much more profitable and a less expensive way to live.[28] In a nice piece of historic coincidence the property was purchased from Captain Henry Waterhouse, who had imported the first Spanish sheep from Cape Town nearly two decades earlier. Hannibal and Maria called their new home the Vineyard because, back in the 1790s, it had been the site of the colony's first grapevines.[29] While Maria established her own household, Hannibal continued to help Elizabeth. There was no shortage of work for them both.

Elizabeth started keeping records in an old book that John had used for keeping accounts in the long-ago days when he was the regimental paymaster. Now that she was working with Hannibal there was a need to share information. Elizabeth used the old register to make fortnightly reckonings: how many sheep in each flock; how many killed, sold or butchered; how many new arrivals at lambing time; which rams were joined to which ewes. In effect, Elizabeth was establishing Australia's first merino stud book. But her management skills did not end there.

She also seems to have learnt from her previous experience to be firmer about collecting debts. There was still very little currency circulating in New South Wales and so it was impossible for Elizabeth to run her businesses on a cash basis. After John left for England in 1809 she essentially became a sole trader, and in 1814 she was in court several times, suing for debt—not only on her husband's behalf, but also in her own name. Elizabeth Macarthur was the only married woman of the period who is recorded as suing in her name alone. It is possible that there were others, but the incomplete marriage records leave the marital status of some female litigants unknown. In allowing Elizabeth's suit, the magistrates of New South Wales had no single English standard to follow. There was great variation between the counties and boroughs, and even within London, on the right of a woman to trade and sue in her own name. Common law gave way to local practices and in New South Wales the legal system swung in Elizabeth's favour.[30]

The precious Spanish rams and ewes, about one hundred of them, were kept close at Elizabeth Farm. The other crossbred sheep, which at the beginning of 1813 numbered 4033, lived with their shepherds on the outlying properties in flocks of about 300, each with four or five rams. With no fences surrounding the outlying pastures, shepherds were a necessary precaution against straying, dingoes and theft. The sheep at Elizabeth Farm were effectively inbred, to maintain purity, but surplus Spanish rams were taken to the properties at Cow Pastures to improve the flocks there. The relative isolation of Cow Pastures ensured that the Macarthur ewes were safe from stray, inferior rams.

As well as the flocks, Elizabeth was overseeing fifty-five horses (including a dozen quality broodmares) and two herds of horned cattle totalling 312.[31] The livestock necessary to feed the household—the dairy animals, pigs and the poultry—were so numerous and so unremarkable as to be not worth including in the record book. But they still needed to be managed, as did the extensive orchards and vegetable gardens. Elizabeth also grew wheat, barley and oats and made hay, not a common practice then but another indication of Elizabeth's forward thinking and farm management acumen. Elizabeth's friend Elizabeth Macquarie (the governor's wife) also cut hay, and the two women seem to have been among the first in the colony to do so.

'We feed hogs,' wrote Elizabeth in 1816, to her goddaughter in England, 'we have cattle, keep a dairy, fatten beef and mutton and export fine wool. A variety of avocations arising from these pursuits keeps the mind pretty busily employed.'[32] Elizabeth was a master of the modest understatement. She travelled so far and so often to oversee her numerous properties that she wore out her barouche (a light, four-wheeled carriage with a driver's seat high in front, two double seats inside facing each other, and a folding top over the back seat). Elizabeth didn't mention the worn-out barouche to John in her letters, but Hannibal wrote to tell him that his aunt was 'much inconvenienced for want of it' and suggested John send out a carriage.[33]

The only indication that John complied with the request lies in a lampooning poem that circulated in the colony at around this time. It described a landau—a carriage slightly larger than but similar to a barouche—with the Macarthur coat of arms (invented by John) emblazoned on the doors. 'Three fair ladies'— Elizabeth and her two eldest daughters—were ridiculed in the poem for admiring those decorated carriage doors with 'exalting pride' despite being the 'humblest, lowest, basest born'. The owners of the carriage were described as 'An expert Staymaker once he, An humble Mantua Maker she'.[34] This seems a sly reference to John's father and brother, with their draper and mercer business in Plymouth. The description of Elizabeth as a mantua maker, or professional dressmaker, is mere slander. Clearly the Macarthur family's successes were not appreciated by all in the colony. All Elizabeth could do was ignore it and, with Hannibal's help, get on with her work.

Elizabeth and Hannibal were not working alone of course. In addition to the convict shepherds, they engaged various labourers, tradesmen and servants on a full-time or an as-required basis. They were also ably assisted by overseer Thomas Herbert, a horseman and ex-convict who worked for them from 1806 until his death in the 1840s.[35] In 1811, Elizabeth had successfully requested the governor grant land to Herbert and to another of her workers. This was the first, but not the last, example of Elizabeth combining kindness with an intelligent view of a long-term advantage. It was in everyone's interest—including Elizabeth's—to reward her best and most enterprising servants. Other servants were encouraged to work hard that they might be similarly favoured and, because the grants were almost always awarded to family men and because their land grants adjoined her own, Elizabeth gained a loyal cohort of neighbours whose families could be drawn on for labour at busy times.[36]

With so many people to supervise, producing fine wool must have sometimes felt like the least of Elizabeth's concerns, but the prices she could obtain locally for beef and mutton were consistently falling as more and more farms were established in the colony.[37] 'My cares are many and anxious', wrote Elizabeth to Eliza Kingdon in Bridgerule.[38] Wool now became critical to keeping her widely dispersed (and expensive) family financially afloat.

17

Frontier Bloodshed

*The savages have burnt and destroyed the shepherds' habitations,
and I daily hear of some fresh calamity.*
ELIZABETH MACARTHUR TO ELIZA KINGDON, MARCH 1816

The bulk of Elizabeth's farming problems lay in getting the wool from the Australian sheep to the English shore.

The first bales of wool she sent to England for sale were well received, but the wool was considered very dirty, contaminated with 'innumerable grass seeds' and 'particles of dead leaves and sticks' as well as 'minute portions of charred wood and bark with which the fleeces abound, especially in dry seasons'.[1] In addition, the fleeces weighed more than they should have because of the quantity of sand they carried. Elizabeth was not satisfied with supplying a degraded product. She initiated a wool-cleaning process (which was further developed and refined by her sons) that rapidly became customary throughout the colonies. It was a sensible and ingenious response to the problem: the sheep were washed before they were shorn.

Almost thirty years later, the process was described in the

diary of another woman farmer, Anne Drysdale, in the Barwon
district of Victoria. Her washing place consisted of long logs (or
spars) placed across a river between two trees. The logs formed
two pens into which 'the sheep are flung & allowed to swim &
while they are there pushed by a forked stick under the middle
spar & men with flat sticks rub off the dirt after which they
swim out by an approach & go dripping & exhausted to join
their companions.'[2] After this ordeal the sheep had a day or
two to recover, as they could still not be shorn 'until the yolk
rises, or the wool becomes greasy'.[3] They also needed time to
fully dry out and woolsheds were purpose-built with a 'skilling
or verandah along one side under which some sheep are to be
placed all night, that they may be ready to shear in the morning,
otherwise they would be so wet with dew that the men could
not begin until 9 or 10'.[4] Drysdale's men, working with hand
clippers (of which there were never enough), could together
shear about 200 sheep in a day.

Elizabeth's wool clip was stored on site, in 'wool houses' she
had built for the purpose. The wool was baled in a press cobbled
together by Hannibal from materials to hand. 'I found a very
fine screw among the Iron-work which came out in the *Argo*,'
he wrote to his uncle, and it 'proves to be the best Press in the
country'.[5] After sorting, the poorest quality fleeces were sold to
the government and sent to the female factory at Parramatta, to
be spun and woven into coarse cloth by the convict women. The
rest was baled, transported to Sydney and (if luck and the weather
held) dispatched to England. The transport costs were high,
but the high level of demand from the English manufacturers
meant there was still a profit to be made.

John being in London to oversee the wool's sale was just what Elizabeth needed. He talked it up, made the right contacts and was able to provide valuable feedback about how to obtain a better price. Hannibal seems to have been in charge of shipping the wool and John exhorted Elizabeth to ensure he took more care to ensure the wool was properly sorted because 'the same Bale contained half a dozen different qualities of Wool'.[6] This made it difficult to price the wool accurately without opening all the bales, at some expense, and thus the price they eventually received was lower than it might have been. John continued with his advice and suggestions in letters to Elizabeth, and despite Hannibal's careful explanations kept sending instructions, such as: 'When Wool is sent in future it should be washed as clean as possible',[7] noting that he 'was much disappointed that the Wool should have come home in such a state'.[8] As if the whole colony didn't have to rely on the one man suitably qualified to sort wool; as if Elizabeth didn't go to enormous trouble to ensure that the wool was presented as well as it could be—amidst the dust and dirt of a colony almost as far as it was possible to be from 'England's green and pleasant land'.[9]

From his exile in England, John suggested to Elizabeth that she cultivate Governor Macquarie. She should sound out his interest in schemes that involved his granting to Macarthur additional land and convict servants—presumably in return for a quiet share of the profits. It is unlikely Elizabeth did anything quite so unsubtle, but she was not above manoeuvring the colony's bureaucracy to her own ends. In 1815 she managed to persuade Governor Macquarie to add an adjacent sixty acres to the Cow Pastures property because she had, as the Governor recorded, 'by mistake built a small Cottage on it'.[10] If it was a mistake, it was a profitable one.

When several of his wife's letters finally arrived all together in 1814, John replied with a litany of his physical and mental complaints, writing 'believe me my Elizabeth the period of my separation from you has been an almost uninterrupted scene of indescribable wretchedness'.[11] He suffered from chronic indigestion, which regularly attacked him 'with considerable violence, with an extraordinary irritation of nerves, and a sort of nervous Gout'. The gout was precipitated by many days of 'such dreadful depression of spirits as no one can conceive'.[12] John believed that he would only improve upon being reunited with his wife in New South Wales, but he wasn't beyond being critical of her reports of their farms.

He ever so *helpfully* pointed out to his wife that 'Many important things escape your memory at the moment of writing—do adopt the practice of making short memos when anything occurs worth repeating'.[13] He went on to provide a list of the sorts of things he wanted to know, such as the terms of sale for a flock of sheep, or the prices received for horses, because 'when I am asked the price of Stock which I frequently am I know not what to say'.[14] At least he had the good grace to finish his letters with phrases full of love, for example: 'it will be the study of my life to requite you for all that you have suffered on my account'.[15] Did she roll a wry eye at such a letter, reading it twice or three times for comfort before folding it up, tucking it safely with the others and getting on with her work?

From 1813 to 1815, the colony suffered though drought, and Elizabeth's work became harder and even less profitable. She asked if one or both of her sons could be sent home to help her but John prevaricated, noting that he would give the matter 'the gravest consideration before I decide'.[16] He evidently decided the boys should stay with him and instead sent out another cargo of goods for Elizabeth to sell. Groceries, straw bonnets and 'Peace Printed Cottons'[17] were hardly fair compensation for the boys she was longing to see. In his accompanying letter John frankly discusses the anticipated profit. That was all very well, but first the cargo had to be unloaded, examined, advertised, exhibited, sold, delivered and accounted for. John also asked for news about the renewal of the 'lease of the Sydney cottage' and noted with approval the additional land grant of swampland near Parramatta that Elizabeth had secured from Macquarie, which made 'a desirable whole of the Farm to secure us from interruption'. He went on to suggest Elizabeth work with Macquarie to negotiate a swap of the Toongabbie farm for more land at Cow Pastures 'but I leave the arrangement entirely to you'.[18] Elizabeth was hard put to find enough hours in her day.

Hannibal helped when he could, but he was attempting to establish his own properties and Elizabeth felt the lack of support. She had, she wrote to her Bridgerule friends, been so long 'deprived of any assistance from any male branch of my family that I cannot say I am comfortable or happy'.[19] During the drought her flock numbers declined significantly, as sheep died or were culled. Once-lush pastures turned golden, then brown, then shrivelled to little more than dust in the face of fierce north winds. Elizabeth looked on in distress as her cattle starved.[20] Rivers dried to a chain of puddles and stock died in the mud, stuck fast in their desperate bid for water. And fire, of course, was an ever-present threat. On hot, windy days all eyes scanned the horizon, checking again and again for any hint of smoke or haze. A fire front could arrive faster than a terrified messenger could ride to warn those in its path. Modern Australian farmers are familiar with the cyclical—although never quite predictable—nature of Australian droughts, fires and rains, but Elizabeth and her farming peers were still learning, and learning the hard way.

They were, of course, not the only ones doing it tough. The Aboriginal people of the Sydney basin had been dispossessed, attacked and terrorised for some twenty-five years, and now with the drought, many were probably hungry too. Tensions rose, and Elizabeth was soon to be surrounded by bloodshed and grief. In May 1814 soldiers shot and killed an Aboriginal boy who was part of a group 'raiding' a field of corn on a farm near Appin, about fifteen kilometres to the southeast of Elizabeth's Cow Pastures properties, but much further by road. One of the soldiers was subsequently speared, and his body was mutilated. A vicious series of attacks and counter-attacks ensued.

English settlers ambushed a camp of sleeping Aboriginal people, killing three children and a woman and then mutilating the dead woman's corpse. Aboriginal men were blamed for killing one of Elizabeth's workers, a convict man described by Hannibal to John as 'your old favourite William Baker',[21] who had been with them almost since they had arrived in New South Wales. Killed also was the wife of one of Elizabeth's shepherds. So were three white children at Bringelly, about halfway between the Cow Pastures and Parramatta. Hannibal noted though, that 'in addition to the Natives numbers of convicts are roving uncontrolled through the country committing all kinds of depredations and I have every reason to believe some of them were concerned with the Natives in the attack'.[22] Anxieties among the settlers rose further with rumours that Aborigines planned an attack en masse at the next full moon, in early June. Terrified women and children were evacuated. In the end, nothing happened that night, but Elizabeth and her neighbours continued to live and work with the worry of attack.

To the forefront of Elizabeth's mind was the fact that these attacks mirrored earlier killings of her own workers. In 1805, a few weeks before John arrived back in New South Wales from his first trip to England, Aboriginal people 'from the interior of the mountains' used tomahawks to kill two stockmen working at one of the outlying Macarthur properties.[23] The mountain Aborigines were considered 'wild', and dangerous, in comparison to the 'friendly' Aboriginal people of the lowlands south of Sydney. The latest rounds of reprisals were also said to have been undertaken by those Gandangarra mountain people.

Governor Macquarie visited the region to attempt an investigation. He learned of the rape of Aboriginal women and decided that Aboriginal payback justice had been satisfied. 'Having had their Revenge in the way they always seek it,' he wrote, 'I am not at all apprehensive of their making any further attacks.'[24] Governor Macquarie clearly knew about Aboriginal payback law and their justice system. He ordered both sides to refrain from further attacks, but even before the proclamation was published the white men who had attacked the sleeping campsite were speared and killed. Macquarie sent out a reprisal party of armed civilians but, after three weeks, the party returned empty-handed.

An uneasy peace, of sorts, was maintained until February 1816. A party of thirty or forty Gandangarra mountain men raided a farm near Bringelly and stole servants' possessions. The following day a reprisal party walked into an ambush, had their muskets wrenched away and were shot at and showered with spears. Four white men were killed, another was speared and the rest were chased back to where they had come from. The next day the Gandangarra warriors raided another farm (this time the frightened settlers reported their numbers at sixty) and again left with everything they could carry. A week later the Gandangarra headed south and attacked Elizabeth's properties at Cow Pastures, killing three men and burning their huts. Once more the women and children living in the area were evacuated and once more a party went in search of retribution. Elizabeth retreated to the relative safety of her home at Parramatta.

The colonist's reprisal party was assisted by Budbury, a Dharawal man of the country south of Botany Bay. The white settlers understood that a fierce enmity existed between the people of the plains, the Dharawal, and the Gandangarra mountain people and they planned to use this to their advantage. As in all things, the reality was much more complex and there was substantial interaction between the two groups. Budbury either deliberately or unaware, led the settlers straight into another ambush: the waiting Gandangarra men rained spears and stones down on the reprisal party, and the settlers fled. It was, reported one man afterwards, a 'wonder a great number of us was not killed, some even threw off their shoes to enable them to run fast...'[25] The defeated white men crept home, terrified of finding their families speared to death although in fact the next few weeks were eerily quiet. But at the end of the month an English woman and her male servant were killed, their corpses 'mangled', and Macquarie felt forced to take action. A fraught situation was to be resolved with hideous and brutal simplicity.

The governor sent out three detachments of soldiers, with orders to capture all Aborigines, and to kill any who failed to surrender. There was no distinction between 'wild' and 'friendly' although each detachment was accompanied by Aboriginal guides and each had a list of the names of Aboriginal men who were wanted for murder. The expeditioners were exhorted to 'use every possible precaution to save the lives of Native Women and Children',[26] but Macquarie also ordered that Aboriginal men who were killed were to be strung up in trees, as a warning to survivors.

One detachment headed north to the Hawkesbury region. Over the course of several raids and false leads they did not see a single Aborigine. A second detachment headed down to Elizabeth's Belgenny Farm in the Cow Pastures region. This group's Aboriginal guide was Tindale, and the colonists considered him a 'Chief of the Cow Pastures Tribe', the Muringong people. He also magnificently failed to lead the detachment to any Aboriginal campsites. A white stock-keeper from the Macarthur estates led the soldiers to an Aboriginal village of seventy huts near Bringelly, only to find the site deserted; the inhabitants had clearly been warned. Not so lucky was a group of Aboriginal people camping on the Macarthur estate itself. In a dawn raid, most of the people managed to flee in the nick of time but the soldiers shot one man, who later died of his wounds, and took a teenage boy prisoner.[27]

Elizabeth's attitude towards Aboriginal people seemed to harden. Like many others in the colony, she moved away from her original conciliatory view, which in the earliest days had seen her welcome the visits of Daringa and her baby. Now that there were substantial sums of money to be gained or lost, now that white people known to her personally had been killed, Elizabeth could only see the original inhabitants as a threat. She shared the colonists general lack of insight about Aboriginal culture, affording it no credence or legitimacy. 'Attempts have been made to civilise the natives of this country,' she wrote from Parramatta to her goddaughter in Bridgerule, 'but they are complete savages, and are as lawless and troublesome as when the Colony was first established. Our out settlements are constantly subjected to their depredations.'[28] That the same could equally be said by Aboriginal people, about the colonists, completely escaped her. Elizabeth, like most of the other white farmers, was far more concerned for her livestock than for the Aboriginal people of the area and felt herself to be 'much oppressed with care on account of our stock establishments at our distant farms, at the Cow Pastures, having been disturbed by the incursions of the natives'.[29]

After the promising beginnings of Governor Phillip's interactions with the Eora people of Sydney Harbour, the Aboriginal people of New South Wales as a group were now, in the minds of the colonists, relegated to sub-human savages. Individuals could (and would) be befriended and respected—even loved—but collectively the Aboriginal people were feared and despised. The

English colonists acted on their fear in the same way as colonial invaders had done the world over—with state-sanctioned murder.

At the time Elizabeth wrote her letter, a third detachment of soldiers, marching due south of Sydney, spent frustrating weeks following false leads and finding no one. Finally they were led, in the middle of the night, to an Aboriginal campsite south of Appin. The campsite, which was on high ground not far from a steep rocky gorge through which the Cataract River flowed, was empty but the fire was still burning. In the subsequent search, the soldiers heard a child cry and the commanding officer immediately 'formed line rank entire' and the soldiers 'pushed through a thick brush' towards the noise. The advancing line of redcoats spotted the fleeing people and opened fire. Some Aboriginal people were killed; some were so badly wounded 'death would...be a blessing'.[30] Others, in their panic and fear, ran right off the cliffs, and fell more than fifty metres to their deaths on the rocks below. The soldiers took two women and three children prisoner and counted fourteen bodies—including women, children, two warriors and an old man. The corpses of the warriors were hauled for more than a mile to a hilltop, where their bodies were hung up in the trees. The men's heads were later sent to the anatomy department of the University of Edinburgh.

The Appin massacre failed to bring peace to the colonial frontier, although violence against Europeans on and around Elizabeth's properties ceased to be reported. Attacks and reprisals continued apace, largely along the edge of white settlement, which at this point had moved to the far side of the Blue Mountains. Macquarie issued proclamations which, in practice, allowed settlers to shoot Aboriginal people with impunity, but in April 1817 he wrote to the colonial secretary in London to say that 'all Hostility on both Sides has long since ceased'.[31] In fact attacks would continue, in various forms, until well into the twentieth century. It seems unlikely that Elizabeth participated in any murderous raids, although other women farmers did. But even if Elizabeth did not herself kill anyone, even if she did not directly order her workers to kill, the killings still occurred on and around her land and to her benefit. She had to believe in the moral superiority of her own people, and her own cause, and conversely in the moral and inhuman degeneracy of Aboriginal people, in order to carry on in her colonial ventures.

Any doubts Elizabeth felt about the family enterprise, any concerns she held as a devout Christian for her own immortal soul, any qualms about killing men, women and children so that her livestock might graze in peace could never, ever be discussed. Who could she tell? The ladies who gathered at Government House to take tea? It was one more coal to add to her smouldering resentment of John, whose actions were the sole reason she was forced to carry such burdens alone. Always and again, her thoughts turned to England and her absent husband and boys. When were they coming home?

18

Prosperity

I cannot even now repress the ardent desire which I have once more to see the place of my birth. So many and so great have been the obstacles that I have never dared to cherish the hope.

ELIZABETH MACARTHUR TO ELIZA KINGDON, DECEMBER 1817

In 1816 Elizabeth turned fifty and the drought broke. John had been absent for seven years, and after the dark times of ceaseless work and dismay, Elizabeth seems to have settled into a manageable, contented routine which included a social life. She wrote to her goddaughter Eliza Kingdon to say she visited and was visited by 'a sufficiency of pleasant, agreeable persons'.[1]

Elizabeth's rapport with the Macquaries continued and her friends included the regimental commander and lieutenant-governor, Colonel Molle, and his wife. Colonel Molle was, according to Elizabeth, 'a most accomplished charming man, who has seen much of the world', and Mrs Molle was 'friendly and affectionate, and pretty conversant with the same sort of knowledge'.[2] Elizabeth's older daughters turned twenty-four and twenty-one in October of that year—more than old enough to manage the household. There are hints in John's letters that daughter Elizabeth still wasn't always entirely well, but he praises Mary for taking on household tasks. John was convinced, he wrote, that such employment was 'better calculated to promote the happiness of the female sex than all the refinements of modern education.'[3] Mary's views on the subject are not recorded, and nor are her hardworking mother's. Little Emmeline was now seven, going on eight, and her supervision and schooling likely fell largely to Mrs Lucas—companion, governess and much-loved family member. She never married, it seems, but instead quietly graduated from Miss to Mrs Lucas as she grew older.

Four years since her ill-fated engagement to John Oxley, Elizabeth's eldest daughter managed to catch the eye of another potential suitor—William Charles Wentworth, son of Darcy Wentworth and convict woman Catherine Crowely. Darcy and Catherine had sailed out to New South Wales in the *Neptune*, along with John and Elizabeth Macarthur, and during that journey had conceived young William. The relationship between the families was uneasy, to say the least. Elizabeth could hardly have been on visiting terms with a convict woman. It is also likely that young William was the author of that mocking poem about the Macarthur ladies and their emblazoned landau but it is almost certain, however, that the Macarthurs wouldn't have known that.

In 1816, while John Macarthur was still in England, William Charles Wentworth (also in England) wrote to his father in New South Wales about 'the passion I have so long entertained' for the oldest Macarthur daughter.[4] In the same letter he also writes that 'I have never confessed it to anyone but Mr McArthur'.

It is entirely possible he never even mentioned his passion to the object of his affections. Wentworth, in his mid-twenties, writes movingly of his feelings and mentions the advantages of the match for both families. Again, as with the proposal from Oxley, there is no record of young Elizabeth's thoughts on the matter, nor of her mother's. Wentworth believed John Macarthur supported his suit, but it all fell through after Wentworth quarrelled over a money matter with the Macarthurs' second eldest son, John. If Wentworth's convict antecedents also told against him in the Macarthurs' eyes, there is no record of it. There *was* a group of free settlers who refused to allow their children to marry the offspring of convicts but there is no evidence the Macarthurs belonged to it, and John Macarthur later, in a private letter, described the groups' attitude as 'illiberal'.[5] Either way, Wentworth took the rejection very hard and the two families remained at arm's length socially, despite regularly seeing each other at various business, political and social occasions.

Knowing from John's letters that the colonial office refused to budge on the matter of allowing him to come home, Elizabeth again suggested to her husband that their youngest sons might come home to Parramatta to help her. By the time John read her letter, though, James had finished school and was working in the counting house of a merchant trading in goods from 'West and East India'.[6] Much to James's relief, he remained there for only a year and, as soon as William finished school too, John Macarthur set off with the two boys on a year-long agricultural tour through France and Switzerland.

They inspected olive groves, vineyards and silk farms and

made enquiries into the manufacture of rapeseed and poppy oils. They turned their attention to irrigation and to improving the boys' French. In Paris they glimpsed Bonaparte, who had escaped from exile on Elba, at the window of the Tuileries. The European tour proved instructive, educational and a tonic to John's 'disorders of the nerves'.[7] The fact that it was also very much cheaper for the three to live on the continent than in England no doubt also played a part in relieving some of John's disquiet. At the age of sixteen James was, wrote John in a letter to Elizabeth from Geneva, growing 'very fast and promises to be a very fine young man. William [now fourteen] continues a little lively fellow and I think will remain so', although John added that William was 'like his Father a little prone to be idle. James on the contrary is slow and persevering.'[8] Elizabeth loved to read about her children, but the letters must have made her feel their absence all the more keenly.

The remittances Elizabeth had been able to send through to John, despite the difficult economic state of the Colony, he gratefully received. 'Edward,' wrote John, 'returned from [soldiering in] America wanting everything', and son John, finished with university and looking to become a lawyer, had to be provided with the means to pursue his legal studies and to buy a place in the Temple (which then, and now, houses barristers' chambers and solicitors' offices). On their return to England in the northern spring of 1816, both younger boys were yearning for their home in Parramatta, but still their father was unable to return without facing, as he wrote to Elizabeth, 'irretrievable ruin'.[9] John was, again, despondent. He wrote candidly about how he might finagle his way home and then suggested Elizabeth should commit the letter 'to the flames'.[10] She obviously did not.

The tide was, however, on the turn. Within a few months John and the boys were quite sure the government was more receptive to the idea of John returning to New South Wales, and James was 'almost crazy with joy at the idea of returning to his home'.[11] John began to plan for his return. He wrote to Elizabeth:

> Will you have the goodness to prepare in the most careful manner you can, a few acres of the Cow Pastures for Seeds, on land out of reach of floods, and likewise eight or ten acres at Parramatta, for the same purpose. We shall find room somewhere for the Vines and Olives I hope to bring out alive.[12]

Elizabeth, familiar with her husband's grand plans and, after all this time, not inclined to believe in his return until it was formally confirmed perhaps did not leap up and immediately order a team to be yoked to the plough.

The wheels of bureaucracy turned slowly for several months before finally one of John's patrons managed to convince the colonial office that the colony of New South Wales would be better off for John's presence in it. Macarthur was allowed to return on one condition: he must concede to the 'impropriety of conduct which led to your departure from the Colony'.[13] John, in spite of everything, would concede no such thing. With his typical stubbornness, he made it more difficult for the colonial office to let him home than should have been the case. More months and letters passed between Macarthur and the colonial office until finally it must have seemed easier for the government to draw a line under the whole sorry episode than to continue the endless obfuscation.

In February 1817 the government offered John Macarthur, along with his sons James and William, free passage home on a convict transport ship. Additional tonnage for implements, stores and a greenhouse full of the cuttings collected during the European tour was also to be provided. Not only had John persuaded the colonial office to let him go home, but he got them to pay for it! He gloated to Elizabeth that 'neither concession nor retraction shall be insisted upon',[14] and he looked forward to telling her all the details in person, when she could 'reward me with those endearments to which I have so long been a stranger'.[15] To complete John's victory, his nemesis, Bligh, died later in 1817 in the knowledge that Macarthur would return to New South Wales without charge.

Elizabeth's second son, John, stayed in England to pursue his legal career. Her husband wrote candidly to her about him:

> For altho' I think him as free from vice, or even irregularity, as any Young Man I ever knew, he is unfortunately very careless, very good natured, and perhaps a little too proud for one who has but little money, and few connections to advance and promote him in Life. From whom he derives these qualities you will be under no difficulty to discover.[16]

These words echo the views of the Bridgerule villagers about John Macarthur himself, when he was a young man wooing Elizabeth. But in this case John was being overly modest about his son, who was probably the brightest of the Macarthur sons and certainly the apple of his father's eye. As John, James and

William prepared to set sail for home, young John was, according to his father, working on legislative changes and was engaged 'in passing an Act of Parliament to open the trade of the Colony and to exempt wool and several articles that I hope to introduce from the payment of duties for a limited time'.[17] Given that young John was still, at the time, studying law rather than fully practising it, perhaps his fond father overstated his son's role, but the fact remains that young John was actively pursuing his family's business interests in England, and playing no small role in their financial success.

Father and younger sons set sail for Sydney via Rio aboard the *Lord Eldon* and arrived in New South Wales on the morning of Tuesday 30 September 1817. John's first question to the pilot, who came aboard to see *Lord Eldon* safely to anchorage, was about his wife. Was she well? Upon hearing that she was, John relaxed a little and had more patience for 'a most annoying adverse wind' which was preventing the ship from moving into the harbour. John sent a brief note, via another boat that met the ship, to his 'dearest best beloved Elizabeth' about his happy exchange with the pilot and flagging that his severe gout would prevent him from rushing home with the boys. But he felt sure the gout would soon pass and 'Home will do more for me than the Doctor—How many dear associations does that word Home create!'[18] Captain Piper also went out to the ship, and James, overjoyed to be back, penned a hasty postscript to the note his father had written.

> Captain Piper is just come on board, we shall set off as soon as possible in his boat, and my father will follow as soon as the heat of the day is over, in his

carriage—Adieu, we shall soon be with you—Your affectionate son JAS. MCA.[19]

Elizabeth was not waiting in Sydney to meet them. Last time John returned she cooled her heels in town for more than five weeks before the ship appeared, so perhaps it was simply a matter of expedience to stay at Elizabeth Farm, continuing to work, and wait for her family to arrive. The joyous end result was just the same.

'I am yet scarcely sensible of the extent of my happiness,' wrote Elizabeth to Eliza Kingdon in Bridgerule, 'and indeed I can hardly persuade myself that so many of the dear members of our family are united again under the same roof.'[20] Emmeline, now aged nine, had not seen her father or brothers since she was a babe in arms. She was 'much engaged in running about, and showing her brothers everything that she can think will amuse them'.[21] In turn, her brothers were able to amaze and delight their sisters as they unpacked the crates they'd brought with them. In addition to the plants, seeds and farming paraphernalia, the boys had collected many fine souvenirs including oil paintings of the European landscapes through which they'd passed and gilt-edged dinner services with complex arrays of plates and servers and tea sets. The wonder was that they found room for it all at Elizabeth Farm, which was still a modest square cottage, and not yet the elegant bungalow it would become.

Elizabeth felt John had hardly changed at all. Whether she found that a good or a bad thing, she doesn't say. But her little boys were now 'fine young men. James six feet high and stout withal, William more slender but evidently giving promise of being stout also'.[22] Both boys were delighted to be home, and

neither expressed any regrets about leaving England behind. But
the more John and the boys discussed their adventures abroad,
the more Elizabeth longed to return to England herself. Now,
surely, she could begin to make plans to visit the home—and
faces—she'd not seen in nearly thirty years. Her mother, aged
seventy, was still living in Bridgerule and Elizabeth's half-sister,
Isabella Hacker, was mother to five daughters (she would go
on to have another two). But Elizabeth's hopes for any reunion
were in vain.

John's optimism about the curative effectives of home did not
last longer than his first southern summer. As mild as he found
the winters in New South Wales, the cooler weather saw a return
of his gout, and along with the pain came the familiar darkness
of spirit. He found it hard even to exert himself enough to write
a letter to Walter Davidson, and when he did he was candid
about his own malaise: 'You have witnessed how much I used
to suffer from mental depression. It is now so much increased
that I often pass weeks, without one cheerful moment, and I
am seldom relieved from this dreadful gloom, except by the
return of acute pain.'[23]

The management of the estates fell, then, to sons James and
William. Hannibal's help was no longer needed, and he and
his wife Maria focused on their growing family and their own
substantial holdings. John very much felt himself to be in charge
and that he was breaking his sons in 'by degrees to oversee and
manage [his] affairs'.[24] But given that he was confined to his
bedroom for weeks at a time, perhaps Elizabeth did not step
back from managing the farms as much as she might have hoped
to. According to their father, the boys appeared 'to be contented

with their lot, but I by no means think them well calculated for it. They have not the sufficient hardness of character to manage'.[25] Of course he was wrong. His sons worked hard and learnt fast, and the whole family's efforts began to pay off. For the next decade or so, the Macarthur family (and, indeed, the whole colony) did exceedingly well, with their main income drawn from the sale of wool. After thirty years of farming, much of it entirely managed by Elizabeth, the Macarthurs were a success.

When James and William weren't working—and, probably, being young men of spirit, even when they were—they amused themselves by riding, shooting, fishing and occasionally visiting the officers at the Parramatta barracks. In 1819 and the years following, the wild cattle at Cow Pastures were finally brought in and yarded. George Johnston's son, also called George and at twenty-nine a superb horseman, was appointed superintendent of government stock and given the task. In the course of his work he engaged in a mad race with one of the Macarthur sons, fell from his horse and was kicked in the chest and killed. John Macarthur wrote of his death as having 'inexpressibly disturbed us all, for he was a most deserving young person'.[26] George's death was a salutary example to all the young Macarthurs but, as it must, life went on.

A year after their return James and William were still regaling their mother and three sisters with amusing accounts of their travels. The household, now full to overflowing with young adults, was well-stocked with, as Elizabeth noted 'an excellent collection of books'. Elizabeth went on to tell her goddaughter that 'we receive most of the new publications from England'.[27] Not one for novels, Elizabeth preferred biographies, history and travel. At one stage she read everything she could about Afghanistan, and then she was similarly intrigued by travelogues about India.[28] The Macarthur family's reading tastes were eclectic, and a stocktake, much later, of the library at Elizabeth Farm revealed hundreds of volumes: the novels of Walter Scott and Daniel Defoe; histories; biographies; poetry (including works by Wordsworth and Burns); classics (including Virgil and Milton); prayers and sermons; almanacs; books about gardening and sheep and architecture; well-thumbed grammars; parliamentary reports; catalogues; tracts; picture books; and the complete works of Shakespeare.

The overcrowding at Elizabeth Farm was addressed by moving James and Edward Macarthur down to Belgenny, in the Cow Pastures region. There they lived in the cottage that their canny mother had 'accidentally' built in 1815. It is possible that this cottage today forms the service wing of Belgenny Cottage (built in 1822).[29] William planted twenty acres (eight hectares) of vineyard, as well as olive trees, with a view to one day producing oil in saleable quantities. And the brothers explored the lands further to the southwest, following the Abercrombie and Wollondilly rivers through the southern highlands to the fertile area north of the present-day township of Goulburn, which was at the time called the Argyle district. Within the next decade the Macarthurs would establish a new estate there, called Taralga.

The collection of Macarthur land grants at Cow Pastures (including Belgenny Farm) were grandly renamed by John as Camden Park, in honour of the Lord who had originally granted the land during John's first trip to England. In naming the property, John was in effect bragging to his colonial peers about his superior connections and patronage. The family had, in name and ambition at least, progressed from a mere *Farm* at Parramatta to the far more genteel *Park*. John was also cannily asserting his ownership over an area that had previously been considered, by the colonists at least, an open common. Governor Macquarie began to provide both the Macarthur boys with further land grants and support in their own names, in open acknowledgment of their explorations and in tacit acknowledgment that James and William were the drivers behind Camden Park's current success. Elizabeth's 'prudent and able management'[30] was acknowledged only by her husband, albeit in a letter to Lord Bathurst. By the early 1820s about a hundred European people lived and worked at Camden Park. It is likely that Aboriginal people lived and worked there too.[31] A hierarchical system of overseers and upper servants allowed family members to keep their distance from the convict workers. As James succinctly put it, 'We find it more convenient not to give orders to the convicts ourselves.'[32]

It was perhaps inevitable that Elizabeth would withdraw from the daily life of the farm work to make way for her sons and husband. But she continued to maintain an interest, and she would later write that she still liked to go out and watch the shearing. If she provided ongoing advice and support to her sons, it was done discreetly, in quiet conversations rather than in the letters that went constantly back and forth between Camden Park and Elizabeth Farm. That her grown-up sons respected her views and opinions is evident from the tone of their letters to her; they are never patronising or terse.

John negotiated a deal with Macquarie to sell rams to the government to establish a wool industry in Van Diemen's Land. The rams left Sydney in February 1820, although of the 312 that were sent, only 181 survived to be distributed among the settlers. Those rams were crossbreds and many were decried as inferior culls, but they were still a cut above any stock in Van Diemen's Land at the time. The Macarthur sheep had an almost immediate effect on flock quality and, despite the fact that John had kept his finest rams safe at home, the crossbreds' arrival marked a turning point in the Van Diemen's Land wool industry. A tradition was established of annual ram sales, held at Elizabeth Farm the day after the Parramatta fair and animal show and advertised in the *Sydney Gazette*.

John Ryrie Graham, an eminent sheepman who in the 1870s wrote *A Treatise on the Australian Merino*, remembered seeing Macarthur sheep in 1826. Weighing in at about thirty pounds each they were very small, smaller than the merinos of Graham's day (which were in turn smaller than modern merinos) and each wore a small leather collar. The fine-woolled sheep were compact, low set and with such short legs that their bodies were close to the ground. Graham believed that at the time he saw them, and for many years after, 'these sheep were undoubtedly the best in the Australian colonies, and could Mr Macarthur have produced three times the number of rams he did produce, they would have met with a ready sale'.[33]

As an old man, though, and with the wisdom of a lifetime spent working with and breeding sheep, Graham admitted that the Macarthur sheep were considered exceptional only because other sheep in the colony were so poor. The much-vaunted fine wool of the Macarthur flocks may have been as much the result of the inadequate native grasses and poor nutrition provided by most of the colony's farms, as it was intelligent breeding. Yet during these heady years the Macarthurs saw a five-fold increase in the quantity of wool they exported, and it sold in London at record prices.

In 1820 the non-Indigenous population of New South Wales was just over 33,000 but by the end of the decade it was 70,000.[34] Britain was slowly realising that the despised penal colony could be a place of rich rewards for anyone with the appropriate entrepreneurial spirit, and respectable free settlers arriving in New South Wales were keen to meet the successful Macarthurs. From the Macarthurs a 'new chum' could receive advice, and introductions and purchase finely bred sheep with which to begin his own wool-growing enterprises. Brothers Robert and Helenus Scott were just such well-connected and well-educated newcomers when in 1822, shortly after arriving, Robert wrote to his mother in England:

> McArthur's name of course you have heard of; he has been here for many years—the leading man of the colony, I must say deservedly: he is a very clever, shrewd, calculating man, with an extraordinary degree of perseverance and foresight, but a man of the most violent passions, his friendship strong & his hatred invincible.[35]

John Macarthur's volatility was becoming more and more evident and there was little, if anything Elizabeth could do to mitigate it.

She did, however, have more time to read for pleasure now, and was able to return her focus to the management of the household at Elizabeth Farm and to the education of ten-year-old Emmeline. Son John, as well overseeing the sale of wool in London and lobbying for parliamentary favours, was responsible for selecting and shipping out all the necessary household and farm goods and implements. In several shipments, he may have failed to meet his mother's high standards because she felt compelled to remind him that everything he sent out for their personal use should be of appropriate quality:

> We wear our things out and therefore wear them long…
> At this distance from the Mother Country mere articles
> of show are ridiculous. Our household linen and clothes
> I contend should be of good quality, both because they
> are better taken care of—are in the end more useful,
> certainly more respectable, and in the object of package
> and freight cost no more than trash.[36]

She makes it clear that from now on she would like supplies, including table linen and napkins, to arrive on a regular, twice-yearly basis. By this point she clearly has her blood up. 'The last cambric muslins [you sent] we were greatly deceived in. Your sisters made them up into dresses, they washed to pieces immediately—injured we suppose in the bleaching.'[37]

Elizabeth's newfound attention to household matters left her older two daughters, especially Mary who had taken up the housekeeping role while her father was away, at something of a loose end. Eldest daughter Elizabeth struck up a correspondence with her mother's goddaughter Eliza Kingdon, who it seems she had not met during her English sojourn with her father a dozen or more years earlier. 'Altho I have not the pleasure, dear Miss Kingdon, of being personally known to you, yet my Mother permits me to hope you will not reject my correspondence.'[38] Miss Macarthur attempted to explain to Miss Kingdon how she and her sisters filled their time. 'We remain out rambling in our woods, or diverting ourselves in our garden until the evening surprises us.'[39] This hardly sounds enough to keep grown women occupied and Miss Macarthur hinted as much in her second letter, noting that 'in the history of our day…there is not much variety'.[40]

Elizabeth did not seem to encourage her daughters to do more—for themselves or for others—or to somehow make more of their lives. It is worth remembering that the villagers of Bridgerule, when vilifying John Macarthur as 'too proud and haughty', also labelled Elizabeth as 'indolent and inactive'.[41] Perhaps they were right. Perhaps Elizabeth, forced by circumstance to be a busy and enterprising woman, may well have preferred the leisurely life she bestowed—or inflicted—on her daughters. We can only imagine, then, the eager anticipation among the Macarthur women of the governor's ball held in January 1819, to celebrate the seventy-fifth birthday of Queen Charlotte. For Elizabeth it was a chance to enjoy herself and relax; for her daughters a chance to get out into the world.

Mrs Macquarie's guest list, a hand-written working document, lists 186 guests. Elizabeth, it seems, did not approve of all the invitees and, as she wrote to her goddaughter, 'I will not say that these assemblies have been very select.' That lack of discernment didn't seem to prevent her attending. The Macquaries ensured the annual Queen's Birthday celebrations were a lavish affair. The ballroom was decorated with coloured lamps and festooned with greenery and flowers. Revellers danced to the music of the regimental band.[42] Eldest daughter Elizabeth was invited too, as were Hannibal and Maria. So was Mrs Lucas, which sheds some interesting light on her status—clearly she was perceived as more than a mere governess or servant. Absent from the guest list, though, is Elizabeth's second daughter Mary. What trouble did that cause in Elizabeth's home?

Mary, when mentioned at all in her siblings' letters, is often described as difficult. Even her mother seemed, at least occasionally, to find her challenging. Mrs Macquarie, following the etiquette of the day, couldn't be expected to include *all* the unmarried younger sisters and the list indicates that, for other families too, only the eldest unmarried daughters were invited.[43] At smaller, less overtly ceremonial occasions Mrs Macquarie entertained Elizabeth and the other ladies of Sydney in the evenings with 'Tea, Coffee, Cards, Music, and a little Dance'.[44] Perhaps poor Mary was at least invited to these.

Mary was the quintessential middle child, who was never the focus of her parents' full attention. When Mary was between the ages of six and ten, her father was in England and her mother was juggling the competing demands of baby William, infant James and managing the farms. Upon her father's return Mary might have expected to see more of her mother, but she may well have felt compelled to compete with her older sister Elizabeth, newly returned from seeing England and the world. Then in 1807 (the year Mary turned twelve), Elizabeth's almost fatal, paralysing illness and long recovery necessarily took precedence. The surprise arrival of another sister, little Emmeline, and the second absence of her father came at a time when Mary was on the cusp of adolescence. Throughout her teen years her needs had to give way to the recovering invalid, the growing baby and her mother's ongoing battle to keep the family farms profitable. Maybe Mary *was* the difficult, prickly girl (and then woman) described in her brothers' letters—or maybe she was simply strong-willed. Perhaps she felt let down by those she loved.

Whatever her thoughts on the matter, Mary was soon to emerge from between her older and younger sisters in a social triumph. In 1823 she married James Bowman, principle surgeon of the colony. According to the *Sydney Gazette* the couple married 'On Tuesday, the 4th November, at her Father's Residence, Parramatta'.[45] James was thirty-seven, Mary nine years younger at twenty-eight; spinsterhood was only narrowly avoided. In a letter to Eliza Kingdon, the mother of the bride perhaps gave away more than she meant to when she noted that Mary had 'broken through the spell of celibacy which seemed to encompass the house'.[46] Was Elizabeth speaking only of her unmarried daughters, or did she include herself? Was it that John was often unwell? Or had Elizabeth and John, over time, grown even further apart?

Doctor Bowman had met John and his sons in 1817, when they sailed back to New South Wales together in the *Lord Eldon*, and John regarded him as 'a most respectable prudent man' and believed that the marriage held 'every rational prospect of happiness'. Ten years earlier, when John vetoed daughter Elizabeth's marriage to John Oxley because of the young man's debts, the Macarthurs had not the funds to rectify the situation, if they even had the inclination. But now, flushed with financial success, John bestowed on Mary a magnificent dowry of 2000 sheep and 200 cattle, with which Bowman declared himself 'perfectly satisfied'.[47] The newlywed couple lived in Sydney at the General Hospital, and James Bowman rapidly acquired, via grants and purchases, an estate of almost 5000 hectares called Ravensworth, about 250 kilometres north of Sydney and about 90 kilometres inland from the port of Newcastle, where miscreant convicts were sent to mine for coal. The former naval surgeon had married very well.

The family's sense of prosperity manifested in several ways. A number of family portraits date from this time, and, shortly after Mary's wedding, in 1824, John Macarthur finished overseeing the building of a new cottage at Elizabeth Farm, downhill from the original homestead. It was an elegant abode of rendered brick in the Colonial Georgian style, with joinery of Australian cedar and floors of ironbark. The new cottage's very first inhabitant could not have been more welcome: it was Captain Edward Macarthur.

Elizabeth's eldest son, now aged thirty-five, returned to New South Wales after an absence of some sixteen years spent soldiering. Elizabeth was overcome, and even two months later wrote that his return was 'so joyful to us that I hardly yet can think of it calmly'.[48] For the first time in the life of her scattered family, Elizabeth had six of her seven living children together in New South Wales. She only needed her second son John, who had not returned from England since he sailed for school at the age of seven, for everything to be perfect. Elizabeth's joy, though, was short lived. Edward did not stay in New South Wales for long, and in less than a year he sailed for England once more. His father, always very hard on his sons, felt he was 'entirely unfitted' for colonial life, and Edward seems to have concurred. He never saw either of his parents again, although they parted amicably and maintained a regular correspondence. John subsequently referred to him fondly as his 'dear Ned'.

Upon Edward's departure Elizabeth's thoughts followed him back to England. Her mother had recently become a widow for the third time. Elizabeth had never liked her mother's third husband, stating candidly to Eliza Kingdon that John Bond 'was always an idler'. It's an odd thing to say to the woman who was but a babe in arms when Elizabeth last saw her and who, along with her brother Reverend Thomas Kingdon, was a good friend to Elizabeth's mother. Perhaps Eliza had said something in her previous correspondence to encourage such frankness. Elizabeth again mused about visiting. 'The powers of steam have now become such in their application to navigation that I know not whether I may not be tempted to re-visit England.'[49] But if she had any true intention she could have sailed with Edward. She assuaged her conscience 'through the generosity of Mr Macarthur' and arranged an allowance for her mother. There seems to have been no correspondence between Elizabeth and her half-sister Isabella, now with seven daughters and, on Elizabeth's side at least, no love lost. 'I think of her poor soul, her poverty, her distress without in the least discovering how her situation can be substantially benefited…for so numerous a Family what can be done? They must learn to earn their own Bread, for our means are not unlimited.'[50] Isabella, about nine years old when she last saw Elizabeth, perhaps thought of her older sister more fondly—Isabella's first child, born in 1803, she named Elizabeth Veal.[51]

Rather than take a trip to England, Elizabeth retired further into the comfort of her family in New South Wales. New colonists, the Scott brothers, wrote again to their mother noting that 'the Macarthurs are the best educated and keep themselves more clear of the mob than any family in the colony'.[52] It is unclear, however, whether the Macarthurs kept 'clear of the mob' by choice or by necessity. Elizabeth was sociable by nature and before John's return from England her letters were full of visits paid and received. Within a year of his return from England, though, John was writing to friends that 'we only visit or are visited by one family'.[53] Even allowing for John's exaggeration, Elizabeth does seem to step back from social engagements during the decade of the 1820s. Although her daughters Elizabeth and Emmeline and Hannibal's wife Maria, as well as Penelope Lucas were raising funds first for the Parramatta Bible Association and then for 'a School, for the Education of Female Servants',[54] Elizabeth was conspicuously absent from the published lists of committee members and subscribers.

Her focus now was on John, and his failing physical and mental health. His depressive episodes were becoming ever more frequent, his outbursts more volatile and unpredictable. As a project took his interest he would begin it with obsessive zeal, only to lose the motivation to complete it. Increasingly quick to anger, John was also becoming paranoid. 'Suspicion had become a habit with him. He could conceive no opposition that was not built on enmity.'[55] There was no chance of Elizabeth taking a trip to England now—John could not possibly travel and she could not possibly leave him behind.

19

Headaches and Public Humiliations

...your dear father has had a severe attack of his old
tormenting complaint, with all the customary attendance
of despondency and low-spiritedness.

ELIZABETH MACARTHUR TO EDWARD MACARTHUR,

17 DECEMBER 1826

Elizabeth was remarkably frank about her husband's 'despondency and low-spiritedness', at least to family members.[1] Writing to her son Edward, aware that he would not soon be receiving a similar letter from his father, Elizabeth apologises on John's behalf. 'I have let your father know I am writing. He only says "Poor Fellows! What have I of a pleasing nature to write to them about?" This is the disease unquestionably.'[2] How astute she was, to recognise his depression as a disease of the mind and therefore not something he could control. So, to the extent that she was able, Elizabeth continued in her role as peacemaker, smoothing over the 'misunderstandings'[3] and soothing her husband when she could. If she appeared outwardly calm, her inner turmoil and stress revealed itself physically—since the time of the rebellion against Governor Bligh, if not before, Elizabeth had suffered severely from 'tormenting headaches',[4] and during this period and beyond they became worse and more frequent.

Bedridden for weeks at a time, morose and despondent, John would then rally and, with his sons James and William, his nephew Hannibal and son-in-law James Bowman, he looked set to take on the world. He was always very proud of his family, proclaiming its wealth at every opportunity. John already had a coat of arms designed for the family. Now the servants were required to wear livery; a gatehouse was built at Elizabeth Farm, where the paved driveway led into the streets of Parramatta; there was a new cottage at Camden Park; and that second cottage at Elizabeth Farm, for family and guests. John oversaw it all, in frenzies of activity interrupted by weeks in bed when depression or his painful gout (or both) struck him down once more. He became a serial litigator, and, just as he had in the 1790s, engaged in a number of complex court cases with various neighbours, businessmen and even the orphan school at Parramatta.

John caught the attention of Commissioner Bigge, who had been sent out from England to formally review the colony. It was as if John couldn't help himself: he complained bitterly to Bigge about Governor Macquarie, despite Macquarie's ongoing warmth and kindness to the Macarthur family. He maintained his intelligent charisma, managing to completely capture Bigge, and the commissioner's subsequent report and recommendations reveal him to be little more than a mouthpiece for John Macarthur and the cause of significant trouble for Macquarie, who was nearing the end of his tenure. Macquarie had supported the emancipists—he felt former convicts held the key to the colony's future—but in doing so he alienated the rich and powerful in both Sydney and London.

In 1821 Macquarie was replaced as governor by Major-General Sir Thomas Brisbane, Edward Macarthur's former commanding officer. Further Macarthur prosperity ensued, although as usual John bit the hand that fed him and Governor Brisbane was eventually subject to vicious Macarthur misrepresentations in London about his administration. Elizabeth, also as usual, blithely ignored her husband's enmities and enjoyed visiting with Lady Anna Maria Brisbane, 'a dear woman; whose nursery was her occupation and delight'.[5] Lady Brisbane gave birth to two children while in New South Wales, patriotically (if not poetically) naming them Eleanor Australia and Thomas Austral. She held intimate weekly dinners, and Elizabeth considered the table 'handsomely set out and served in a manner superior to anything we have yet seen in the colony'.[6] After dinner Lady Brisbane played the piano and sang, and her sister played the harp. Elizabeth, in her usual manner, had found a friend in the new governor's wife. But it was not a friendship that could last.

Brisbane was recalled by the colonial office in London after only a few years, replaced in 1825 by Sir Ralph and Lady Eliza Darling. It was a recall helped along by John Macarthur's complaints and London connections. To Brisbane's annoyance, even before he found out about the recall through official channels, Macarthur told him all about it—he had heard of Brisbane's recall through his well-connected son John. Whether or not Elizabeth was aware of her husband and son's machinations, she was very sorry to see the Brisbanes go. 'These changes are very painful to me, who am too advanced in life to look forward with any satisfaction to making acquaintances,' wrote Elizabeth to Eliza Kingdon. 'I shall always particularly regret parting with

Lady Brisbane, and her Sister Miss Macdougall, more amiable, more unaffectedly right minded persons we must not expect to succeed them.'[7] Elizabeth did, of course, befriend Lady Darling and the pair enjoyed going for drives or, as Elizabeth wrote in a letter to her son, taking 'an airing together in the barouche'.[8] Was it mere coincidence that John Macarthur quarrelled most fiercely with the families with whom his wife's affections lay? Or, conversely, were Elizabeth's friendships deliberately nurtured to counteract her husband's inevitable clashes?

In 1826 John devised a grandiose plan to sail to and from Europe via China and Bengal, for none-too-clear trading purposes. Elizabeth, writing to Edward and very much aware of how embarrassing John's appearance in London might be to both her eldest sons' careers, pictured 'to myself your great consternation'[9] when they heard of his father's plan. 'We none of us liked the thought,' Elizabeth went on, 'and were exceedingly pleased when he abandoned the idea. It made a great talk and clatter here for a time.'[10] In the end, Edward and his brother could rest easy: their father soon changed his mind.

Indeed, the number of times he changed his mind was part of the problem. Even Governor Darling noticed:

> In a former Letter, I mentioned some of the thousand projects he had in view…There is no exaggeration in this, however extravagant it may appear; the whole Plan was entered in a Book, from which he read the details to me. These schemes, however, were all abandoned for the more practicable one of going to South America for the purpose of introducing and improving the breed of Asses! Like the others, this project had its day, and is now no longer heard of.[11]

In another letter, Governor Darling related with some horror that John had freely boasted that 'he had never yet failed in ruining a Man who had become obnoxious to him'. The Governor went on to describe John Macarthur as 'a Man of strong passions, and observes no medium in anything. He is equally ardent in his exertions to serve as he is to injure.'[12] Within weeks he again wrote dubiously of Macarthur: 'He is now like a wayward Child, and remains at home brooding, but I expect is not altogether idle.'[13]

True to type, John was not idle at all and this time Elizabeth was directly affected by his actions. Buoyed with successfully constructing the second cottage at Elizabeth Farm, he engaged in another building project. In 1799 he had purchased twenty-two hectares on the shores of Cockle Bay (today's Darling Harbour). Now he arranged to build a stately home there, called Pyrmont. The ground had barely been cleared when he decided to also renovate the main cottage at Elizabeth Farm—the family's home. John began the work with enormous enthusiasm and, according to his wife, too many workmen. 'The important improvements your dear father mentions,' Elizabeth explained in a letter to Edward, 'are little other than delusions.' There had been at least fifty different plans, she complained, and goodness knows how many artists consulted and partly employed. Elizabeth's dear husband had 'ground marked out in different ways, over and over again—foundations dug out—all sorts of litter and rubbish and still no building begun—whether it will [begin] I cannot tell.' Elizabeth believed more money had 'been flitted away than it would have cost to put up the building. Your poor Father cannot do anything in a quiet orderly way.'[14]

Elizabeth could see the folly in John's actions, but she was powerless to stop him. The days were long since past when she was able to mitigate his wilder schemes. She eventually moved to Sydney, living with her daughter Mary at the hospital, having been firmly told 'that if I return your dear father will not proceed.'[15] This period of marital separation might have been a mere convenience: Elizabeth moved to Sydney simply to avoid the bustle and discomfort of the renovations. But it seems firm evidence of further friction in Elizabeth and John's relationship. From this point on they were often apart, and Elizabeth's letters refer more and more candidly to John's deteriorating mental health.

Elizabeth enjoyed herself in Sydney; there was a constant stream of family and other visitors. Youngest daughter Emmeline, now twenty, was especially fond of her brother James, despite (or perhaps because of) the ten-year age gap. The two often travelled together between Parramatta, Camden and Sydney. On one occasion, a Mrs Abel came to visit and Elizabeth was able to report (in a letter to Edward) that she 'has been amusing Mary and I with an account of two or three parties she has been at this week, one at Mrs Jones'—a ball and supper. A strange mixture of finery, ostentation and vulgarity—according to her account.'[16] Elizabeth had not lost her ear for the telling phrase.

While she was staying in Sydney in 1826 with her son-in-law, Doctor Bowman and her daughter, Mary, Elizabeth (at the age of sixty) became a grandmother for the first time. Mary Bowman gave birth to a healthy boy she named Edward. Little Edward was, of course, the apple of his grandmother's eye and she regularly mentioned him in her letters to her sons Edward and John. By the end of that year she could write 'Your sister and your young nephew Edward are well. The little man has some teeth and is growing fast. The Doctor [Bowman] is well also and desires his kindest regards.'[17] In yet another letter she describes a Macarthur family visit (which she did not attend) to see Maria and Hannibal Macarthur at their Parramatta property, the Vineyard. In time the Vineyard would boast a fine, two-storey Georgian house, but in the late 1820s John Macarthur's nephew and his wife were still living in the original small cottage. When Elizabeth's family visited, two of Hannibal's brothers were expected any day from England; Maria Macarthur a few weeks earlier had given birth to her eighth child; and Maria's sister-in-law, also staying at the Vineyard with her family, had just given birth to her seventh son. 'You may imagine,' wrote Elizabeth, 'the Vineyard cottage was well peopled. They must be as thick as hops.'[18]

Across the river from the Vineyard, at Elizabeth Farm, John harried the men who did not labour fast enough, while Elizabeth's daughters Elizabeth and Emmeline, and Penelope Lucas, shunted from room to room as the work progressed. Periodically work would stop for weeks, leaving the family to make do in a half-finished house. At times John would change his mind about something, and demand the work be done over again. Eventually he called a halt to the work at Pyrmont, and had sandstone from the site transported to Parramatta for the new verandah at Elizabeth Farm.

It would have been much more convenient for everyone, including the harassed workers, if the family at Elizabeth Farm could have moved into the cottage just down the hill, where

Edward had stayed during his brief visit. But that home was currently occupied, rent free, by Thomas Hobbes Scott, the newly appointed archdeacon and former secretary to Bigge (who wrote the damning report about Macquarie). That Scott should be appointed archdeacon almost immediately upon assuming holy orders was somewhat irregular and he was not well-loved in the colony, even though he had only recently arrived. Nor did John Macarthur's patronage promote his cause, although Elizabeth now and into the future considered him 'our dear kindhearted friend'.[19] In 1827 Scott moved out, and a grateful Mrs Lucas moved in. Perhaps for the first time in her life (she was now fifty-nine years old) she had a home of her own. She called the cottage Hambledon[20] and she would live there, dining each afternoon at the main house with the family, until her death in 1836.

Elizabeth stayed several months in Sydney before she returned to live at Parramatta. Her humble little cottage had been 'transformed' wrote James, 'by our Father's fertile genius into an elegant and commodious residence'.[21] James was quite right. The renovated house had become a long low and very beautiful bungalow with a library, a conservatory and a formal dining room. The kitchens, storehouses, cellars, offices and staff quarters were located behind the house on the southern side—conveniently close but separate to ensure safety in case of fire as well as a modicum of privacy for the family. A deep, north-facing verandah flagged with the enormous sandstone pavers from the family property at Pyrmont was bookended with inviting little sunrooms. From there, Elizabeth could sit and look out across her garden, or step straight out onto the carriage circle. With no second floor, the new house was by no means a grand home by the standards of the colony, but it was perfectly designed and proportioned. Its modesty seems to have reflected Elizabeth's tastes, rather than John's, although there is no evidence that she had a hand in the design.

With the house at Elizabeth Farm finished, John may have felt at a loose end, but he was also engaged with the new Bank of Australia, the management of his agricultural and financial affairs, and his various court cases and litigations. And it didn't end there. James and William Macarthur were appointed magistrates as, in a short-lived and much less successful exercise, was their unpredictable father. But the chief concern of the family in the mid to late 1820s was the Australian Agricultural Company.

The company was a joint venture floated in London and funded by British and colonial interests. Its main aim was to breed and profit from sheep, although olive groves and vineyards were also envisaged. Essentially the company sought to replicate the successful model of Camden Park and, in an early example of overt corporate citizenship, the company's plans spoke of strengthening the local economy by introducing innovative methods and industries to the colony—while profiting the shareholders, of course. All was conceived on a grand scale. Shares were offered to the value of one million pounds and land grants of a million acres were promised, on the outskirts of the settled districts.

It was no surprise that Camden Park should be the model— the man behind the establishment of the Australian Agricultural Company was Elizabeth's son John. Investors included eight Macarthur family members, twenty-seven members of the

British parliament and others in London and New South Wales. The first Board of Directors included several of young John's friends; and a committee of management established in New South Wales included his brother James, his cousin Hannibal and his brother-in-law James Bowman.

The company would eventually prosper—it still exists today—but it got off to a decidedly shaky start. James Macarthur foresaw many of the likely problems from the beginning and was only induced to join the company because of a sense of duty towards his father and older brother. Bitter feelings were directed towards the family when Macarthur and Bowman sheep were sold to the company at premium rates, with some describing it as fraud. In 1827 James visited the company lands at Port Stephens, about 200 kilometres north of Sydney, and was dismayed by the swampy ground, the mismanagement, and the agent's 'disgusting' familiarity with the local Aboriginal women.[22] The man was soon dismissed and was replaced, to the amazement of the colonial newspapers, by John Macarthur himself. Nobody in the family was able to dissuade him.

Early in 1828, James set sail for England to explain the company's precarious financial situation to the directors there, while his father set off for Port Stephens. 'The energy of his measures,' reported the *Sydney Gazette*, 'produced an electrical shock and acted medicinally for the settlement.'[23] According to the paper, 'The old gentleman'—as they referred to John—'rises before the sun and continues actively employed till between two and three the next morning.'[24] But while the settlement at Port Stephens may have improved, the fortunes of the Australian Agricultural Company did not.

Throughout the colony, sheep were at this time afflicted by drought and disease and John's frenzied efforts made little difference. By 1829 the directors in England sent out their own agent to take control, and the Macarthurs largely stepped back, and away.[25] James tried to counteract the monopoly effect of the company, by ensuring, for example, that not all the best Macarthur sheep were sold to it and that enough were kept back for at least some to be sold to other farmers. He argued about it with his father, writing that 'it is better we should suffer in a pecuniary point of view than save money at the expense of reputation, and of friends'.[26] John Macarthur's reputation, despite his brief efforts at Port Stephens, fell further still and the *Sydney Gazette* opined that James was already 'much more esteemed' than his father.[27]

In the late 1820s John succumbed 'to the most gloomy apprehensions' and suffered the 'peculiar and sudden disturbances' to which the family were becoming accustomed. Elizabeth wrote: 'He suffers excessively and even more than we can well judge is certain, but it is the mind preying upon the body, and disturbing its proper functions.' Elizabeth's attentions, however, were fully focused on her daughter Mary, who had more to contend with than the demands of her small, firstborn son. Mary's husband, Principal Surgeon James Bowman, was a man who made an excellent first impression. Governor Macquarie had at first praised Bowman for his 'assiduous and humane attention' to the convicts and for his 'mild, gentleman-like manners and accomplishments'.[28] But by the time of his departure, Macquarie gauged Bowman as an arrogant man of whom his successor should beware. His medical practices were sound, but his personal practices were not. Shortly after his first son's birth (if not before) James Bowman began an affair with a former convict woman, Mrs Hart. He was found out, and Mary was distraught, but then things got even worse.

Mrs Hart had fallen pregnant with Bowman's child, and her husband, Thomas Henry Hart, who had been in prison in Port Macquarie for nearly three years, sued Bowman for criminal conversation (adultery) and compensation of £2000. The case 'excited a vast interest', and in December 1828 it seemed like the whole of Sydney turned out for the trial.[29] Hart's lawyer had the crowd eating from his hand right from his opening statement. He made much of the salaciousness of the case, freely using terms like 'aged sinner', 'guilty' and 'debauch'. The courtroom crowd was delighted. When the witnesses were called, the show got even better. One after another Mrs Hart's servants and lodgers lined up to testify about how often, and how regularly, Doctor Bowman visited with Mrs Hart. How Mrs Hart stepped out on Doctor Bowman's arm—'up Pitt Street towards the race course together'. How the two would disappear into an upstairs room and not re-emerge for an hour. Mrs Hart's sister-in-law was particularly damning, relating a vivid tale of marching upstairs to bang on and kick the locked door, loudly demanding that the guilty pair emerge. Bowman's lawyer, Miss Elizabeth Macarthur's former suitor Mr William Wentworth no less, was hard pressed to make a cogent argument in his client's defence. He tried to undermine the witnesses; he clutched at technicalities; he contradicted himself; and finally, he took the time-honoured route of maligning Mrs Hart. None of it worked.

Bowman was found guilty and Mr Hart was awarded damages

of £50 and costs. Mary Bowman's marriage never recovered, although the couple went on to have four more children. They remained unhappily together for twenty years, until Bowman's sudden death in 1846. The excruciatingly embarrassing exposure of the trial was no doubt hard on Elizabeth, but perhaps even more so on John, that proud and haughty man. However, the family simply closed ranks and carried on. Elizabeth's letters, before and after the trial, don't mention it at all. Just days after the trial there was further bad news: James and William's former tutor, Huon de Kerrillieu, was missing, apparently lost on the way to visit his son's property at Campbelltown. He was never seen again. It was surely a quiet Christmas at Elizabeth Farm.

The government census of 1828 lists thirteen servants at Elizabeth Farm: a Scottish gardener, a coachman, a butler (improbably named James Butler, aged twenty-seven), two grooms, a cook, four labourers (three of them Irish Catholics), two maidservants (Jane Mead, thirty-eight, and Margaret Shepherd, sixty-one) and a Muslim footman called John Bono, from southern India.[30] The gardener and the footman had both arrived in the colony as free men but all the others were ex-convicts or were still serving their time, and all reflect, albeit within the class-conscious context of the times, the family's open-minded approach to employees. Penelope Lucas was also listed on the Macarthurs' census paper but, like each of the family members, there was no employment descriptor beside her name. The newspapers of the day would report that the Macarthur family was exemplary for its 'kindness and liberality to servants and dependants'.[31] The same census records the Macarthurs as owning, in total, about 43,000 acres (17,000 hectares). Theirs was the largest single holding in New South Wales, except for that of the Australian Agricultural Company.[32]

The Macarthurs held grazing land at Camden and Argyle, Elizabeth Farm, a town allotment in Parramatta and several in Sydney, and the Pyrmont estate consisting of twenty-two hectares of unimproved land on Darling Harbour. Their livestock included nearly 14,000 sheep, 172 horses and some 200 cattle. John worried about the family's financial position, yet throughout the 1820s Macarthur wool regularly sold at prices their agent described as 'extraordinary'.[33] Even when the 'high dry, blighting winds'[34] of drought struck again in the late 1820s, the family was making a net profit from the wool of £2000 a year. In the 1830s they would make more than twice that amount annually. And that's without adding in the profits from the sale of wheat, cattle, rams and horses. But while John complained of the poor prices fetched by his livestock, he would, in the next breath, begin some new and expensive building campaign. His ups and his downs, his manias and his depressions point towards the condition that a modern-day psychiatrist would call bipolar disorder.[35] Yet John continued to engage in business, public and social events while his increasingly worried family watched on.

Around this time, John and Elizabeth attended a ball at Government House, to celebrate the king's birthday. The *Sydney Gazette* reported with glee (and not a little malice) that John Macarthur 'was attended by his body-guard of aboriginal natives, whose uniform consists of scarlet shirts, blue trowsers, and yellow handkerchiefs. This guard of honour was armed with long spears...we scarcely know the day when he looked so cheerful.'[36] Mrs Phillip Parker King, Hannibal's sister-in-law, reported the spectacle somewhat differently: 'Mrs Darling gave a most splendid Ball...to which Mr M'Arthur made all his family go, Hannibal was also there...The dresses of some of the ladies were magnificent. Mr M'Arthur astounded everyone by bringing in three natives from Port Stephens, dressed in red shirts and white trousers, they staid a little while and when their curiosity was gratified, departed. Mr M'Arthur had only returned from Port Stephens the night before'.[37] No honour guard, no uniform. Just John Macarthur showing his friends from Port Macquarie the curious customs of the colonists in Sydney. It seems that John Macarthur had sunk so low in the regard of the colony's first newspaper that the editors felt free to mock him.

All Elizabeth could do was carry on in the face of John's ever declining mental health, distracting herself with her children and grandsons. Mary's second son, James, was born in 1829, and her eldest child, Edward Macarthur Bowman, was then almost three. In one letter to Edward in London, Elizabeth noted that 'young Edward MacArthur, [is] no inconsiderable personage amongst us, I assure you. He really is a very fine boy and just now is at a very engaging age.'[38] Little Edward's Bowman heritage was thus, if only for a moment, completely erased. But Uncle Edward in London had some news of his own.

In 1830 Lord Cholmondeley appointed his good friend Edward Macarthur as a secretary in the Lord Great Chamberlain's office, a position that came with much prestige and an apartment in the House of Lords. George Horatio Cholmondeley and Edward Macarthur had first met eighteen years earlier in Sicily, in 1812. Edward, then twenty-three, was there as a soldier and George, twenty, was holidaying his way around the continent on his grand tour. There was much gossip about George being homosexual. One contemporary diarist described him as 'a young man of effeminate manners, not promising much manliness of character'.[39] No one seemed surprised that his two marriages (his first wife died) were childless. George's aristocratic father loathed him, and did everything he could to disinherit him. It's possible that Edward and George were lovers. They were certainly good friends, and Edward regularly visited George at his estate in Cheshire. Elizabeth, on hearing of Edward's new job, was delighted and like mothers throughout time, thought well of the people who thought well of her son. 'We congratulate you on your appointment,' wrote Elizabeth. 'Your friend the Marquis certainly has shown you very marked attention. I should think him a kind and good man.'[40] Edward obviously thought him so, too. He would later send his mother a portrait of Cholmondeley.

When she wrote those lines, Elizabeth was staying at Belgenny Farm, within the wider Camden Park estate. She'd been there for two weeks already and planned to stay for two or three weeks more. Away from Parramatta (and John, who 'was low and complaining'), Elizabeth remarked that she felt better than she had in some time and she was delighted with all the improvements to the farm. 'William [is] very busy with sheep shearing and harvesting', which had been delayed due to rainy weather. The river had previously run too high to wash the sheep safely but at least there was 'an abundance of grass'. James, still overseas, had sent out a new wool classer from Germany, the 'unobtrusive and modest' Mr Koeltz, who seemed 'very much pleased with the wool and very much surprised at its uniform good character'. Elizabeth painted a glowing picture of the wool house she had ordered built more than a decade earlier, with 'every bin full up to the beams with fleeces even to crowding, all evenly and neatly piled and covered with cloths to prevent dust from soiling its present purity of appearance'.[41] No wonder the wool house was full—in 1830 they sheared 17,000 sheep at Camden and would export 40,000 pounds (18,000 kilograms) of wool.[42] The 'very manifest improvement in the wool' was a 'source of solid satisfaction to us all' wrote Elizabeth, and she paused for a moment to count her blessings. 'My heart dilates with thankfulness to Almighty God, the Giver of all Good.'[43] She didn't give a jot for the fine house her husband planned to build at Camden Park but was happy in the 'little cottage… neatly kept'.[44]

Elizabeth wrote glowingly of William's industry: '[He] has so beneficially devoted his time and been so successful in planting and propagating to a very great extent trees, plants, and flowers from almost every part of the world.' Together, mother and son, her hand tucked in the crook of his arm, took delight in walking through William's extensive gardens. Voluble and erudite, William, now thirty years old, could identify each plant by its common and Latin names and its place of origin, and could discuss with his mother the ease—or otherwise—by which the specimen had been propagated. Elizabeth's responding questions and prompts reflected her own passion for gardening.

Many of the plants had been sent over by her sons in England 'and it is with sweet recollections as we pass each tree or flower of yours that we converse of you [Edward], of John and the other dear absentee [James].' Practical Elizabeth also noted her satisfaction with the various garden pathways which were 'so well drained and gravelled that you may walk in the garden immediately after very heavy rain without soiling your shoes—something rare in this new country'. Aware that James was about to sail home, Elizabeth expressed her sadness that Edward wasn't coming home too: 'we should have rejoiced to welcome you home again.'[45]

She thought often of her absent sons. Writing to her husband in Parramatta from their Belgenny Farm in her only surviving letter to him, Elizabeth remembered 'Our dear and beloved sons—their images seemed to hover around me, when I retired to rest. God bless them—and strengthen them in those virtuous dispositions and honourable qualities, which you have at an early age impressed upon their minds and imparted to them, by example.'[46] She seems to write this without any sense of irony, given John's often less than honourable and virtuous disposition. She goes on in a companionable tone. 'I hope you have recovered from the oppression you were suffering from yesterday', she writes, and then, 'I had something of it myself'.[47] The stoic Elizabeth was also, it appears, subject to feeling low. Typically pragmatic though, she blames it on a change in the weather. She ends the short note in the standard salutation of the day: 'Believe me to be, my dearest Macarthur, Ever your affectionate wife, E. Macarthur.'[48] She signed off her letters to her sons in a similar way. If Elizabeth found peace in her absences from John it is also clear that he, as difficult as she knew him to be, always remained in her heart.

Back in England James spent time with his brother John, and travelled with him to Paris, sending back books, parasols, bonnets and other articles for his sisters. Then in early 1831 James farewelled his older brothers Edward and John, and set sail once more for New South Wales and home. He had a swift voyage and arrived in New South Wales in April. On 23 April, Elizabeth wrote to her son John, whom she hadn't seen since he went to England to school, aged seven. James's return, full of news about his brothers, had clearly reminded Elizabeth how much she longed to see them both, and John especially. 'I need not tell you how happy the return of dear James, after a three year absence, made us.' She thanked John warmly for the gifts he had sent for her, bracelets 'and other ornaments...I shall think of you when I wear them, not that I needed these emblems, to help you live in my remembrance'. John had also sent out a small portrait of himself. 'I cannot recognise the boy I parted with in 1801,' wrote Elizabeth poignantly, but several people confirmed to her that it was indeed a good likeness 'so that I must suppose it to be so and I am very glad to have it.'[49]

John would never read his mother's words. Two months after James's departure John died—probably following a stroke—in London, aged thirty-seven, four days before his mother wrote her final letter to him.

20

The End of a Marriage

*The fountain of my Eyes, which I believed to have
been nearly dry, have been opened anew.*
ELIZABETH MACARTHUR TO EDWARD MACARTHUR, 17 MAY 1834

When Edward's grief-stricken letters arrived, in September
1831, Elizabeth was in Sydney, caring for her daughter Mary,
who had just given birth to her third child. Elizabeth bore the
terrible news of her son's death with a resigned fortitude, but
everyone was deeply worried about how John would take it.
He was confined again to bed with an attack of gout so severe
that he needed assistance to dress. James and Emmeline, also
in Sydney, drove with their mother back to Parramatta, and
William joined them there from Camden. Emmeline had never
met her brother John, and his sisters barely knew him, but the
whole family entered into a long period of mourning.

John confounded his family's expectations by accepting
the news with 'manly fortitude, blended with tenderness' and
'tempered with such Christian resignation to God's dispensation'
that William, writing about the scene to Edward, said that

'no words of mine can express how much I revered him'.[1] John tried to hide the depths of his sorrow from Elizabeth and, as he recovered from his gout, he was once again out and about, attending meetings of the Legislative Council and making new plans for a grand family home at the Camden Estate. 'Poor dear John,' he wrote to Edward. 'How often do I suffer when alone, indulge in a bitterness of grief no language can describe and this is perhaps more intense because I find it necessary to conceal from your dear mother what I feel.'[2]

Elizabeth wasn't fooled. She knew how very deeply John's feelings ran for his son. And she grieved too, in her quiet way. 'How often my thoughts dwell on our loss, and on you, my dear Edward. I must not tell, nor will I give way to feelings of sorrow and regret, which can be of no avail.'[3] Her husband had no such qualms. John spoke constantly about his beloved son, reading and rereading aloud all his letters. Elizabeth bitterly resented her husband's behaviour, feeling that he was indulging his sorrow 'at the expense of ours in talking of the dear departed continually'.[4] Their son's death further deepened the fault line in their marriage, with neither feeling they could lean on the other for support.

Elizabeth wrote as often as she could to her sons in England, whenever a ship was about to leave for England. In an age when the 'enormous charge of postage'[5] was paid by the recipient, based on distance travelled and letter size, Elizabeth attempted frugality by crossing many of her letters—writing across the page from left to right in the usual way and then turning the page at a right angle to write more lines across the existing ones. She seems to have written them on the fly, noting thoughts down as they enter her mind and then apologising. 'This my dear sons you will say is a proper old woman's gossipy letter.'[6] In fact there is little or no gossip, and rarely a bad word to say about anyone. Elizabeth's letters, especially after her son's death, are full of warmth and love and family comings and goings.

John Macarthur seems to have favoured his son John over Edward, and probably over James and William too. John was the child with the shining intellect, with the burgeoning London career, with the parliamentary connections. It was John who was directly responsible for the successful prices received for Macarthur wool in English markets, John who established the Australian Agricultural Company, and John who whispered in all the right ears to ensure land grants and other perks flowed to Macarthur family members. As a father, John Macarthur loved all his children, but he was unlikely to have been subtle about any favouritism. Within a few days of his brother's death, Edward told his parents that he wished he had been the one to die instead of John, given that Edward's own life was 'less valuable than was his'.[7]

It was now up to Edward to take on the role of family agent and fixer, and he was quick to point out that it meant 'my destinies now seem fixed in England'.[8] Edward was in no hurry to return to New South Wales. In the months following his brother's death, a worried Edward wrote constantly from London to Parramatta. As the eldest son and his father's heir, he assumed a patronisingly formal tone towards his adult siblings. 'My dear Brothers and Sisters,' he wrote, 'It becomes your duty to bear up against this heavy calamity and to comfort and console our dear parents. Be assured that in all things I will do my duty here. I feel assured you will do yours at home.' The question was, though, in the face of their father's worsening mental state, what did duty entail?

John Macarthur was continuing to give his family plenty of cause for concern and seemed to have entered a state of mania. Elizabeth wrote to Edward:

> It is the old story. Setting a variety of wheels in motion, with a <u>Steam Engine</u> power—planning—building— making believe to do so at least, digging up the Earth— altering—directing, driving about at all hours changing his mind continually and in short keeping his family in a perpetual worry.[9]

John became more and more restless, barely sleeping, walking out for miles and, with no regard for propriety, talking to anyone he encountered. It was clear to Elizabeth that John laboured 'under a divergence of mind'.[10] She had seen it before, but in the past John's problems had not been quite so exposed to the world.

John soon fell completely into the abyss of paranoia. He accused Elizabeth of infidelity, his daughters of theft, and thought James and William had fled into the countryside. He claimed his son-in-law, Doctor James Bowman, was trying to poison him (which, given the quality of nineteenth century medicines, may not have been far from the truth) and took 'a most unaccountable dislike to our friend Mrs Lucas'.[11] In a frenzied climax at Elizabeth Farm, he rampaged through the house with pistols and swords. Doctor Anderson was fetched from the hospital in Parramatta. He was 'a very worthy man', who had been visiting John daily and who, according to Elizabeth, 'quite understands the nature of his complaints'.[12] John was eventually restrained and, in consultation with their doctors, the family confined him within three rooms of the newly renovated house, where he was looked after by longstanding and trusted servants.

Elizabeth, peremptorily ordered out by John, stayed in Sydney with Mary and her family, while her other daughters moved in with Penelope Lucas at Hambledon Cottage. Elizabeth bore her husband's capricious demands with calm resignation—she would do whatever was necessary to help maintain his peace of mind and if that meant staying away from him then, as she wrote to Edward, 'such is life'.[13] John, although remaining confined, soon recovered his equanimity. He was in good physical health, Elizabeth was told, and appeared 'cheerful and not at all unhappy'.[14] Elizabeth and her children made the heartbreaking decision to have him declared insane.

Elizabeth had long anticipated John's breakdown: 'I cannot say that the blow—severe as it is—has come upon us without long previous apprehensions that sooner or later, that mighty mind, would break down and give way.'[15] In Sydney she kept to herself and stayed within the family circle: walking in the newly planted Botanical Gardens; taking carriage rides with Mary and the grandchildren; accepting some callers but declining to visit in return. John recovered enough to visit his wife, just for the day, and Elizabeth thought him better 'but still too restless'.[16] Although she remained optimistic about John's recovery, Elizabeth did not, then or indeed ever, make a return visit. Her marriage was effectively over. It is impossible to know whether the separation was simply a matter of acquiescing to John's capricious demands, or because Elizabeth had finally had enough. Either way, it was a difficult time for everyone.

James and William, appointed as John's guardians, took it in turns to stay at Elizabeth Farm. James, especially, found it emotionally gruelling. His father would rail against him, wrote Elizabeth to Edward, with 'all the bitterness which your poor father can readily call to his aid'.[17] But when James, hurt and distressed, left to return to Camden, his father would then demand his return. He wanted James with him all the time.

Almost a year after his initial confinement, there was some sense that he might be improving—and Elizabeth dared hope she could return home. John was able to walk into Parramatta, and there talk rationally and calmly with those he met. But he continually invited strangers home to dine with him, much to James's dismay. One of his Bowman grandsons, little James, 'was taken to see his poor grandfather', wrote Elizabeth to Edward, and, much to everyone's relief, 'was kindly received'.[18] But the improvement did not last, and Elizabeth and John did not reconcile. John continued to believe his family was conspiring against him, and he was causing havoc within the house.

In 1833 the family decided to move him to Belgenny Farm. One of the men John had stopped to chat with a few months previously witnessed his removal and, shocked and upset, wrote with alarm to the newspaper. When he had last met with John in the street:

> I never in my life saw him look better, or converse more rationally, and he told me he was every day hoping to resume full management of his affairs. [And yet] passing through Parramatta a few days since, I was astonished to find that Mr John McArthur was hurried off to Camden

against his will, the poor man loudly protesting against the violence.[19]

This meddling, anonymous 'Observer' called for an immediate inquiry. The family was, understandably, rather put out. James visited the newspaper editors to explain the situation and, according to Elizabeth 'they all behaved very well'.[20] They apologised for inquiring into a private matter, and John Macarthur's illness was not mentioned in the press again.

Despite John's apparent unwillingness to remove to Belgenny Farm, Elizabeth reported to Edward that she had been told he was 'there enjoying himself very much, taking great interest in the building, the garden and horses. I do not hear that he makes any enquiries or notices anything relative to the sheep'.[21] Elizabeth did not visit him. In the privacy of his estate at Camden Park, away from interactions with strangers, John regained his physical health and, in the later part of the year, was once more fully lucid. He took a lively interest in the building of the new family home although in practice it was William who oversaw the day-to-day operations.

John also recognised that the Camden property was no longer quite the jewel in the Macarthur crown. Overgrazing and drought had taken a toll on the quality of the grasslands. John's will, which distributed the various Macarthur properties among his sons but marked Edward as the heir and chief beneficiary, now needed to be revised to ensure that James and William were still treated fairly. But John had drafted and signed his will before his sons assumed guardianship over him. In order to revise it now, James and William would have to revoke their guardianship and restore their father's legal rights. Was John well enough for them to take the risk? To their credit, James and William maintained the guardianship arrangement and refused to allow their father to change his will in their favour, even as friends advised them against doing so. They trusted that Edward would treat them fairly. Despite these ongoing concerns John, for the time being, relaxed at Belgenny Farm into a better, calmer state of mind.

With John at Belgenny, Elizabeth was finally—after an absence of more than a year—able to 'return to dear home' at Parramatta.[22] Before she moved back to Elizabeth Farm, her youngest daughter Emmeline (now twenty-six) spent some time putting the house 'in better order', perhaps to spare her mother the full evidence of John's destructive outbursts. The emotional turmoil of John's illness had taken its toll on Elizabeth, and once she returned to Parramatta she was increasingly unwilling to leave home. 'I have plenty of exercise within the limits of our own estate and the looking about the gardens and grounds annexed keeps me amused,' she wrote to Edward, 'but the effort is to make visits abroad and the apprehension of coming in contact with strangers I have not been able to combat.'[23] All those curious people asking after John, all the excuses she made on his behalf—it was too much. Easier by far to stay at home and receive visits only from those who knew her—and understood her current circumstances. 'People in the world would think this is a foolish feeling,' continued Elizabeth 'and perhaps it is so.'[24] But there was little she could do about it.

Elizabeth took comfort in her friendship with Penelope Lucas, and in her garden at Elizabeth Farm, which by all accounts included an impressive collection of plants from around the world. Edward regularly sent her seeds and seedlings, including a sample of corn. Penelope Lucas, knowing full well how much her friend liked to discuss her sons, would without fail comment upon the little corn plantation when they walked together in the grounds. There was a decorative pond near some willows and native cypresses, and although the water remained a little muddy, Elizabeth hoped it would clear when some rain fell.

Elizabeth's eldest daughter, now known as Aunt Eliza, had an interest in the garden too. 'She has a fine collection of bulbs from the Cape,' wrote Elizabeth to Edward.[25] Portugal laurel, hydrangea, iris—the garden was 'very full of large & beautiful flowers…but the pride of the garden just now is the Magnolia'.[26] Explorer Thomas Mitchell had spent a night at Elizabeth Farm in 1831, before setting out on one of his expeditions, and he wrote about its gardens: 'There I saw the first olive tree ever planted in Australia; the Cork-tree in luxuriance; the Caper growing amongst the rocks, the English Oak, the horse chestnut, broom, magnificent mulberry trees…[and a] great variety of roses growing in beds, also climbing roses.'[27]

At sixty-seven, Elizabeth had for some time suffered from slightly inflamed eyes and was beginning to find it difficult to write to her children as often as she might like. Her eyes ached and she could not always see clearly enough to trim the end of the quill she used for writing. Edward sent out a pair of spectacles which, as Elizabeth wrote back, 'answer exceedingly well'.[28] She preferred to write by day, but sometimes wrote to Edward of an evening:

> It is now candlelight, and I know you will hardly be able to make out my scribble…Emmeline is at the same

table with me, writing to you also. She is not quite well, but nevertheless she writes. Elizabeth and our friend Mrs Lucas are in the adjoining room chatting with Dr Anderson and your little nephew and namesake has just been to kiss grandmother and Aunt Emmeline and bid goodnight.[29]

Elizabeth did not keep herself in total isolation. John's nephew Hannibal, his wife Maria and their many children still lived just across the river and the two families were in regular contact. Her old friend Betsy Marsden visited, accompanied by her grown-up daughter. And Anna King, wife of the former governor King and mother to Hannibal's wife, Maria, had returned to New South Wales after a twenty-four-year absence. She became a frequent visitor to Elizabeth Farm. 'She desires her kind love to you,' wrote Elizabeth to Edward. 'She is very active and visits about in a most wonderful way for an elderly person.' Mrs King was then sixty-nine—only a year older than the tongue-in-cheek Elizabeth.

Immediately prior to Mrs King's arrival in New South Wales, Elizabeth was thinking about whether her friend would 'be pleased with this altered community'.[30] Elizabeth considered the colony wonderfully changed, with 'ships arriving and departing continually. It has started forward into a degree of importance I had never expected to see it attain. Two or three stage coaches leave Sydney every day to Parramatta and one to Liverpool.'[31] But in her current, troubled state of mind, there was so much rapid change in the community 'that I could hardly feel myself at home in it. It is literally by keeping at home that I do feel at ease'.[32] In March 1834 Elizabeth put away her fears long enough to travel to Sydney, to stay again with Mary. She wrote to Edward to say, 'Yesterday your dear sister Mary was safely delivered of a fine little girl!'[33] Finally a granddaughter, after three boys. Not that Elizabeth in any way resented those little boys, noting in the same paragraph that the second eldest, James, 'is a very merry active little fellow full of frolic and merriment'.[34]

Hannibal Macarthur, with his mother-in-law's arrival, not to mention the recent birth of his and Maria's eleventh child, finally decided to commence 'building a house on a very extensive scale and next to the present cottage'.[35] The new house would be a two-storey building of Georgian Regency design, with a Doric colonnade along the ground floor. It very much resembled the house John had been building (and revising, and changing his mind about and revising again) at Camden Park since the mid-1820s. John's enthusiasm for the new house, which would become the grand family seat, was such that he moved from the cottage at Belgenny into one of the partially completed wings. The family had 'never known him in such good health—he eats, sleeps and looks well'.[36] Of course, it couldn't last.

In March, at about the same time as his first granddaughter was born, John descended again into illness and mental collapse. He was once more restrained, this time confined to the farm cottage at Belgenny. There, on 11 April 1834, John Macarthur died. It was three years, almost to the day, since his son John had passed away and two years since he had seen his wife.

Details of John's final days are scant and the actual cause of his unexpected death is unclear. The newspapers of the day barely mentioned John Macarthur's passing, and he was buried quickly and quietly at Camden Park, not in a churchyard but on a rise opposite and about a mile away from the still-unfinished grand house. More and more the colonial settlers were aping the English aristocracy by establishing family burial grounds within their own estates and in time John's wife and children would be buried beside him. Elizabeth did not attend her husband's funeral, but that was not unusual—funerals were routinely, at this time, male-only events.

Instead she stayed at home and wept. It was five weeks before she could bring herself to write to Edward. 'I had fondly indulged myself with the hope,' Elizabeth wrote to her son, 'that it would have pleased God to restore the dear departed to a more sane state of mind & that he might have been at peace with his family.' It was not to be. Now that 'the shock arising—or rather increased by the suddenness of the event, is in some measure subsided', she could only take consolation in her faith: 'Thy will be done on Earth blessed God as it is in Heaven.'[37]

John Macarthur's will, written in 1828, bequeathed Elizabeth Farm and all its contents to Edward. Elizabeth, as John's wife, was to have the use of the property, and the contents, during her lifetime. He also left her his shares in the Bank of Australia and an annuity, to be charged on the estate. Similar annuities were provided for his unmarried daughters, and £100 each to the Bowmans and Mrs Lucas. John stipulated that his 'esteemed friend Penelope Lucas spinster of Parramatta [was] to reside in the house and premises wherein she now lives during her life or so long as she shall think fit.'[38] If Mrs Lucas were to leave, or die, then his eldest daughter Elizabeth was to have the use of Hambledon Cottage. Everything else—all of his considerable property and stock—was divided between Edward, James and William Macarthur. In an era of the primacy of the male first-born, John's will seemed to Elizabeth and her family to be entirely appropriate and, anyway, in day-to-day terms, nothing changed. James and William continued to manage all the various estates on behalf of the whole family, with the profits pooled and drawn down only as required to meet everyone's relatively modest living expenses.

Edward, in England, continued to be sent funds representing his share and he continued to do his best to fill his dead brother's role as family agent. He procured the annual order of shoes for the family in Parramatta, ordered a riding habit for Emmeline and chose coloured muslins for his sisters' summer dresses. He regularly sent out books, periodicals and furniture. There was occasionally some talk of his returning to New South Wales but, in his mother's lifetime at least, it never eventuated.

Aware that his brothers had shouldered the entire burden of their father's illness and that he was continuing to live in comparative ease as a result of their efforts, Edward did his best to cultivate powerful friends in England, who could further benefit the family, by bestowing gifts from New South Wales. A pair of black swans for his good friend Lord Cholmondeley; another pair for the duke of Portland. Brightly feathered parrot skins also made most acceptable presents, and Emmeline arranged to send him some more.

Edward had lobbied for a baronetcy for his father (which as eldest son he would inherit) but was unsuccessful. In a letter replying to Edward's request, Lord Aberdeen noted that Edward's father had 'earned the appropriate reward of an ample fortune' and implied that, under the circumstances, that was more than enough.[39] Like his father and brother before him, Edward inspected the Macarthur fleeces arriving in England and pronounced them too dirty, not well presented, and with the colours too mixed. And as their mother had done before them, battling with dust and dirt and drought, Edward's brothers duly ignored his advice.

Elizabeth continued to stay at home, receiving visitors but declining to pay them calls in return. She was not one to mope, and her eldest daughter reported that she was 'quite well and in better spirits than could have almost been hoped for',[40] but Elizabeth was in the habit of sparing her family her true sorrows. It was not until January 1835, some eight months after John's death, that she could bring herself to travel down to Camden Park. In the wake of their father's death, James and William were planning to sell off several hundred acres of land to create a township, which would also be called Camden, near where the Cow Pastures bridge crossed the Nepean River. By 1840 the first 100 half-acre (2000-square-metre) allotments were for sale. But in the mid-1830s there was not even an inn nearby; colonial travellers passing through to places further inland routinely stayed with William and James. Elizabeth, still unable to face encounters with strangers, stayed away until she could be sure of her privacy. 'I want to be quiet and alone when I make this first visit—which must excite feelings I would not forego but of too solemn nature for publicity,'[41] she wrote, though she also said she regretted missing the shearing.

When finally, in January, Elizabeth did make the journey to Camden Park, she was accompanied by her daughter Elizabeth and her grandson Edward Bowman, now nearly nine. They stayed for three weeks. James came up from the properties at Argyle, further inland, and little Edward's Uncle William went to some lengths to amuse and divert the boy, presumably so that Elizabeth could have some time alone. The fine new two-storey house, built a mile or so behind and out of sight of the farm buildings of Belgenny, was all but finished and Elizabeth admired it very much. 'It is a handsome building,' she wrote to Edward, 'more of a Classic character than any other I have seen—spacious on the ground floor and indeed sufficiently so on the Chamber floor.' But she couldn't help thinking of her husband, so much the originator of the building and very present in every detail, who didn't live to see it finished. Then one thought led to another and she ached for her missing children. 'I cannot pursue this train of thought' she told Edward, 'you may be sure when weeping over his tomb I thought of and prayed for you also my dear son.'[42]

In time a memorial stone was erected above John's resting place, which includes mention of the first little James who Elizabeth lost in 1797, before his first birthday. Her grown-up son John had his own tombstone at St Martin-in-the-Fields, in London. No stone, though, for Elizabeth's first little girl, who died on the voyage out from England and was buried at sea.

While she was staying at Camden Park, Elizabeth missed—probably deliberately—a vice-regal ball and some lively meals at the Vineyard. Hannibal's brother-in-law, Captain Phillip Parker King (son of Anna Josepha and the former Governor King; brother to Hannibal's wife) was the former commander of schooner HMS *Adventure*. In company with another ship, King and the crew of *Adventure* had spent the years 1826 to 1830 charting the coasts of Peru, Chile and Patagonia, with King earning a promotion to post-captain along the way. In 1832 he had returned to his properties and wife Harriet in New South Wales (in a now familiar story, Harriet had been managing them in her husband's absence). Now, on 12 January 1835, the *Adventure* was anchored in Port Jackson with that sister ship: HMS *Beagle*. The two vessels were in the fifth year of a scientific sailing expedition, and one of the scientists on board was twenty-six-year-old Charles Darwin.[43]

Darwin admired the bustling city of Sydney, but the great numbers of convicts and the limited number of bookshops (made worse because, apparently, those existing sold a low class of book) led Darwin to fear that Australia 'with such habits and without intellectual pursuits...can hardly fail to deteriorate and become like...the United States'.[44] He took a quick journey across the Blue Mountains to the newly settled Bathurst region, returning to attend a ball hosted by the governor on 26 January, to celebrate the forty-seventh anniversary of the First Fleet's arrival at Sydney Cove.

Darwin was fascinated by the Australian wildlife but less impressed with the young ladies. Lunching with Hannibal Macarthur and his family at the Vineyard he heard, much to his patriotic horror, otherwise 'very nice looking young ladies exclaim "Oh, we are Australians and know nothing of England!"'[45] Darwin was equally disappointed in the state of the colony's society, noting that: 'The whole population, poor and rich, are bent on acquiring wealth; amongst the higher orders wool and sheep grazing form the constant subject of conversation.'[46] Given that most of the 'higher orders' Darwin spoke with were

Macarthurs, his observations are hardly surprising.

After her three weeks at Camden Park, Elizabeth returned home to Elizabeth Farm, no doubt to hear all about the visitors, now sailing for Hobart Town (Darwin's expedition would take more than a year to return to England). Despite her grievous losses, Elizabeth, of course, carried on. Her daughter Mary and the Bowman family moved out of their rooms at the Sydney Hospital and into the fine new home called Lyndhurst that they'd built on nearly 40 hectares at Glebe, at the edge of the Sydney township. It looked across Blackwattle Bay to the Rocks area of Sydney Town. But within a year of their move Doctor Bowman was for some reason removed as inspector of colonial hospitals and, although he continued to receive his official salary for a further two years, the Bowman family may have begun to regret their expensive show home. In August Elizabeth had further cause for worry: her daughter Emmeline caught the measles, although she recovered to be, in her eldest sister's opinion, in better health than she had been for years.[47]

Then in October 1835 Elizabeth suffered a further blow: her old friend Betsy Marsden died. Elizabeth turned to her sons at Camden Park for solace and in November she arrived for a longer visit. Despite losing Betsy, Elizabeth was recovering her equanimity and was less worried about socialising. For this visit she was accompanied by the latest governor, Lieutenant-General Sir Richard Bourke, and his married daughter, Anne, who wrote to her brother that 'Old Mrs Macarthur and Emmeline went up [to Camden] and made it very pleasant'.[48] Elizabeth described Anne as 'a frank, lively little woman quite free from affectation and I should think very warm hearted. She has a delightful voice and having had the advantage of good tuition she sings most enchantingly.'[49] When the governor and his daughter departed, Penelope Lucas came to stay for three weeks, followed by little William Bowman and his Aunt Eliza. Elizabeth returned to Parramatta in early 1836 'much better for this excursion' and 'blessed with good health'.[50] It was just as well because in 1836 Elizabeth lost two more stalwarts.

The first loss was only temporary. Her son James sailed once again for London, this time to talk to Edward about the family business and to obtain a large loan to buy more land near Camden Park. He also wanted to find himself a wife, although on his last trip to England he had noted to his father that all the young ladies he met, through his brother John, were 'in circles far too high to suit a Society so peculiar as ours'.[51] James also worried about the dangers of marrying an English woman, who would be a virtual stranger, without the benefit of long previous acquaintance.

The second loss was far more difficult to bear. Mrs Lucas, esteemed and loved by the whole Macarthur family, passed away, aged sixty-eight. In time, someone—surely it was Elizabeth—arranged for a memorial to be erected in St John's Church, Parramatta. A female figure engaged in teaching children is depicted in a delicate marble carving. Beneath is a loving inscription:

> To the memory of
> PENELOPE LUCAS,
> More than thirty years resident in this colony,
> Who, having contributed to its welfare by the
> Example of her active life and benevolence,

Dying, bequeathed great part of her property
For the promotion of religious education
In this community.

In unavailing sorrow for her loss
This tablet is erected
To commemorate her great worth
And humble reliance for salvation,
Not on her own but on her Redeemer's merits.
She died in 1836, aged 68 years.

Elizabeth wrote to Edward with much understatement that she would, 'miss the solace of friendship the last of so many years'. In that same letter to Edward, written late in December 1836, Elizabeth thanked him for writing with discretion and care 'about the death of my aged parent'.[52] Elizabeth's mother Grace Bond had died too, aged eighty-nine.

Grace was only nineteen when Elizabeth was born and forty-two when her daughter sailed for New South Wales. She never saw Elizabeth again. Perhaps that was not so unusual at that time, although Elizabeth certainly had had the means to visit, if not the will. Does it signify that none of Elizabeth's daughters was named Grace? Some brief excerpts of Elizabeth's letters to her mother survive, but none written by mother to daughter. We can never know how they truly felt about one another. Grace was buried by the Reverend Thomas Kingdon—brother of Elizabeth's old friend Bridget—in the churchyard at Bridgerule, beside her third husband John Bond. Her first husband and her infant daughter Grace shared a grave nearby.

Less than a year later, the whole New South Wales colony was plunged into mourning when the news arrived of the death of King William IV, son of beleaguered 'mad king' George III. The king died in June 1837, having ruled for only seven years. William IV was succeeded by his niece, who had just turned eighteen. Her name was Victoria.

21

Family Feuds

This poor old residence is endeared to me by many associations.
I should be grieved to see it and the gardens neglected.

ELIZABETH MACARTHUR TO EDWARD MACARTHUR, 5 MAY 1838

Two weeks before Victoria's coronation in June 1838, in a London buzzing with celebration preparations, Mr James Macarthur Esq. married Miss Emily (Amelia) Stone. Finally, there was some happy news for Elizabeth and her family.

The bride was thirty-two years old, the groom thirty-nine. It was clearly a match entered into with prudence. Miss Stone's extended family (wealthy bankers, most of them) had been known to the Macarthurs for nearly twenty years, and Miss Stone's dowry, a neat £10,000, was nothing to be sneezed at. Yet there is also every suggestion that the couple held genuine feelings for each other. Emily's sister, writing about losing her sibling to New South Wales, correctly predicted James 'will fill up the place of a sister as well as a husband, he seems to enter so completely into all her feelings'.[1] The former tenant of Hambledon Cottage, archdeacon Thomas Hobbes Scott, officiated at the wedding and he wrote to Elizabeth immediately afterwards to tell her of his great pleasure in performing the ceremony. Emily was, he told her, 'one of the most amiable young women this country contains. She is in every way worthy of him and he of her.'[2] The marriage would, in fact, be a long and happy one. The couple set out on a honeymoon tour of Scotland and England before departing, in November 1838, for New South Wales.

The newlyweds sailed aboard the *Royal George* and were accompanied by 102 labourers and their families, all destined for Camden Park. The workers, including six families from Dorset and another six from Kent, were the latest in a long line of skilled immigrants from England and Germany to be selected and supported in their passage out to New South Wales by the Macarthurs. Convict transportation to New South Wales would cease in 1840 but the Macarthurs had already seen the value in selecting and importing their own workforce. Edward, having lost his plum position at court with the ascension of Queen Victoria and at something of a loss about what to do with himself, missed his brother's wedding. He was in Germany recruiting winemakers and their families to work in the Camden Park vineyards. In the past his brother John had done the same, in England and on the continent. Edward's trip meant that he and James never really did speak frankly about the family business, although upon his return James assured Elizabeth that all was well in that regard.

The German families arrived in New South Wales in early 1838, and Elizabeth wrote about them to Edward. 'I saw them all last night…and was highly pleased with their appearance and demeanour.'[3] Various delays meant the families did not arrive at Elizabeth Farm until seven o'clock in the evening, but 'we had a supper ready for them and I saw men, women and children comfortably arranged on either side of the long table'. Afterwards Elizabeth and Emmeline spoke with the foreman and another man and their two wives in the drawing room. The emigrants set out early the next morning for Camden Park, all, according to Elizabeth, 'well and cheerful'. Drays carried the baggage; the children and one adult travelled in 'a convenient Braking carriage' and presumably the others walked.

Elizabeth knew Edward would 'be most solicitous to hear of these poor people', given that he had 'taken so active a part in procuring at no small expense of time and trouble families so interesting to our colony, and as such we trust will be beneficial to ourselves more immediately'.[4] As always, Elizabeth was interested in the wellbeing of the colony, but far more interested in the wellbeing of the Macarthurs. Under their five-year contract, the German winemakers built a crescent row of cottages at Camden looking out over the vineyards and a lagoon. They planted apple trees, and each family had 'a cow or two, a garden, and poultry in abundance'.[5] These German families would successfully introduce Rhine Riesling into Australia. In time their children, along with those of the English emigrant families and presumably the children of the emancipated convict servants, would attend a school on the estate. Long before the township of Camden was established, the Camden Park estates were a village unto themselves.

Elizabeth began to mention her own health more often in her letters, although usually describing illnesses only as long or short. She delighted in her grandchildren, but in 1838 the Bowmans began to struggle financially, and they left their grand Sydney home to live at their country estate Ravensworth.[6] It seems that Elizabeth never visited them there. She longed to see Edward again, and most of her letters to him during this period contain at least a line or two wistfully wondering when he might return to New South Wales. Yet it is clear that she is trying hard not to nag and in each letter she rephrases the question, noting that 'various persons' keep asking when he might be back or telling him how much she 'regretted his change of mind with respect to revisiting the colony.'[7]

Elizabeth was an old woman now and regularly referred to herself as such. So, when James and his bride arrived in New South Wales in March 1839, Elizabeth was nervous. 'I cannot but feel considerable anxiety lest the country and habits of the community may disappoint my daughter-in-law', she wrote to Edward. 'Assuredly this Colony in very many instances is too flatteringly depicted which makes me fearful where expectation has been much raised in the mind.'[8] And if the colony disappointed her daughter-in-law, perhaps James's aged and unsophisticated mother—still at heart that girl from the remote Devonshire village—might be a disappointment too.

Elizabeth need not have worried. The new couple stayed for a short time at Hambledon Cottage while the furniture, china and household goods that had travelled out with them were installed in the big new house at Camden Park, which was to be their permanent home. Elizabeth found Emily to be every bit as amiable and friendly as had been reported, and they would ever after regard one another with affection. James's brother William may well have also been nervous about Emily, given how close the two brothers were, but again Emily loved everyone her husband loved, and William would live, for the rest of his life, happily at Camden Park with Emily and James. A year after arriving at Camden Park, in May 1840, Emily gave birth to a daughter. She was named, of course, Elizabeth.

William, perhaps spurred on by the happy example of his brother, may have looked for a wife of his own at around this time. Apparently he cautiously proposed to Kate Macarthur, one of his cousin Hannibal's daughters. But Kate was then only a teenager and William was in his late thirties, and she turned him down. Shortly afterwards she announced her engagement to Patrick Leslie, who subsequently complained of William disliking and discriminating against him out of jealousy:

> I saw the game he was playing long before he asked Kate but I was never afraid of him as a Rival even with his wide & broad domains—This will explain the whole of their coolness to me but it must explain it to no other single person for Kate would not think it right to let it be known.[9]

Patrick Leslie was the nephew of Walter Davidson who was in turn the nephew of John Macarthur's patron and friend Sir Walter Farquharson. Arriving in the colony at the age of nineteen, Leslie had ambitions to emulate the pastoral success of the Macarthurs, but when Leslie fell out with his uncle, James and William Macarthur took Davidson's side, while Hannibal Macarthur and his family took Leslie's.

When Kate Macarthur and Patrick Leslie eventually married in 1840, in a lavish ceremony with eight bridesmaids, Elizabeth declined to attend the ceremony and the jolly luncheon held afterwards at the Vineyard. No one thought the worse of her for that, given her age and her often precarious health, but perhaps there was more to her absence. Emmeline and William Macarthur arrived so rudely late that they met the wedding party as it emerged from church and they left the luncheon as early as they could. Family feuds are always complex, but Pat Leslie was a brash young man who, like many young men, was inclined to assume that any problems could only be the fault of others. Soon after Kate and Patrick's wedding, his brother George Farquhar Leslie married Kate's sister, Emmeline Maria—no doubt further entrenching family battlelines.

Far more compelling than any hurt feelings of William's was the economic context of the late 1830s and the 1840s. The colony's economy had slowed, and most of the pastoralists—including both Macarthur families—had fallen into debt. Prices for wool, livestock and grains plummeted. William was diversifying into wine and horticulture and although wealthier colonists across the eastern seaboard would, now and into the future, source the plants in their gardens from his annual catalogue, it was hardly enough to replace the lost wool income.

Worse, the Macarthurs were no longer considered the leading breeders of merino sheep and their ram sales declined accordingly. Over time the family had concentrated their breeding efforts on the fineness of wool to the neglect of other features. Others had begun to breed sheep that were hardier, larger, with denser fleece and a longer staple. William was asked by John Hughes, a visiting pastoralist, why he bred such sheep when his own sheep, in a similar climate and landscape, yielded nearly double the money per fleece. William replied with an air of hauteur that his family 'bred the pure blood'. Hughes replied that 'in South Australia we bred for pure money', which William described 'as a Yankee way of looking at it'.[10] The Macarthurs' days of pre-eminence in sheep breeding were fading fast.[11]

In the meantime, Mary Bowman and her husband, now with five children, teetered on the edge of bankruptcy and were quietly supported financially by William and James. Elizabeth and her daughters Elizabeth and Emmeline lived frugally, as they always had anyway, and allowed their annuities to fall into arrears. Edward, still at a loose end in London, wrote yet again to his brothers, to complain and advise. His mother, though, remained unaware of the growing tensions.

Under the terms of their father's will, Edward was entitled to half the net profits (after the annuities had been paid) and James and William were to receive a quarter each. But the brothers had agreed that, with James and William continuing to work in the field as it were, the net profits would be shared equally—one-third each. Edward insisted, however, on retaining ownership of half the stock and of all the land bequeathed to him and, with his usual tin ear, sent a high-handed directive about the sale of the Pyrmont property. His letter arrived just as the preparations for Kate's marriage to Patrick Leslie were in full swing, and a disappointed William was in no mood to prevaricate. He poured out all his resentments into a long and bitter reply to his older brother: 'The tone & substance of [your previous] letter have given me great surprise & concern. I think we have cause to feel aggrieved by them.'[12] William then proceeded to set out his many grievances.

Since arriving back in New South Wales almost twenty-three

years ago 'I have been engaged the entire period in the active management of the property; during several years of which, & those most disastrous ones, with the entire weight of the concern on my shoulders. I have scarcely ever been ten days at a time absent from them during the whole time.'[13] It would have been far better for his own financial interests, William explained, if he had withdrawn from the family pastoral concern and established his own properties. He certainly felt that he'd had the right to do so and 'had fairly earned it'.

> I had for years performed a degree of drudgery to which not every one in my place would have submitted during so long a period. I had to teach myself the difficult trade of wool sorting. Up to 1831, every fleece, every flock of sheep was sorted at great pains by me. It formed nearly constant occupation of a very irksome kind for two or three months of every year. I should have preferred hard labour in the field. I never shrank from it not uttered a word of complaint because I knew it was necessary but I have often performed it with aching eyes, amidst all sorts of interruptions & discomforts, which a sense only that it was for the good of all would have induced me to submit to.'[14]

What had Edward been doing in the meantime? 'I do not put this as a reproach,' wrote William reproachfully,

> but merely to point out, that whilst we were devoting the best years of our lives to the interests of a group concern & sacrificing without a murmur the opportunities never to return of realizing our independence for ourselves, you were pursuing your own separate profession; the

very means of your advancement in it being in a great
degree the fruit of our exertions. Will it be either just
or generous in you to take advantage of this now? [15]

William went into some detail about conversations he'd had
with their father about the disposition of the estates, carefully
pointing out that when their father had been lucid late in 1833
he and James had steadfastly refused to allow their father to
alter his will in their favour, even though their father John had
'frequently lamented' what 'he called an <u>act of injustice</u> towards
us'. The emphasis was William's and he was not above twisting
the knife a little harder. 'I will not dwell upon the distressing
periods (with reference to our Father's health) of 1830 & 1832
to 1834, but I do think it hard that because we did not neglect
our duty then, we should, by your means, be made to suffer for
it now.'[16]

William told no one of this letter and kept it without sending it for over a year, hoping the situation—and Edward's
attitude—would improve. Neither did. Edward, unaware of
his brother's building animosity, was concerned by the lack of
regular financial reports and distrusted his brothers' prudence
and business abilities. The colony fell into a severe economic
depression and the conditions could not have been worse for
breaking the brothers' partnership. William, though, could see
no alternative.

In 1841 he finally brought his concerns, his letter of more
than a year before and Edward's earlier letters, to Elizabeth's
attention. She, hitherto unaware of the growing hostilities,
felt the rift very deeply and told Edward so in no uncertain
terms. Her next letter to him, full of cold anger, distress and

disappointment, also carefully articulates the sense of family solidarity and ambition upon which she based the work of her entire adult life.

> My dearest Edward, I have carefully perused the accompanying letter, [ie William's] and can fully concur in the <u>accuracy</u> and <u>truth</u> of the statements in it. Often has your dear and respected father held conversations with me…hoping and praying…that our children would be satisfied with the disposition of his property, and that his greatest consolation was founded on the belief that the family were so strongly united in the bonds of mutual confidence and affection—and in the desire to carry out his plans for the general good as would lead them hereafter to act, each individual, for the benefit of the whole, and for the attainment of the objects he had through life ardently devoted himself to rather than for any views of individual or separate advantage. I do assure you, my dearest Edward, this dissatisfaction of yours has given great pain—I was only apprized of it a short time since and only within the last two days saw your letter announcing your displeasure, which was to me as an Electrical Shock having been assured by James on his last return from England in answer to my Enquiry that all had been arranged with you in accordance with the proposed plan submitted to me before he left the colony and in the justice and propriety of which I entirely agreed. I certainly did strenuously urge you to come out and <u>see</u> for yourself…knowing how impossible it is to judge of the state of things without seeing…this I still urge you to do, as the proper course in every point of view, for it will enable you, if you prefer returning to England to speak from your own knowledge, and thereby

add great weight to your <u>statements</u> and <u>representations</u> in behalf of the Colony.[17]

Although the brothers eventually managed to reach agreement about the management of the family properties without breaking the partnership, theirs was an uneasy truce. Edward did not visit the colony, and William would not write to Edward again until 1845, leaving all correspondence to James. Elizabeth, though, could not hold a grudge against her beloved son and her subsequent letters to Edward revert to her usual warm and loving tone.

In early 1842 Elizabeth again travelled down to Camden Park, this time staying for about three months. For some of her visit her daughter-in-law Emily and son James were in Sydney, with James attending his duties as a member of the Legislative Council, to which he had been appointed in 1840. But Elizabeth was perfectly happy staying with William. Yet again she delighted 'in seeing daily all the interesting farming operations', and, in what must have been a relief to Edward, wrote in an affectionate style to tell him all about it. 'Sheep washing and shearing, wool sorting and packing. Hay making and wheat harvest—all I am thankful to say satisfactorily completed.'[18] Elizabeth also spoke highly of her daughter-in-law Emily, whom she considered 'affectionately attached to James, to his interests, and to those of the family generally, hospitable and courteous to all practicing at the same time a laudable economy'.[19] Even better than Emily, though, was Elizabeth's healthy eighteen-month-old granddaughter, 'the little Elizabeth' who was 'a very interesting child' who prattled away with a sweet temper 'not at all spoilt by over indulgence'.[20] Except, perhaps by her fond grandmama.

Elizabeth returned to Parramatta in April but was home for only a week when the unthinkable occurred: her daughter Elizabeth died suddenly. She was only forty-nine years old. Her death fell on 19 April—the anniversary of her brother John's death eleven years earlier.

Elizabeth's daughter's body was taken to Camden Park, where she was buried near her father. The cause of her death is not known, but if she was weakened by her childhood illness in some way, it had not affected her ability to serve on the committee of Parramatta's school for servant girls, or to go for long walks, or to spend hours working in the garden. Her death was a shock to her mother and family. Six months later Elizabeth was still suffering. 'She I trust in God is happy,' wrote Elizabeth to Edward, 'still I mourn, and tears flow when I think of her many virtues, her unaffected piety, her sweet disposition—to me she was the most devoted of daughters but I must not proceed in this strain, and therefore for a few minutes I will lay down my pen.'[21] Elizabeth had now lost four children. It was a heavy burden for a seventy-five-year-old mother and a widow, even one as mentally strong as Elizabeth Macarthur.

Rather than stay at Elizabeth Farm and dwell on her sorrows, Elizabeth distracted herself by travelling to Sydney to see Mary and her family, recently returned to Lyndhurst from their Ravensworth property in the Hunter Valley. Surely she did not expect peace and quiet in a household of children, but shortly after her arrival there was an extraordinary 'explosion'.[22] Son-in-law Doctor Bowman, no longer drawing a salary and with his capital sunk into the fine Sydney house and Ravensworth, had made a series of unfortunate investments and was now threatened with foreclosure by the Bank of Australia. Mary, and the wider Macarthur family, were entirely in the dark about the extent of his debts, making the revelations all the more shocking. Even Mary's enormous dowry was entirely swallowed up, and Mary was furious about it all.

'I leave you to imagine the dismay this has caused,' wrote Elizabeth to Edward. She tried to encourage Mary towards acceptance of her lot, but 'poor Mary whose lofty spirit can <u>ill</u> brook reverses is little prepared to submit with Christian forbearance'.[23] Mary told her mother in no uncertain terms that if the crisis had been caused by the will of God then she would have submitted without a word but given that her whole family was now at risk thanks to the 'most unwarrantable and ill judged speculation' of her husband, Mary was indignant and resentful.[24] Her brother William would later claim, as men often do about angry women, that she went slightly mad.[25]

James and William Macarthur undertook, however, to bail Bowman out. At a cost of £6000 and much trouble, they took over the management of his estates. Although they repaid his most pressing debts, the bank gave them a mere five years in which to pay off the rest. Edward, at this point still fighting with his brothers about the management of their own estates, was livid. Mary became overwrought and unwell, so her mother stayed on to lend a hand. Lyndhurst would be sold at the end of 1843 and until then Elizabeth frequently stayed at the house with Mary.

Elizabeth kept her beloved grandchildren out from under their mother's feet by taking them for rides in her carriage. One of their favourites was to drive into the Domain, in the heart of Sydney town, to hear the military band play on summer afternoons. While the children listened to the music, Elizabeth enjoyed chatting to the many people she knew there. The regimental commandant never failed to pay his respects, nor did the many ladies of Elizabeth's acquaintance. A former military colleague of Edward's would often ride over to ask after her son. Elizabeth, ever the horsewoman, watched the major's mount with a smiling eye. 'His horse is always endeavouring to get close to the stand of the Military Musicians—it is quite laughable to observe the animal.'[26] On other days she and the children drove to Mrs Macquarie's Chair, an outlook point that then as now offers a fine view over Sydney town and the harbour. Despite her advancing years, Elizabeth was still active: on one January day she and the children walked some four kilometres from Mrs Macquarie's Chair southwards to Woolloomooloo ('What a name!'[27] remarked Elizabeth) then eastwards over the hill at Potts Points, around Rushcutters Bay to Darling Point.

In the brief intervals when Elizabeth returned to Elizabeth Farm, there was yet more socialising. She rarely attended dinners and balls, but there seems to have been a steady stream of visitors to Elizabeth Farm. Elizabeth had, a few years earlier, told Edward that 'dear ancient Parramatta' was now 'quite the fashion to admire as an antiquity in respect to the date of the Colony—and the old Cottage, Garden and Grounds attract great attention from most strangers'.[28] The latest governor, Sir George Gipps, and his wife were frequent visitors, and Elizabeth grew to like them both very much. Emmeline was on excellent terms with Lady Gipps, regularly visiting her informally and often a guest at Government House receptions. But Lady

Gipps wasn't the only attraction at Government House for Emmeline. Henry Watson Parker, Lady Gipps' cousin and Governor Gipps' private secretary, caught Emmeline's eye. In 1842, shortly after her sister's death, Emmeline and Henry, both aged thirty-four, announced their engagement. But if the happy couple expected congratulations, they were sorely mistaken. The Macarthur family, Elizabeth included, were appalled. All visiting to Government House ceased immediately.

The 'Dear Old Lady'

*[Elizabeth Farm is a] home endeared to me by its having been my
abode so many years and in a variety of circumstances—some indeed of a
very painful nature—and others of serene happiness—and surrounded
by many blessings conferred upon me for which I pray to God I may be
sufficiently thankful.*

ELIZABETH MACARTHUR TO EDWARD MACARTHUR, 31 MAY 1849

Elizabeth may have had words with Lady Gipps, furious at her
for encouraging the unsuitable match, although the family's
reasons for rejecting Parker as a suitor are not at all clear. James
and his wife Emily described Parker as penurious, which was
to some degree true given he only had his modest salary to
live on. His father in England was well off, but, as a fourth
son, Henry's expectations of an inheritance were probably low.
Elizabeth admitted that Parker's reputation was sound but found
him bad tempered and narrow minded. She wrote to Edward,
as the head of the family, seeking guidance—her concerns were
ostensibly all about Emmeline's happiness. 'I feel horrified and
apprehensive when I look forward—fearful for the happiness of
the poor thing, the youngest and most cherished and indulged.'[1]

Was it Emmeline's happiness she was fearful for though, or
her own? In an 1829 letter to Edward, Emmeline had responded

to his request for details of home life with a searing insight into her daily life:

> Every day occurrences of this place cannot possibly interest you and as for home details an account of the stupid monotonous life we lead would give you the horrors—I certainly envy you when I read your letters from Italy and Switzerland—so interesting—so captivating to a poor unsophisticated Australian![2]

More to the point, with her sister Elizabeth's death it was now entirely clear to Emmeline (and her family) that the care of her elderly mother would fall to her. So the timing of her engagement was perhaps not at all coincidental and nor, perhaps, was her family's refusal to allow it.

Elizabeth had, some fifteen years earlier, refused on Emmeline's behalf, another offer of marriage. In 1827 Saxe Bannister, then attorney-general of New South Wales, had suggested to John Macarthur a match between himself and the then nineteen-year-old Emmeline. John consulted with Elizabeth, and they were of one view when John replied, firmly, in the negative. As far as Elizabeth was aware, Mr Bannister and Emmeline 'had never been thrown into each other's company nor could we discover the least partiality other than that of a very general nature. We none of us dropped the least hint to her, not thinking it necessary as Mr Bannister was so soon to quit the country.'[3]

Henry and Emmeline were forced to wait for nearly a year, until the family heard back from Edward. It seems little wonder that with Emmeline pining in Parramatta, Elizabeth spent much of her time in Sydney. Of course Elizabeth could consent to the wedding without Edward's approval, but perhaps she privately hoped that in the time it took to receive Edward's reply, Emmeline's affection for Henry would wane. For once, though, Edward said the right thing and sided with his younger sister. Perhaps he hoped to annoy his brothers at the same time. He reminded his family that Emmeline had reached an age when she was fully capable 'or ought at least to be of judging with discretion herself'.[4] He then asked some pointed questions about whether James had allowed her annuity to fall into arrears.

The family duly allowed the marriage to go ahead and in November 1843 the couple was wed. The governor and his wife travelled from Sydney especially to attend. James gave the bride away, Hannibal's youngest daughters were bridesmaids (the family feud was obviously not so deep as to preclude them), and the church at Parramatta was crowded with spectators. Elizabeth did not attend the church service, although whether she was unwell or still unwilling to face so many strangers is unclear. She was certainly well enough to receive guests afterwards at an elegant breakfast at Elizabeth Farm. Governor Gipps and his wife did their best to mend bridges by making themselves very agreeable and assuring Elizabeth of the bridegroom's 'worth and integrity of character'.[5] The vice-regal couple then returned immediately to Sydney, graciously allowing the newlyweds a brief honeymoon at the governor's Parramatta residence.

The Macarthur family now wondered how best to care for Elizabeth, who was in her late seventies. There was some pressure for her to move to Camden Park, where she would have the benefits of living with family. There would also be the financial benefit of not maintaining a second household at Elizabeth

Farm. The Bank of Australia, of which John Macarthur had been a founder and where Hannibal was still a director, had just spectacularly failed. Elizabeth had become a shareholder on John's death and she may have incurred a direct loss. And the family as a whole was still suffering financially. Another long drought had meant that both the quality and quantity of wool shipped to London declined during this period. An auction was held to disperse some seventy or so of the family's horses but many failed to find buyers.[6] Small-time suppliers to the family, like the miller who provided their flour, went bankrupt and, in a domino effect, hit the family with serious losses. Mary's family continued to require support. And large loans from London—to fund the expansionary activities of James and William into the Argyle and Murrumbidgee regions—were incurring ever increasing rates of interest.

Elizabeth voluntarily went without her annuity and in her will renounced all rights to arrears. She explained to Edward that although they could produce most of the necessities of life, as well as wine, fruit and dairy products, 'still there is the lack of money to pay wages and to purchase tea, sugar and cloathing'.[7] Meat and grain were selling so cheaply 'that it does not pay the grower'.[8] Without mentioning it to James and William, Elizabeth asked Edward to discreetly enquire about the allowance she paid to her half-sister Isabella Hacker in Bridgerule, and to find out whether it might be appropriate to allow it to lapse. After the death of her mother some seven years earlier, Elizabeth had ensured that her mother's allowance flowed to Isabella, who had since emigrated to Prince Edward Island, Canada, with her husband and at least one of their seven daughters.[9] Edward's enquiries led to the allowance being gradually withdrawn. Elizabeth had hoped to continue the allowance for the rest of her sister's life but, as she explained to Edward, 'such has been the money embarrassments here that I have been fearful to incur any expense'.[10]

A year later, much to Elizabeth's surprise, Isabella sent a letter—the first and last Elizabeth ever received from her. Isabella thanked Elizabeth for all her help over the years, which had been of great assistance, and hoped the affairs of New South Wales would soon mend. In a letter to Edward, Elizabeth noted that Isabella's letter was well expressed 'but very ill spelt…much did your dear father lament that no education was bestowed upon her'.[11] It was more than fifty years since Elizabeth had seen Isabella but she fell easily into the role of the finger-pointing elder sister.

Although the Macarthurs remained asset-rich, their cash-flow problems continued, with William many years later vowing that he would never again wish to live through the events of the decade following 1842. The immediate problem of Elizabeth's care was resolved by Emmeline and Henry. The couple moved into Elizabeth Farm, and Henry Parker—perhaps pointedly— paid all the farm's upkeep costs. It was at first a temporary arrangement, but it would continue for the rest of Elizabeth's life. Elizabeth became fond of Henry, and appreciative of his kindness.

Emmeline and Elizabeth took 'carriage exercise' almost every day, and Elizabeth continued to take great pleasure from walking in her garden. Emmeline wrote to Edward in 1844, providing an intimate vignette:

Our dear Mother goes regularly to church with us when the weather will permit—receives the Sacraments and joins us again at evening prayers which we have in the dining room—& sometimes the tradespeople employed by the family come & with the Servants Cottagers and their children we have quite a little congregation.[12]

In late July of that year, Elizabeth's old friend Anna King died at the Vineyard. She was a year older than Elizabeth, and about to turn eighty. Surely Elizabeth could not help but reflect on her mortality, and pray for a peaceful end when her own time came.

In late 1844 Elizabeth went to Camden for two months, staying there for Christmas and, accompanied by her son William, returning to Parramatta in January. Within a few days of Elizabeth's arrival home, her Bowman grandsons were brought up from Sydney by their Uncle Henry. A 'very, very merry' dinner ensued which Elizabeth and William obviously enjoyed. Two days later, Elizabeth and the Parkers attended church for the 26 January Anniversary Day celebrations—it was fifty-seven years since the First Fleet arrived at Sydney Cove, and, as Elizabeth remembered well, thirty-seven years since the overthrow of Governor Bligh. But he was long gone and, despite it all, Elizabeth's family had persevered. It was with some satisfaction that she sat with Emmeline and Henry in a very full church, and made room for two young Marsdens, whom she described as 'fine youths'.[13] Hannibal and his many family members sat in a pew nearby, and all in the congregation could hear the distant Sydney guns, firing a salute.

Elizabeth, even in her old age, retained a shrewd understanding of the world around her and continued an active interest in current affairs and the expanding colonial frontier. Her great-nephew James Macarthur, Hannibal's son, had in 1840 explored the Australian alps and travelled south through Gippsland with Polish scientist Sir Paul Edmund de Strzelecki. It was Strzelecki who climbed Australia's highest peak and named it—after the Polish democratic leader, Tadeusz Kosciuszko. Hannibal's younger brother, Charles, a captain in the Royal Marines, estab-lished the first white settlement at Port Essington, in 1838, in what is now the Northern Territory. Ludwig Leichhardt, the Prussian naturalist and explorer, travelled with his party nearly 5000 kilometres overland from Moreton Bay (now Brisbane) to Port Essington in 1844–45. Leichhardt returned to Sydney where his long-time correspondent and friend, William Macarthur, welcomed him to Camden Park so he could work on preparing his journals for publication. Later, Leichhardt visited Elizabeth at Parramatta. He was 'a very modest and most intelligent person,' wrote Elizabeth to Edward, 'and by no means spoilt by his being made so much of a Lion since his return'.[14] Edward continued to send Elizabeth books and periodicals, so she could stay up to date, but now there was also a good library in Sydney.

Edward, serving in the army once more and transferred to Ireland, sent his mother newspapers from Dublin as well as from London. Elizabeth duly scoured the library shelves for books about Ireland and, in line with Edward's sympathies, was much distressed about the sufferings of the Irish people. 'What an unhappy and maybe ill-used country!!!' she wrote. The plight of the Irish stayed on her mind for some time and, ever practical, she took 'some solace in reflecting that the bitter cold of winter was then passed away and the season of harvest approaching'.[15] This was, however, at the height of the potato blight and for many there would be no harvest.

As happy and engaged as she was, Elizabeth was not immune to the pain of further loss. In 1845 Mary Bowman, again at Ravensworth, fell from a verandah and broke her leg. She couldn't walk for many months and her family feared she may never regain the full use of her leg. She would later claim that her husband was 'selfish and to me harsh and cruel' and that the only respite she had from his bad temper was while a member of her family was visiting.[16] Was that another reason Elizabeth stayed so often with her daughter in Sydney? She confessed that Mary's 'was not a happy married life at any period for any length of time'.[17] Perhaps tellingly, no one mentions exactly how Mary fell from the verandah.

One year later James Bowman suffered an apoplectic fit and died. Mary did not seem sorry, writing to her mother to say that 'disappointments of many kinds, falsehood and ill-treatment have changed me' and that she had not expected 'to be left as I am, a beggar in all things'. She thought that if she took care of the children and behaved as a wife should, then surely her husband would fulfil his side of the bargain and take care of 'worldly things', only to discover too late that he had 'gambled all away, so disgracefully'.[18]

Elizabeth feared that Mary's reaction to his death was not quite seemly. 'I cannot arrive at any conclusions with respect to the feelings of poor Mary,' Elizabeth wrote to Edward. 'Let us hope they are such as becomes a Christian and erring Mortal.'[19] Although Mary recovered and was able to walk again, she and her eldest son were unable to carry on with the farming ventures, and in 1848 Ravensworth was sold. Mary and her children moved to Camden Park to be supported by James and William.

Elizabeth also worried about, and feared for, Emmeline. She and her husband, both aged thirty-five when they married, suffered enormously in the years following their wedding. A son was stillborn, and a daughter born prematurely died soon after birth.[20] Elizabeth praised Henry's care of his wife in these dark times, writing to Edward to say that 'nothing can be more tender and affectionate than his conduct'.[21] During at least one of Emmeline's 'painful disappointments'—probably a miscarriage—Elizabeth was herself unwell and unable to provide her daughter with care and support. Instead, Elizabeth found herself an invalid, although her recovery was 'greatly accelerated by the use of a warm Bath placed near my bedside, into which I was assisted twice a day for several weeks and attended like an infant—nothing can have exceeded the affectionate attention of our dear Emmeline and her no less kind Husband'.[22] In late1846, in the wake of Emmeline's losses and Elizabeth's unidentified illness, their doctor recommended a change of air. Hannibal was pleased to offer them the use of his marine villa at Watsons Bay. Hannibal had purchased the property from the original Robert Watson—pilot, harbourmaster and lighthouse keeper—a few years earlier.

In January 1847 Henry Parker hired a steamship to take his precious passengers and their luggage direct from the Elizabeth Farm wharf on the Parramatta River right down through the long harbour past Sydney to Watsons Bay—a picturesque cove on the sheltered, Port Jackson side of the South Head peninsula.

An Aboriginal community lived beside the lagoon at nearby Camp Cove, and the small European community at Watsons Bay was made up of fishermen, pilots, sailors and their families. Elizabeth noted with pleasure that there was 'a goodly number of children and plenty of young voices'.[23] Hannibal, for reasons Elizabeth could never discover, called his little villa Clovelly. The villa is long gone but Clovelly Street remains, as does Robertsons Park, which once formed the villa's grounds. From the cove the ground rises gently towards the narrow spine of the peninsula. The house sat well up the hill, with one side facing Military Road. Elizabeth was able to sit at the other side of the house and look back across the harbour towards Sydney while 'breathing in as much of the sea air as I conveniently can'[24] and watching Emmeline swim.

Elizabeth was soon going for walks again, with the aid of a stick and accompanied by Emmeline and Henry. They made their way around the point to Camp Cove, or climbed the short rise behind the villa. Elizabeth wrote that 'by a singular Gap in these stupendous Rocks which form the South Head, you are at once open to the Ocean without'.[25] It is indeed a spectacular view from that gap, with a tumble of rocks to the left leading to the South Head of the harbour, and to the right a long vista of sandstone cliffs falling to the surf below. And ahead are the open waters of the Pacific Ocean.

What did Elizabeth think about while looking out to sea, that small elderly woman in whom love and ambition and sheer force of will had combined to create a dynasty? In a chair brought up for her especially, Elizabeth liked to sit and see the ships arrive at the heads, watch the pilot boats go out to meet them and then to follow their progress up the harbour. It was hard to believe that the mighty Port Jackson, now so full of comings and goings and so famously described by Elizabeth's friend Governor Phillip as 'the finest harbour in the world, in which a thousand sail of the line may ride in the most perfect security', had ever, since the arrival of the First Fleet, lain empty of ships.[26] But Elizabeth had seen it so.

Throughout the summer Elizabeth and the Parkers entertained a string of visitors. All five of the young Bowmans came to stay, as did Doctor Anderson, who had treated John Macarthur at his worst. Anderson had remained a family friend and had for some years been living at Hambledon Cottage. William, who had been ill at Camden Park, arrived looking thin but cheerful, and his mother took pleasure in watching him regain his health through a steady diet of fresh fish, oysters and sea bathing. Many of the Watson Bay fish he caught himself, in company with Emmeline and Mr Parker, in a small boat from which he could see his mother sitting happily on the villa's verandah. Occasionally Elizabeth ventured out with them on short excursions to various parts of the harbour. Then, in March 1847 she and the Parkers returned to Elizabeth Farm much refreshed by their holiday.

Governor Gipps and his wife had returned to England the year before, to be replaced by Sir Charles Augustus Fitzroy and his wife Lady Mary. Elizabeth had yet another vice-regal couple to befriend. Lady Mary, adept with the needle and with a fine eye for design, amused herself by creating patchwork quilts. She employed a technique still in use today: paper piecing. Hundreds of paper templates were cut, then the fabric was basted on top of the paper, then each hexagon was whip-stitched to those adjacent. According to family lore, Elizabeth started making a hexagon quilt too and it's entirely possible the women worked on their projects while they visited each other. In early December 1847, there was a wedding at the Vineyard, for yet another of Hannibal and Maria's six daughters, and the vice-regal couple were pleased to attend. But four days later Lady Mary, aged fifty-seven, was killed.

She had climbed into her carriage at Government House in Parramatta, ready to be driven to Sydney by her husband. But he had barely taken the reins when the horses bolted and charged along the driveway, which curved down a hill. The barouche overturned and smashed against a row of oaks that lined the drive. Lady Mary suffered a fractured skull and died almost immediately; her husband survived with only minor injuries. The Macarthurs were shocked, as was all of Sydney: thousands of people came to pay their respects and there were more than eight hundred mourners in the funeral procession.[27] The patchwork coverlet Lady Fitzroy was working on remains unfinished to this day—the colours of her basted hexagons still quite bright, having spent a century and more tucked in her sewing bag. Elizabeth didn't finish her own quilt either but at some time Emmeline, or perhaps her granddaughter Elizabeth, finished it for her. Every now and again Elizabeth Macarthur's quilt is displayed as the rare and beautiful museum piece it has become.

Lady Mary's accident cast a pall over the Macarthur households, but there was more bad news to bear. The liquidation of the Bank of Australia in 1843 had hit Hannibal, as one of the bank's directors, particularly hard. In 1848 he was 'obliged to bend to the storm and to pass through the Insolvent Court'.[28] He was declared bankrupt, and he and Maria went first to their son-in-law's home in Braidwood and then later to Moreton Bay, where one of their married daughters was living at a property called Newstead. Hannibal had kept up appearances so carefully that his financial failure came as a complete surprise to Elizabeth and her family. Even if they had wished to provide financial support, though, it was beyond them. They were so deep in debt that Elizabeth's family hadn't even been able to help Mary to retain Ravensworth. The Vineyard was sold to a Catholic archbishop and within a few years renamed Subiaco. It became a Benedictine convent and school for young ladies. Henry Parker managed to buy Hannibal's villa, Clovelly, at Watsons Bay. Hannibal sold it to him for £450, having originally paid £1800 for it. Such were the effects of the economic crisis—or the bonds of family.

Parker completely refurbished the house and planted the Moreton Bay figs and Norfolk Island pines that can still be seen today. In January 1849 he once again hired a steamship to collect his wife and mother-in-law from Parramatta and carry them to the harbour-side retreat. The family was worried enough about Elizabeth's health and advancing years that their party included Doctor Anderson. The journey was quite a logistical exercise. They carried so much baggage that a luggage boat was towed behind the steamship, which left the wharf at Parramatta at noon. By three o'clock they called in at Sydney Cove, where William Macarthur and Captain Phillip Parker King joined the flotilla. At Watsons Bay the resident pilots and their boat crews were happy to lend a hand with the unloading, and so by six o'clock the villa's residents were seated at dinner, while William and Captain King returned to Sydney on the steamer. By ten o'clock Elizabeth had retired for the night, in one of her son Edward's comfortable old field beds. Unsurprisingly, she thought of him 'not a little'.[29]

Again, Elizabeth enjoyed her months beside the sea. Emily and James Macarthur came to visit, with their only child, Elizabeth, now almost nine years old, and her two youngest Bowman cousins. With their grandmother, they all set out on a long excursion by boat along Middle Harbour, then a remote reach of Port Jackson, and didn't return to Watsons Bay until sunset. Elizabeth, now eighty-two, still relished her walks and sightseeing at the Gap. She enjoyed talking with the fishermen and pilot crews. She also befriended an elderly couple who lived in a cave, their home 'built up a little in front and divided into two or three apartments kept orderly and very clean'.[30] The couple were born in Devon, like Elizabeth, and she often walked over to their cave residence to reminisce with them. A newspaper article of 1903 featured Watsons Bay, describing the 'bachelor camp' of fishermen who still lived in that cave—really not much more than a deep overhang. Those men believed the earliest white inhabitants of the site had been 'Billy Taylor and his old lady'.[31]

When the holiday was over, Elizabeth was pleased to return to the familiar rhythms of Elizabeth Farm. In her beloved home she could comfortably receive her regular stream of visitors. Her own children and grandchildren, of course, but also the grown-up children of the many friends of her youth. During

1849, Mary's daughter Isabella contracted scarlet fever and was sent from Camden Park to be cared for in isolation at Elizabeth Farm. Mary and her daughter stayed in a tiny spare room called the Oak Tree Room and, from a couch squeezed into the room for the purpose, Mary nursed her little girl through the illness.[32] In the course of a day Elizabeth might stroll in her garden, discuss the state of the orchard with the head gardener, and then retire to write a letter or two while there was still daylight enough to do so. She still regularly wrote to Edward in Ireland, and to Emily, James and William at Camden Park—letters that confirm that her mind remained bright even as her body faded. Late each afternoon, as she had done her whole life, Elizabeth changed for dinner and joined her family in prayer before eating a meal made from the produce of her own gardens and farms.

In the summer of 1850, aged eighty-three, Elizabeth was strong enough for a third stay at Watsons Bay, yet frail enough to ensure that she and the Parkers again travelled in the company of Doctor Anderson. As a young woman, Elizabeth had written from Sydney to her friend Bridget Kingdon about 'a Bay near the Harbour's mouth' where she and her new Sydney acquaintances 'passed the day in Walking among the Rocks, and upon the sands very agreeably'. Elizabeth spent time that long-ago day remembering her friend and 'I looked carefully for some shells for you',[33] but she could find none better than Bridget might find herself on the English beaches near her father's vicarage. Now, sixty years later at the same beach, Elizabeth's thoughts still returned to Bridgerule. The scenes of her youth and childhood, Elizabeth remarked, could not 'be easily forgotten, nor will the memory of dear friends departed, nor of those that still remain, once my young playfellows, be effaced from memory while it pleases God that I retain that faculty'.[34]

Little is known of Elizabeth's final illness beyond the bald fact that she suffered a stroke and, on 9 February 1850, in the company of her daughter Emmeline and her friend Doctor Anderson, she died.[35]

Elizabeth's death cannot have been unexpected but that it occurred at isolated Watsons Bay, in the summertime, presented an immediate and pressing problem. Perhaps, from among the Watsons Bay community, a ship's carpenter was quickly able to build a simple coffin for her. With the roads in and out of Watsons Bay still rudimentary at best, Elizabeth's body was most likely taken to Sydney by steamer, accompanied by Henry Parker and Doctor Anderson, and possibly by Emmeline too. From Sydney surely a swift messenger was dispatched to Camden Park to break the grim news and to confirm that Elizabeth would be buried beside her husband and eldest daughter, in the family graveyard on the rise opposite Camden Park House. In that hard hilltop soil, at the hottest time of the year, men laboured with picks and shovels to create a final resting place while a wagon bearing her little body made the slow journey from Sydney. There is no record of any kind of public funeral for Elizabeth, so we must merely assume that, in line with the customs of the day, Mary and Emmeline did not attend, and were instead represented by James and William, who listened to the local reverend intone the familiar words and watched as their mother's coffin was lowered into the ground.

William planted the graveyard with tall, exotic palms which in time could be seen from the grand house his father designed and where Elizabeth's descendants still live. The woman who, with her arrival in the colony in 1790, represented all the complexity, optimism and pragmatism of the antipodean colonial experiment, died a mere year before the discovery of gold would change everything again.

There was nothing inevitable about the Macarthurs' success. Plenty of others with similar ambitions failed to do so well. The secret to their achievements was a combination of skill, good timing, and—mainly—the combined efforts of the family. Having first John, then their grown-up sons, as agents and catalysts in England proved a boon to the Macarthurs' ability to sell wool, lobby for regulatory change and receive additional land grants. Having the capable Elizabeth on hand to oversee the family business ventures in New South Wales for a total of twelve years while her husband and sons were overseas was equally crucial to the subsequent success of their enterprise. The family fortune was then cemented by the efforts of the second and third generations.

Months after Elizabeth's death, her daughter-in-law Emily wrote to an aunt in England: 'little can I tell you how much I have missed the dear old lady.'[36] And that image of Elizabeth Macarthur, as genteel lady, as helpmeet to John Macarthur's genius or—erroneously—as some sort of social-climbing society matron has somehow been the picture that has endured in the Australian imagination.

Australian history has been, until recently, very much the history of white men working—as farmers, as soldiers, as miners, as explorers. Women and other outsiders were largely written out, as if they were merely peripheral to the *real* story. In the history of Australian farming, though, women very much *were* the real story. Elizabeth Macarthur is only one of many women who were—and are—crucial to the family farming enterprise. In her ambition, her fortitude and her love for her family she was just like many other strong and intelligent farm women.

Elizabeth was a real-life Elizabeth Bennet who married a Wickham, instead of a Darcy—albeit a Wickham who loved her as much as he was able. She is interesting not because she was some sort of paragon, but because she was in fact so very typical. She was an ordinary English country woman who fell in love with a difficult man and, as a result of his decision to sail to New South Wales, she lived an extraordinarily interesting life.

Her successes, and those of women farmers like her, truly deserve to be one of the iconic stories of Australian history.

Epilogue

Elizabeth Macarthur left a lasting legacy. Her children and their children continued the building of Australia's agricultural industry and contributed to some of the key events in our history.

Sir Edward Macarthur (1789–1872)

A year after his mother's death, and with international interest in the colony surging because of the 1851 discovery of gold, Edward returned to New South Wales as deputy adjutant-general of the army in Australia. In 1854 he was promoted to colonel and moved to Melbourne, just in time to have to deal with the protesting gold miners at Eureka. In the days following the short but bloody rebellion Edward and his commander-in-chief, Sir Robert Nickle, travelled up to Ballarat, talked with the miners and advised that martial law be withdrawn.

In 1855 Edward took over command of the British forces in Australia. When Governor Hotham died, Edward, in 1856, became for almost a year the acting administrator of the newly formed colony of Victoria. Edward continued to disagree with his brothers' farming and financial management practices, and in 1858 their partnership was dissolved. Elizabeth Farm now belonged entirely to Edward.

In 1860 Edward returned to England, and in 1862 was knighted. In that year, at the age of seventy-three, he married Sarah Smith Neill, the daughter of one of his regimental colleagues. Edward died ten years later, leaving Elizabeth Farm to his brother William although stipulating that his wife Sarah should have a lifetime interest in it. Lady Sarah Macarthur, who in her widowhood regularly fired off letters to William Macarthur about the management of 'her' estate, died in 1891.

Mary Bowman née Macarthur (1795–1852)

Mary, widowed and penurious, died at Camden in April 1852 at the age of sixty-six. She had five children:

Edward Bowman (1826–1872) became a botanical collector. He travelled Queensland sourcing specimens, for Baron Ferdinand von Mueller among others, and discovered several new plant species. He never married.

James Bowman (1829–1871) also never married but seems to have spent his life at Camden. For a year or two in the mid 1860s he was Edward Macarthur's agent at Elizabeth Farm.

William Bowman (1831–1878) and Frederic Bowman (1836–1915) both married and had large families. With the assistance of their Macarthur uncles, they established themselves on properties in Queensland.

Isabella Bowman (1843–1883) was married in 1858. Her husband, James Kinghorne Chisholm, was one of nine sons born to politician and pastoralist James Chisholm MLC. Isabella and James had seven children[1] and properties at Narellan, near Camden Park.

Sir William Macarthur (1800–1882)

For the rest of his long life William lived at Camden Park, briefly with Mary and, after she died, with her children, and always with James and Emily and their daughter, Elizabeth. At the time of their mother's death, William and James held eleven thousand hectares at Camden, with stock worth £47,500 and more than twenty thousand hectares elsewhere, including land on the Abercrombie River and leases along the Lachlan and Murrumbidgee rivers.

William introduced dairying at Camden, continued to breed horses and cultivated extensive orchards. He was also a successful vigneron, and by 1850 the vineyard at Camden was producing over sixty thousand litres of red and white wines and brandies each year. He also became president of the New South Wales Vineyard Association. In 1855 he travelled to France as New South Wales commissioner at the International Exhibition in Paris, with a highly regarded display of Australian timbers. William was knighted in 1856, awarded the *Légion d'honneur* and in February 1861 was made an honorary member of the *Société Impériale Zoologique d'Acclimatation*.

He was appointed to the New South Wales Legislative Council in 1864, where he would serve until the year he died. He was a trustee of the Free Public Library, vice-president of the Australia Club, president of the Agricultural Society of New South Wales, and a member of the senate of the University of Sydney. But William's true passion was botany. The gardens at Camden Park were his extensive laboratory. He experimented with propagation, crops, irrigation systems and an ingeniously heated greenhouse. He developed more than sixty new camellia varieties. William died at Camden Park on 29 October 1882.

James Macarthur (1798–1867) and his wife Emily Macarthur née Stone (1806–1880) also lived and worked at Camden Park for the rest of their lives. In the late 1840s and through the 1850s James was elected member for Camden in the various incarnations of the early New South Wales legislature. Emily took a lead role in managing the Camden estates. In 1859 James resigned from parliament and refused the knighthood offered to him by Governor Denison. From 1860 to 1864 James, with his wife and daughter, toured England and Europe, representing New South Wales at the International Exhibition in London in 1862. In 1866 he was nominated to the New South Wales Legislative Council. In March 1867 he became president of the Agricultural Society of New South Wales but died suddenly shortly afterwards at Camden Park on 21 April.

Elizabeth Macarthur Onslow (1840–1911) was James and Emily's only child. She enjoyed painting, and many of her watercolours of Elizabeth Farm survive to this day.[2] In 1867, she married naval officer Captain Arthur Onslow. They had eight children, of whom five sons and one daughter survived to adulthood. In January 1882 Captain Onslow died unexpectedly, leaving Elizabeth a forty-one-year-old widow, her youngest child barely a year old. In October that same year her Uncle William, the last surviving and youngest of John and Elizabeth's sons, died too. The newly widowed Elizabeth Onslow inherited all the Macarthur family properties (although by then Elizabeth Farm had been sold).

Elizabeth Onslow became the active head of the estates. She established an innovative and award-winning dairying complex at Camden Park. Later she added a piggery and experimented in the production of silk. She was involved with local charities as a benefactor and patron, including the Camden School of Arts, the Society for the Prevention of Cruelty to Animals, and the Camden Agricultural, Horticultural and Industrial Society, which held the first Camden Show in 1886. In 1897 she donated the clock and bells of St John's Church, Camden. She is also credited with creating the St John's Mothers' Union, a precursor to the Camden Red Cross branch established in 1914.

In 1899 Elizabeth converted Camden Park Estate into a private company, with her children as shareholders and directors, retaining Camden Park House and 390 hectares as her own private property. She compiled and curated a selection of family letters and records, a task that her daughter Sibella would eventually finish, culminating in a massive tome called *The Macarthurs of Camden* (first published in 1914).

Elizabeth Macarthur Onslow died while visiting England, in April 1911. She was seventy-one years old. Her descendants own, and live at, Camden Park—still a productive dairy farm.

Emmeline Emily Parker née Macarthur (1808–1888) and Henry Watson Parker (1808–1880)

The Parkers continued to live at Elizabeth Farm until 1854 when, after a dispute with Emmeline's brother, Edward, they moved permanently to their house at Watsons Bay. Henry was a member of the New South Wales Legislative Council and, in 1856, he was elected member for Parramatta in the Legislative Assembly. In

October of that year he became premier of New South Wales, a position he held until September 1857. He was knighted in 1858.

In 1862 the Parkers moved permanently to England, where Henry stood unsuccessfully against the man who became Prime Minister, William Gladstone, in the British elections of 1868. Henry Parker died in 1881, leaving an estate worth a whopping £140,000. Emmeline was almost eighty when she died and was buried in England, in May 1888. Her mother's journal, recording John and Elizabeth's voyage from England to New South Wales in 1790 and the only document we have today written in Elizabeth's own hand, was found among Emmeline's possessions and sent back to her Australian relatives at Camden Park.

Hannibal Hawkins Macarthur (1788–1861) and Maria Macarthur née King (1793–1852)

Following his bankruptcy in 1848, Hannibal and Maria lived in southern Queensland with one of their married daughters. In 1852, Hannibal was appointed police magistrate. Later that year, Maria died, aged fifty-nine. Hannibal was so affected by her death that he suffered a physical breakdown and resigned from the magistracy. He returned to England in 1853, where he died at Norwood on 21 October 1861. He was seventy-three years old.

Elizabeth Farm

After Emmeline and Henry Parker moved out of Elizabeth Farm in 1854, Edward's agent William Allport and his family moved in. They stayed until 1863, when Allport was dismissed and Edward's nephew, James Bowman, became the agent. By

1865 the property was quite dilapidated and Edward decided to lease it out, repainting and making a few minor repairs before doing so. For the next ten years and more, the various lessees also failed to maintain the farm's thousand acres, resulting in broken fences, unkempt laneways and paths, and pasture full of weeds and scrub. The house was little better: termites were taking their toll. The badly leaking shingled wooden roof was covered with galvanised iron, which inadvertently but happily preserved the old roof for posterity.

In 1881 the Macarthur family sold Elizabeth Farm for £50,000 to Septimus Alfred Stephen. He subdivided the thousand acres (400 hectares) into quarter- and half-acre blocks (leaving Hambledon Cottage and the original house on slightly larger blocks) and sold the lot. The first buyer paid £6000 for the original house but soon leased it out. Elizabeth Farm continued to deteriorate. Over the next twenty-five years the old house saw numerous owners and tenants and was, at various times, a boarding house and a glue factory.

In 1903, the now-derelict house and its six acres (2.5 hectares) was sold to school teacher and headmaster William Swann for £550—effectively for the value of the land alone. Swann was well aware of the history of the house and convinced of its importance to Australia's cultural heritage. He set about repairing it for his large family, who moved in during 1905. William Swann died a few years later, in 1909, but his wife, Elizabeth, and unmarried daughters continued to live in the house for the rest of their long lives. Believing themselves to be mere custodians, the Swann women cherished the house but did little to change the building. In 1968 the Swanns sold their house to a trust set up expressly for Elizabeth Farm's preservation. The house and gardens have since been restored and remain in public hands.

Camden Park House

The Macarthur-Stanham family continue to live in Camden Park House, which is still surrounded by William Macarthur's extensive garden; now the largest intact nineteenth century garden in New South Wales.

Belgenny Farm

Belgenny Farm remained the home farm of the Camden Park Estate until 1973. It was purchased by the New South Wales government in 1984, and it has the oldest collection of farm buildings in Australia.

Macarthur memorials

The Elizabeth Macarthur Agricultural Institute is the New South Wales state government's quarantine and biosecurity facility. The institute also manages a flock of some 250 sheep—direct descendants of the Camden Park merinos. The flock has been maintained as an inbred, closed bloodline for 200 years.

Elizabeth Macarthur High School is a selective and community high school. The school serves the Narellan area, near Camden Park. Elizabeth's family is also memorialised in many place names throughout New South Wales. The Australian electoral division of Macarthur, which encompasses the area around Camden Park, was named after Elizabeth and John Macarthur. A small township west of Melbourne is also called Macarthur and was named, in 1857, for Elizabeth's son General

Edward Macarthur, as was Macarthur Street in East Melbourne.

In 1966, when Australia converted to decimal currency, John Macarthur was featured on the two-dollar note. The note was issued until 1988, when it was replaced by the two-dollar coin. In 1995 Elizabeth Macarthur was commemorated on a collectors-edition five-dollar coin, part of a set celebrating colonial Australia.

Acknowledgments

Writing a book is not nearly the solitary activity I imagined it might be.

The Australian literary community provided me with solid support and vital networks. Writers Victoria introduced me to a whole new world of writers and writing. My shortlisting for the Hazel Rowley fellowship provided much needed validation and motivation. I spent two weeks in the Blue Mountains at Varuna, as the recipient of a residential fellowship. In Canberra I was accepted into the ACT Writers Centre's HARDCOPY professional development program for writers. This program, and the marvellous people I've met through it, was my literary launch pad.

In 2014 I visited Elizabeth Macarthur's birthplace: Bridgerule. I could not have received a warmer welcome. My thanks to all I met, including Rose Hitchings, who was almost as excited as I was to find the gravestones of Elizabeth Macarthur's parents and sister. Diana Green who generously shared her knowledge, pictures and research. The owners of the Glebe—now a beautiful B&B, but once the home of Elizabeth's best friend Bridget Kingdon. David and Vivienne Hale, owners of Lodgeworthy Farm (where Elizabeth Macarthur was born), who kindly invited me into their home, shared their information about Elizabeth and provided the most delicious afternoon tea. The spritely octogenarian, Mr Bowden, who showed me through St Bridget's church and then rang the church bells for me. And last and best of all, Bridgerule local Sheila Cholwill who invited me, a complete stranger, into her home and spent days showing me around the village. Sheila and her husband Colin's generosity and thoughtfulness will stay with me for a very long time.

In the course of writing this book it became very clear to me that people who love books are my kind of people. Every single librarian I came across was unfailingly helpful. Perhaps the collective noun should be a kindness of librarians. At Sydney Living Museums Jacky Dalton and Jacqui Newling were lovely. My grateful thanks also to Edwina and John Macarthur-Stanham. Through my online blog (Adventures in Biography) I made many new bookish friends, who were lavish with their support and information. Shout outs to fellow bloggers Whispering Gums, ANZLitlovers, the Australian Legend, and A Biographer in Perth. Special mentions to Dr Marion Diamond at Historians Are Past Caring, family historian Roger Kingdon, and to biographer Bernice Barry—who all were incredibly generous with their information, insights and expertise.

Special thanks to my agent Jacinta di Mase, my editor Jane Pearson and my publisher at Text, Michael Heyward. You were all willing to take a punt on me and in so doing changed my life.

Thank you to my brilliant day-job colleagues at ACIG (www.acig.com.au): Gerard Colla, Euan Lockie, Linda Hall, Tom Dale, Jo Lim, Tracey Hind and Erin Louis. You make working a pleasure and you provided unwavering support and enthusiasm for the book, even when my own motivation flagged.

The encouragement of friends, family and colleagues also made a big difference. Few of you stepped inside my home, or welcomed me into yours, without gently asking how the book was going—which meant more to me than you might imagine. Many thanks to all my friends, old and new. Particular commendation to Jane McKenzie, whose willing participation in my Sydney research adventures truly helped me over the line, and to Samantha Comte, for always being there for me.

And thank you most of all to my wonderful husband Tim and our beautiful children: Charlie, Will and Ashlee. I could never have done it without you.

Select Bibliography

American Psychiatric Association, *Diagnostic and Statistical Manual of Mental Disorders*, Fifth Edition, American Psychiatric Association, Arlington, VA, 2013.

Atkinson, A., *The Political Life of James Macarthur,* PhD thesis, 1976.

Atkinson, A. 'John Macarthur Before Australia Knew Him', *Journal of Australian Studies*, No 4, Melbourne, June 1979.

Atkinson, A., *Camden: Farm and Village Life in Early New South Wales*, Oxford University Press, Melbourne, 1988.

Atkinson, A., *The Europeans in Australia: A History,* Volume One, Oxford University Press, Melbourne, 1998.

Atkinson, A., 'The Moral Basis of Marriage', *Push from the Bush 2*, Melbourne, 1978.

Australian Dictionary of Biography, National Centre of Biography, Australian National University, <http://adb.anu.edu.au/biography>.

Australian Meteorological and Oceanographic Journal, No. 58, 2009.

Badger, J., 'The Lamentable Death of Lady Mary Fitzroy', *Journal of the Royal Australian Historical Society*, Sydney, December, 2001.

Barani, *Sydney's Aboriginal History*, <http://www.sydneybarani.com.au/>.

Bassett, M., *The Governor's Lady: Mrs Philip Gidley King*, Melbourne University Press, Melbourne, 1992.

Bickel, L., *Australia's First Lady*, Allen & Unwin, Sydney, 1991.

Binney, K.R., *Horsemen of the First Frontier (1788–1900) and The Serpents Legacy*, Volcanic Productions, Sydney, 2005.

Blainey, G., *The Tyranny of Distance*, Sun Books, Melbourne, 1980.

Bown, S., *Scurvy: How a Surgeon, a Mariner, and a Gentlemen Solved the Greatest Medical Mystery of the Age of Sail*, Thomas Dunne Books, New York, 2003.

Bradley, W., *A Voyage to New South Wales: The Journal of Lieutenant William Bradley R.N. of HMS Sirius 1786-1792*, Australian Digital Collections, University of Sydney.

Bridgerule Parish Registers—Baptisms, Marriages, Burials, transcribed by J. Upton. http://www.genuki.org.uk/big/eng/DEV/Bridgerule.

Broadbent, J. and Hughes, J., *Elizabeth Farm Parramatta: A history and a guide*, Historic Houses Trust of NSW, Sydney, 1984.

Broadbent, J., *The Australian Colonial House: architecture and society in New South Wales 1788-1842*, Hordern House, Sydney, 1997.

Brooke, A., & Brandon, D., *Bound for Botany Bay: British Convict Voyages to Australia*, National Archives (UK), London, 2005.

Brown, A.J., *Ill-Starred Captains: Flinders and Baudin*, Crawford House, Adelaide, 2000.

Carruthers, F., *The Horse in Australia*, Knopf, Sydney, 2008.

Clarke, P., *A Colonial Woman: The Life and Times of Mary Braidwood Mowle*, Allen & Unwin, Sydney, 1991.

Clarke, P. & Spender, D. (eds), *Life Lines: Australian Women's Letters and Diaries 1788 to 1840*, Allen & Unwin, Sydney, 1992.

Clendinnen, I., *Dancing with Strangers*, Text Publishing, Melbourne, 2005.

Cochrane, P., *Colonial Ambition: Foundations of Australian Democracy*, Melbourne University Press, Melbourne, 2006.

Cohen, L., *Elizabeth Macquarie: Her Life and Times*, Wentworth Books, Sydney, 1979.

Coleman, D. (ed), *Maiden Voyages and Infant Colonies*, Leicester University Press, London, 1999.

Collingridge, V., *Captain Cook: The Life, Death and Legacy of History's Greatest Explorer*, Ebury Press, London, 2003.

Collins, D., *An Account of the English Colony in New South Wales 1788 to 1801*, 1802, <http://gutenberg.net.au/ebooks/e00011.html>.

Connor, J., *The Australian Frontier Wars 1788–1838*, UNSW Press, Sydney, 2002.

Currey, J., *David Collins: A Colonial Life*, Melbourne University Press, Melbourne, 2000.

Dando-Collins, S., *Captain Bligh's Other Mutiny*, Random House Australia, Sydney, 2007.

Daniels, K., *Convict Women*, Allen & Unwin, Sydney, 1998.

Davidoff, L. & Hall, C., *Family Fortunes: Men and Women of the English Middle Class*, 1780–1850, University of Chicago Press, Chicago, 1987.

Day, M., *Voices from the World of Jane Austen*, David & Charles, Cincinnati, 2006.

De Vries, S., *Strength of Spirit: Pioneering Women of Achievement from First Fleet to Federation*, Millenium Books, Sydney, 1995.

De Vries-Evans, S., *Pioneer Women Pioneer Land: Yesterday's Tall Poppies*, Angus and Robertson, Sydney, 1987.

Dictionary of Sydney, <https://dictionaryofsydney.org>.

Duffy, M., *Man of Honour*, Macmillan Australia, Sydney, 2003.

Dyer, C., *The French Explorers and Sydney*, UQP, Brisbane, 2009.

Egan, J. (ed), *Buried Alive: Sydney 1788–92 Eyewitness Accounts of the Making of a Nation*, Allen & Unwin, Sydney, 1999.

Elder, B., *Blood on the Wattle: Massacres and Maltreatment of Aboriginal Australians since 1788*, 3rd Edition, New Holland Publishers, Sydney, 2003.

Ellis, M.H., *John Macarthur*, Angus and Robertson, Sydney, 1978.

Estensen, M. (ed), *The Letters of George & Elizabeth Bass*, Allen & Unwin, Sydney, 2009.

Evatt, H.V., *Rum Rebellion*, Angus & Robertson, Sydney, 1975.

Falbe, J., *My Dear Miss Macarthur: Recollections of Emmeline Maria Macarthur 1828–1911*, Kangaroo Press, Sydney, 1988.

Flannery, T. (ed), *The Birth of Sydney*, Text Publishing, Melbourne, 1999.

Flannery, T. (ed), *The Explorers*, Text Publishing, Melbourne, 2000.

Flynn, M., *The Second Fleet: Britain's Grim Convict Armada of 1790*, Library of Australian History, Sydney, 1993.

Frost, A., *Botany Bay Mirages*, Melbourne University Press, Melbourne, 1995.

Gammage, B., *The Biggest Estate on Earth: How Aborigines Made Australia*, Allen & Unwin, Sydney, 2011.

Geraghty, R.C.R., *A Change in Circumstance: Individual Responses to Colonial Life*, thesis, University of Sydney, Sydney, 2006.

Graham, J.R., *A Treatise on the Australian Merino*, Clarson, Massina & Co, Melbourne, 1870.

Grimshaw, P., Lake, M., McGrath, A., Quartly, M., et al., *Creating a Nation*, McPhee Gribble, Melbourne, 1994.

Groom, L., *A Steady Hand: Governor Hunter & His First Fleet Sketch Book*, National Library of Australia, Canberra, 2012.

Hadlow, J., *The Strangest Family: The Private Lives of George III, Queen Charlotte and the Hanoverians*, William Collins, London, 2015.

Hill, S., *Paper Houses: John Macarthur and the 30-year Design Process of Camden Park*, PhD thesis, University of Sydney, Sydney, 2016.

Hirst, J.B., *Convict Society and Its Enemies*, Allen & Unwin, Sydney, 1983.

Hirst, J.B., *Sense and Nonsense in Australian History*, Black Inc, Melbourne, 2006.

Hirst, J.B., *Freedom on the Fatal Shore: Australia's First Colony*, Black Inc, Melbourne, 2008.

Historical Records of New South Wales (HRNSW), Vol. 1 and 2, <http://gutenberg.net. au/ebooks12/1204171h.html#ch-69>

Holmes, K., et al., *Reading the Garden: The Settlement of Australia*, Melbourne University Press, Melbourne, 2008.

Hughes, J., *The Macarthurs: A Brief Family History*, Historic Houses Trust NSW, Sydney, 1984.

Hughes, J., *John Macarthur and the Wool Industry*, Historic Houses Trust NSW, Sydney, 1984.

Hughes, J., 'The Macarthur Collection: Its Contribution to Australian Historiography', Elizabeth Farm Bicentennial Seminar, 24 October 1993.

Hughes, J. (ed), *The Journal and Letters of Elizabeth Macarthur 1789–1798*, Historic Houses Trust NSW, Sydney, 1984.

Karskens, G., *The Colony: A History of Early Sydney*, Allen & Unwin, Sydney, 2009.

Karskens, G. and Waterhouse, R., 'Too Sacred to Be Taken Away: Property, Liberty,

Tyranny and the Rum Rebellion' [online]. *Journal of Australian Colonial History*, Vol. 12, 2010.

Keneally, T., *A Commonwealth of Thieves*, Anchor Books, New York, 2007.

Kercher, B., *Debt, Seduction and Other Disasters: The Birth of Civil Law in Convict New South Wales*, The Federation Press, Sydney, 1996.

Kerr Forsyth, H., *Remembered Gardens: Eight Women and Their Visions of an Australian Landscape*, Melbourne University Press, Melbourne, 2006.

King, H., *Elizabeth Macarthur and Her World*, Sydney University Press, Sydney, 1980.

King, J. & King, J., *Phillip Gidley King: A Biography of the Third Governor of New South Wales*, Methuen Australia, Sydney, 1981.

Kingdon, A.S., *The Kingdon Family: A Second Look*, self-published, 1974.

Kingdon, R.D., *The Origin of the Kingdons*, Brown Dog Books and The Self-Publishing Partnership, Sydney, 2017.

Kloester, J., *Georgette Heyer's Regency World*, Arrow Books, London, 2005.

Lancaster, G., *The First Fleet Piano: A Musician's View*, ANU Press, Canberra, 2015.

Lavery, B., *Jack Aubrey Commands: An Historical Companion to the Naval World of Patrick O'Brian*, with Peter Weir, Conway Maritime Press, London, 2003.

Levi, J.S. & Bergman, G.F.J., *Australian Genesis: Jewish Convicts and Settlers 1788–1850*, Rigby, Adelaide, 1974.

Macarthur-Onslow, J. W., 'Told Me by Sir William Macarthur, My Great Uncle', in *Recollections* by J. W. Macarthur–Onslow, AIATSIS Library.

Macarthur-Onslow, S., *The Macarthurs of Camden*, Rigby, Adelaide, 1973.

Macarthur Papers, First and Second Collections, Mitchell Library, Sydney.

Marsden Online Archive, <http://www.marsdenarchive.otago.ac.nz/MS_0176_001>.

Massy, C., *The Australian Merino*, Viking O'Neil, Melbourne,1990.

McCalman, I. (ed), *An Oxford Companion to the Romantic Age: British Culture 1776–1832*, Oxford University Press, Oxford, 1999.

Morgan, S., *Bombay Anna*, University of California Press, Los Angeles, 2008.

Mrs E., *Advice to a Young Lady in the Colonies*, Greenhouse Publications, Melbourne, 1979.

Mundle, R., *Bligh: Master Mariner*, Hachette, Sydney, 2010.

Mundle, R., *Flinders: The Man who Mapped Australia*, Hachette, Sydney, 2013.

Naval Chronicle, Vol. XXII, July–December, 1809.

Nicholas, F.W. & Nicholas, J.M., *Charles Darwin in Australia*, Cambridge University Press, Cambridge, 2008.

O'Brian, P., *Joseph Banks, A Life*, The University of Chicago Press, Chicago, 1993.

Pascoe, B., *Convincing Ground: Learning to Fall in Love with Your Country*, Aboriginal Studies Press, Canberra, 2007.

Pembroke, M., *Arthur Phillip: Sailor, Mercenary, Governor, Spy*, Hardie Grant Books, Melbourne, 2013.

Philbrick, N., *In the Heart of the Sea: the epic true story that inspired Moby Dick*, Flamingo, London, 2000.

Phillip, A., et al, *The Voyage of Governor Phillip to Botany Bay*, <http://freeread.com.au>

Porter, R., *English Society in the Eighteenth Century*, Penguin Books, Melbourne, 1988.

Rees, S., *The Floating Brothel*, Hodder, Sydney, 2001.

Reynolds, H., *Frontier*, Allen & Unwin, Sydney, 1996.

Reynolds, H., *Forgotten War*, NewSouth Publishing, Sydney, 2013.

Roberts, B. (ed), *Miss D & Miss N: An Extraordinary Partnership*, Australian Scholarly Publishing, Melbourne, 2009.

Robinson, P., *The Women of Botany Bay*, The Macquarie Library, Sydney, 1998.

Russell, P., *For Richer, For Poorer: Early Colonial Marriages*, Melbourne University Press, Melbourne, 1994.

Russell, P., *Wish of Distinction: Colonial Gentility and Femininity*, Melbourne University Press, Melbourne, 1994.

Smee, C.J., *Born in the English Colony of New South Wales 1788–1800*, self published, 2009.

Stapleton, E., *Anna Josepha King: Governor King's Wife*, St Mary's Historical Society, Sydney, 1981.

Stone, L., *The Family Sex and Marriage in England 1500–1800*, Harper & Row, New York, 1977.

Summers, A., *Damned Whores and God's Police*, Penguin Books Australia, Melbourne, 1994.

Tench, W., *1788: A Complete Account of the Settlement at Port Jackson*, Text Publishing, Melbourne, 2009.

Tench, W., *A Complete Account of the Settlement at Port Jackson*, J. Nichol, 1793 <http://gutenberg.net.au/ebooks/e00084.html>

Tomalin, C., *Jane Austen: A Life*, Viking, London, 1997.

Tuckey, J.H. (James Hingston 1776–1816), *Account of a Voyage to Establish a Colony at Port Phillip in Bass's Strait*, 1805, <http://www.spiffa.org/early-writings-on-australian-timbers.html>.

Vickery, A., *The Gentleman's Daughter: Women's Lives in Georgian England*, Yale University Press, London, 1998.

Walsh, D. (ed), *The Admiral's Wife: Mrs Phillip Parker King*, The Hawthorne Press, Melbourne, 1967.

Walsh, R. (ed), *In Her Own Words: The Writings of Elizabeth Macquarie*, Macquarie University Press, Sydney, 2011.

Wannan, B., *Early Colonial Scandals: The Turbulent Times of Samuel Marsden*, Lansdowne Press, Melbourne, 1972.

Wantrup, J., 'The Voyage of the First Fleet', *The La Trobe Journal*, No. 41, Autumn, 1988.

Whitaker, A., *Distracted Settlement: New South Wales After Bligh*, Melbourne University Press, Melbourne, 1998.

Whitaker, A., 'Mrs Paterson's Keepsakes: The Provenance of Some Significant Colonial Documents and Paintings', *Journal of the Royal Australian Historical Society*, 1 Dec 2004.

Wright, C., *Beyond the Ladies Lounge: Australia's Female Publicans*, Melbourne University Press, Melbourne, 2003.

Yarwood, A.T., *Samuel Marsden: The Great Survivor*, Melbourne University Press, Melbourne, 1977.

Notes

Letters to and from Elizabeth Macarthur, and between her immediate family members, can be found in the Macarthur Papers, First and Second Collections, Mitchell Library, Sydney. The sources for other letters and documents are provided in the notes below.

Transcripts of some of the Macarthur letters can be found in:

Hughes, J. (ed), *The Journal and Letters of Elizabeth Macarthur 1789–1798*, Historic Houses Trust of New South Wales, Sydney, 1984.

Macarthur-Onslow, S. M., *The Macarthurs of Camden*, Rigby, Adelaide, 1973 (first published 1914).

1. The Lost Comforts of Home

1   Elizabeth Macarthur to her mother Grace Leach, 18 March 1781, Macarthur Papers, Mitchell Library, Sydney.
2   Elizabeth Macarthur's Journal, undated, Macarthur Papers, Mitchell Library, Sydney.
3   Elizabeth Macarthur to her mother Grace Leach, 8 Oct 1789.
4   Collins, *An Account of The English Colony in New South Wales 1788 to 1801*, published 1802, subsequently Reed, Sydney 1975, Chapter X.
5   Tench, *A Complete Account of the Settlement at Port Jackson*, J. Nichol, 1793, Chapter VII.
6   Collins, *An Account of The English Colony in New South Wales*, Chapter X.
7   Tench, Chapter VII.
8   Collins, *An Account of The English Colony in New South Wales*, Chapter X.
9   Captain William Hill to Samuel Wathen, 26 July 1790, *Historical Records of New South Wales*, Vol. 1, Part 2, p. 369.
10 Rev Johnson to Mr Thornton, July 1790, *Historical Records of New South Wales* Vol. 1, Part 2,—Phillip, p. 386.
11 Extract from a letter, *Historical Records of New South Wales* Vol. 1, Part 2,—Phillip, p. 767.
12 Rev Johnson to Mr Thornton, July 1790, *Historical Records of New South Wales* Vol. 1, Part 2,—Phillip, p. 386.
13 Collins, *An Account of The English Colony in New South Wales*, Chapter X.
14 Rev Johnson to Mr Thornton, July 1790, *Historical Records of New South Wales* Vol 1, Part 2,—Phillip, p. 387.
15 Tench, Chapter VII.

16 Collins, *An Account of The English Colony in New South Wales,* Chapter X.
17 Tench, Chapter VII.

2. An Ill-advised Marriage

1   Episcopal Visitation Returns 1779, viewed online, 2 September 2013, <www.foda.org.uk/visitations/1779/Chanter232B/Bridgerule.htm>.
2   Bridgerule Baptisms 1754–1812, transcribed by J. Upton, viewed online, 25 Feb 2011, <genuki.cs.ncl.ac.uk/DEV/Bridgerule/Baptisms1754.html>.
3   Devon Freeholders Book, 1741, viewed online, 11 February 2011, <www.foda.org.uk/freeholders/QS7/20/blacktorrington.htm>.
4   Bridget Kingdon to Elizabeth Macarthur, 15 September 1799.
5   Bridgerule Baptisms 1754–1812, transcribed by J. Upton, viewed online, 25 February 2011, <genuki.cs.ncl.ac.uk/DEV/Bridgerule/Baptisms1754.html>.
6   King, *Elizabeth Macarthur and Her World*, Sydney University Press, 1980, p. 4.
7   Undated handwritten note in the Macarthur Papers, Vol. 10, A2906.
8   Davidoff and Hall, *Family Fortunes: Men and Women of the English Middle Class, 1780–1850*, The University of Chicago Press, 1987, p. 105.
9   Atkinson, 'John Macarthur before Australia Knew Him', *Journal of Australian Studies* No. 4, Melbourne, June 1979, p. 25.
10 Plymouth Data, viewed online 13 February 2011, <www.plymouthdata.info/Roads-Streets-Fore%20Street%20DEV.htm>.
11 Atkinson, *Journal of Australian Studies*, No. 4, p. 28.
12 *Ibid.*, p 26.
13 Ellis, *John Macarthur*, Angus and Robertson, 1978, p. 6.
14 Devonport Online, viewed online, 13 February 2011, <devonportonline.co.uk/historic_devonport/transcriptions/1791_directory.aspx>.
15 Atkinson, *Journal of Australian Studies*, No. 4, p. 29.
16 *Ibid.*
17 *Ibid.*, p. 30.
18 *Ibid.*
19 James Macarthur to Roger Thierry, 24 February 1859, as cited in Atkinson, *Journal of Australian Studies*, No. 4, p. 31.
20 Elizabeth Macarthur to Eliza Kingdon, March 1816.
21 Porter, *English Society in the Eighteenth Century*, 1988, pp. 190–92.
22 Elizabeth Macarthur to Bridget Kingdon, 1 September 1798.
23 Bridget Kingdon to Elizabeth Macarthur, 15 September 1799.
24 Atkinson, *Journal of Australian Studies*, No. 4, p. 33.
25 Elizabeth Veale conveys to James Vowler, gent of Bridgerule, 8 closes called Two Broad Parks, Longmoore and Longland. Conditions: no timber to be taken. Consideration £340. Viewed online, 25 February 2011, <http://www.a2a.org.uk/search/documentxsl.asp?stylesheet=xsl\A2A_doc.xsl&i=0&com=1&nbKey=2&keyword=Elizabeth+Veale+Spinster&properties=0601>.
26 Stone, *The Family, Sex and Marriage in England 1500–1800*, 1977, p. 46.

27 Watercolour on ivory miniature, reputedly Elizabeth Macarthur, 1785–1790, viewed online, 1 March 2011, <acms.sl.nsw.gov.au/item/itemDetailPaged.aspx?itemID=431535>.

28 Vickery, *The Gentleman's Daughter: Women's Lives in Georgian England*, 1998, p. 40.

29 Elizabeth Macarthur to Bridget Kingdon, 1 September 1798.

30 *Portrait of John Macarthur*, c. 1850s, Artist unknown, oil, viewed online 1 March 2011, <www.sl.nsw.gov.au/events/exhibitions/2008/politicspower/images/2.html>.

31 King, *Elizabeth Macarthur and Her World*, 1980, p. 7.

32 Bridgerule Marriage Register 1754–1837, viewed online, 11 Feb 2011, <genuki.cs.ncl. ac.uk/DEV/Bridgerule/Marriages1754.html>.

33 Atkinson, *Journal of Australian Studies* No. 4, p. 33.

34 *Ibid.* The letter was dated 10 March 1789.

35 Hill, 'Macarthur, Sir Edward (1789–1872)', *Australian Dictionary of Biography*, Volume 5, 1974, pp. 122–23.

36 Stone, *The Family, Sex and Marriage in England 1500–1800*, p. 35.

37 Vickery, *The Gentleman's Daughter: Women's Lives in Georgian England*, 1998, p. 45.

38 Stone, *The Family, Sex and Marriage in England 1500–1800*, p. 504.

39 King, *Elizabeth Macarthur and Her World*, 1980, p. 9.

40 Ellis, *John Macarthur*, 1978, p. 10.

41 Flannery (ed), *The Birth of Sydney*, 1999, p. 49.

42 Wantrup, 'The Voyage of the First Fleet', *Latrobe Journal* No. 41, 1988, pp. 30–34.

43 Elizabeth Macarthur to her mother, Grace Leach, 8 October 1789.

3. Honour and a Small Victory

1 British National Maritime Museum, scale model, viewed online, 25 April 2017, <http:// collections.rmg.co.uk/collections/objects/66321.html>.

2 Flynn, *The Second Fleet: Britain's Grim Convict Armada of 1790*, 1993, p. 33.

3 Rees, *The Floating Brothel*, 2001, p. 59.

4 Lavery, *Jack Aubrey Commands: An Historical Companion to the Naval World of Patrick O'Brian*, 2003, pp. 29–30.

5 Internet Family History Association of Australia, viewed online, 25 April 2017, <www. historyaustralia.org.au/ifhaa/ships/2ndfleet.htm>.

6 For convict numbers, refer to *Historical Records of New South Wales*, Vol. 2, p. 432.

7 Duffy, *Man of Honour*, 2003, p. 31.

8 *Historical Records of New South Wales*, Vol. 2, p. 427.

9 Elizabeth Macarthur's shipboard journal.

10 *Ibid.*

11 *Historical Records of New South Wales*, Vol. 2, p. 428.

12 Ellis, *John Macarthur*, 1978, p. 18.

13 As cited in Flynn, *The Second Fleet*, 1993, p. 38.

14 Devonport Online, viewed online, 13 February 2011, <www.devon.gov.uk/localstudies/111166/1.html>.

15 Ellis, *John Macarthur*, 1978, p. 19.

16 Flynn, *The Second Fleet*, 1993, p. 38.

17 Duffy, *Man of Honour*, 2003, pp. 36–40.

18 Elizabeth Macarthur's shipboard journal.

19 Flynn, *The Second Fleet*, 1993, p. 65.

20 Elizabeth Macarthur's shipboard journal.

21 *Ibid.*

22 Flynn, *The Second Fleet*, 1993, p. 38.

23 *Ibid.*, p. 36.

24 *Ibid.*, p. 39.

25 *Ibid.*

26 *Ibid.*

27 Elizabeth Macarthur's shipboard journal.

28 Flynn, *The Second Fleet*, 1993, p. 33.

29 Elizabeth Macarthur's shipboard journal.

30 *Ibid.*

4. From the *Neptune* to the *Scarborough*

1 Flynn, *The Second Fleet*, 1993, p. 59.

2 *Ibid.*, p. 61.

3 Elizabeth Macarthur's shipboard journal.

4 *Ibid.*

5 *Ibid.*

6 *Ibid.*

7 All Darcy Wentworth references from the *Australian Dictionary of Biography*, viewed online, 25 April 2017 <http://adb.anu.edu.au/biography/wentworth-darcy-1545/text3917>.

8 Flynn, *The Second Fleet*, 1993, p. 34.

9 Letter written by Rev Johnson, in Flannery, *Birth of Sydney*, 1999, pp. 101–102.

10 Elizabeth Macarthur's shipboard journal.

11 *Ibid.*

12 Flynn, *The Second Fleet*, 1993, p. 33.

13 *Ibid.*

14 Elizabeth Macarthur's shipboard journal.

15 *Ibid.*

16 Flynn, *The Second Fleet*, 1993, p. 56.

17 *Ibid.*

18 Bown, *Scurvy: How a Surgeon, a Mariner, and a Gentlemen Solved the Greatest Medical Mystery of the Age of Sail*, 2003, p. 19.

19 *Ibid.*

20 *Ibid.*, pp. 20–21.

21 *Historical Records of New South Wales*, Vol. 2, p. 751.

22 Elizabeth Macarthur's shipboard journal.

23 *Ibid.*

24 *Ibid.*

25 *Ibid.*

26 *Ibid.*

27 *Ibid.*

28 *Ibid.*

29 *Ibid.*

30 *Ibid.*

31 *Ibid.*

32 *Ibid.*

33 *Ibid.*

34 *Ibid.*

35 *Ibid.*

36 Elizabeth Macarthur to her mother, Grace Leach, 20 April 1790.

37 Elizabeth Macarthur's shipboard journal.

5. The Tempestuous Southern Ocean

1 Elizabeth Macarthur to her mother, Grace Leach, 10 April 1790.

2 *Ibid.*

3 Flynn, *The Second Fleet*, 1993, p. 25.

4 Mundle, *Bligh: Master Mariner*, 2010, p. 207.

5 Rees, *The Floating Brothel*, 2001, p. 180.

6 *Ibid.*

7 Collingridge, *Captain Cook: The Life, Death and Legacy of History's Greatest Explorer*, 2003, p. 341.

8 Flynn, *The Second Fleet*, 1993, p. 44.

9 *Ibid.*, p. 70.

10 Rev Johnson, in *Historical Records of New South Wales*, Vol. 1.

11 *Historical Records of New South Wales* Vol. 1, p. 438.

12 Elizabeth Macarthur to her mother, Grace Leach, 10 April 1790.

13 *Ibid.*

14 *Ibid.*

15 *Ibid.*

16 *Ibid.*

17 Elizabeth Macarthur's shipboard journal.

18 Flynn, *The Second Fleet*, 1993, p. 59.

19 Elizabeth Macarthur's shipboard journal.

20 Flynn, *The Second Fleet*, 1993, p. 59.

21 *Ibid.*

22 Rev Johnson to Mr Thornton, July 1790, *Historical Records of New South Wales*, Vol. 1, Part 2–Phillip, p. 386.

23 Collingridge, *Captain Cook*, 2003, p. 176.

6. Heavenly Bodies, Botany and Piano Lessons

1 There are about 29 clan groups of the Sydney metropolitan area, referred to collectively as the Eora Nation. Barani: Sydney's Aboriginal History, viewed online, 11 Jan 2018, <http://www.sydneybarani.com.au/sites/aboriginal-people-and-place/>.

2   Tench, *1788: A Complete Account of the Settlement at Port Jackson*, 2009, p. 168.

3   Clendinnen, *Dancing with Strangers*, 2005, p. 99.

4   *Ibid.*, p. 101.

5   Elizabeth Macarthur to Bridget Kingdon, 7 March 1791.

6   *Ibid.*

7   *Ibid.*

8   Collins, *An Account of the English Colony in New South Wales*, August 1790, 1802.

9   Edward Macarthur was baptised at St Phillips, Sydney, on 1 April 1791. Smee, *Born in the English Colony of New South Wales 1788–1800*, 2009.

10 Elizabeth Macarthur to Bridget Kingdon, 7 March 1791.

11 *Ibid.*

12 *Ibid.*

13 *Ibid.*

14 As cited in Clendinnen, *Dancing with Strangers*, 2005, p. 155.

15 Tench, *1788*, 2009, p. 183.

16 Viewed online, 1 May 2016, <http://www.abc.net.au/news/2015-06-30/arthur-phillip-five-surprising-things/6580852>.

17 Elizabeth Macarthur's shipboard journal.

18 Elizabeth Macarthur to her mother, Grace Leach, 18 March 1791.

19 Elizabeth Macarthur to Bridget Kingdon, 7 March 1791.

20 Elizabeth Macarthur to her mother, Grace Leach, 18 March 1791.

21 Macarthur-Onslow, *The Macarthurs of Camden*, 1973, p. 20.

22 Elizabeth Macarthur to Bridget Kingdon, 7 March 1791.

23 Elizabeth Macarthur to her mother, Grace Leach, 18 March 1791.

24 Tench, *1788*, 2009, p. 178, also, Collins, *An Account of the English Colony in New South Wales*.

25 Elizabeth Macarthur to Bridget Kingdon, 7 March 1791.

26 Tench, *1788*, 2009, p. 179.

27 As cited in Clendinnen, *Dancing with Strangers,* 2005, p. 117.

28 *Ibid.*, p. 120.

29 Elizabeth Macarthur to Bridget Kingdon, 7 March 1791.

30 *Ibid.*

31 *Ibid.*

32 *Ibid.*

33 *Ibid.*

34 *Ibid.*

35 *Ibid.*

36 *Ibid.*

37 Tench, *1788*, 2009, footnote pp. 163–164.

38 Tench, *1788*, 2009, pp. 165–166. Clendinnen, *Dancing with Strangers,* 2005, pp. 172–173.

39 Tench, *1788*, 2009, footnote p. 166.

40 Elizabeth Macarthur to Bridget Kingdon, 7 March 1791.

41 *Ibid.*

42 Dawes' notebooks were considered lost until in 1977 they were discovered in the Library

of the Royal Society in London (*Australian Meteorological and Oceanographic Journal*, No. 58 (2009) pp. 83–98).

43 Elizabeth Macarthur to Bridget Kingdon, 7 March 1791.

44 *Ibid.*

45 *Ibid.*

46 *Ibid.*

47 *Ibid.* Tench, *1788,* 2009, p. 151.

48 *Ibid.*

49 *Ibid.*, p. 234.

50 Elizabeth Macarthur to Bridget Kingdon, 7 March 1791.

51 Elizabeth Macarthur to her mother, Grace Leach, 18 March 1791.

52 Frost, *Botany Bay Mirages*, 1995, p. 218.

53 Tench, *1788,* 2009, footnote, p. 102.

54 *Ibid.*, p. 239.

55 *Ibid.*, p. 236.

56 *Ibid.*, p. 243.

57 *Ibid.*, p. 242.

58 As cited in Clendinnen, *Dancing with Strangers*, 2005, p. 49.

59 Hunter, as cited in Egan, (ed), *Buried Alive: Sydney 1788–92 Eyewitness Accounts of the Making of a Nation*, 1999, p. 227.

60 Collins, *An Account of the English Colony in New South Wales*, Part V, Ch. 12.

61 Elizabeth Macarthur to Bridget Kingdon, 7 March 1791.

62 *Ibid.*

63 Collins, *An Account of the English Colony in New South Wales*, April 1791.

64 Elizabeth Macarthur to her mother, Grace Leach, 18 March 1791.

65 Dictionary of Sydney, viewed online, 11 January 2018, <https://dictionaryofsydney.org/entry/parramatta>.

66 Collins, *An Account of the English Colony in New South Wales*, July 1791.

67 Elizabeth Macarthur to Bridget Kingdon, 7 March 1791.

68 Elizabeth Macarthur letter to England, extract, 18 November 1791.

69 *Ibid.*

70 Collins, *An Account of the English Colony in New South Wales*, July 1791.

71 *Ibid.*

7. A Change in Fortune

1 Shaw, 'King, Phillip Gidley (1758–1808)', *Australian Dictionary of Biography*, viewed online, 14 September 2012, <http://adb.anu.edu.au/biography/king-Phillip-gidley-2309/text2991>.

2 Elizabeth Macarthur letter to England, extract, 18 November 1791.

3 *Ibid.*

4 *Ibid.*

5 Bassett, *The Governor's Lady: Mrs Phillip Gidley King*, 1992, pp.112–114.

6 Elizabeth Macarthur letter to England, extract, 18 November 1791.

7 Collins, *An Account of the English Colony in New South Wales*, October 1791.

8   Shaw, 'King, Phillip Gidley (1758–1808)', *Australian Dictionary of Biography*, viewed online, 14 September 2012, <http://adb.anu.edu.au/biography/king-Phillip-gidley-2309/text2991>.

9   Elizabeth Macarthur letter to England, extract, 7 December 1791.

10 Tench, *1788*, 2009, p. 210.

11 As quoted by Lt Ball, in Egan, *Buried Alive*, 1999, p. 267.

12 Tench, *1788*, 2009, p. 225.

13 Collins, *An Account of the English Colony in New South Wales*, December 1791.

14 As quoted in Egan, *Buried Alive*, 1999, p. 282.

15 Collins, *An Account of the English Colony in New South Wales*, December 1791.

16 Egan, *Buried Alive*, 1999, p. 283, see also Grose's entry in *Australian Dictionary of Biography*.

17 As cited in Egan, *Buried Alive*, 1999, p. 283.

18 Collins, *An Account of the English Colony in New South Wales*, p. 144.

19 Queensland Museum, viewed online 2 November 2012, <www.qm.qld.gov.au/Find+out+about/Histories+of+Queensland/Transport+Maritime+History/HMS+Pandora>.

20 Collins, *An Account of the English Colony in New South Wales*, p. 151.

21 *Ibid.*, pp. 151–153.

22 Grose to Phillip, 4 October 1792, *Historical Records of Australia*, I, i, p. 381.

23 Phillip to Grose 4 October 1792, *Historical Records of Australia*, I, i, p. 381.

24 *Ibid.*

25 *Ibid.*

26 Phillip to Dundas, 14 Oct 1792, *Historical Records of Australia*, I, i, p. 398.

27 Collins, *An Account of the English Colony in New South Wales*, p. 160.

28 *Ibid.*

29 Ellis, *John Macarthur*, 1978, p. 50.

30 *Ibid.*

31 *Ibid.*

32 Collins, *An Account of the English Colony in New South Wales*, Ch. XIX.

33 *Ibid.*, pp.164–165.

34 *Ibid.*, Ch. XIX.

35 *Ibid.*

36 *Ibid.*

37 Phillip to Dundas, 4 October 1792, as cited in Egan, *Buried Alive*, 1999, p. 298.

38 As cited in Ellis, *John Macarthur*, 1978, pp. 58–59.

39 Elizabeth Macarthur letter to England, extract, incorrectly dated 21 December 1793 (correct date March 1793).

40 Flannery, *The Birth of Sydney*, 1999, p. 118.

41 Elizabeth Macarthur letter to England, extract, incorrectly dated 21 December 1793 (correct date March 1793).

8. Elizabeth Farm

1   Elizabeth Macarthur letter to England, extract, 22 August 1794.

2   Elizabeth Macarthur to Bridget Kingdon, incorrectly dated 1 September 1795 (correct date September 1798).

3   *Ibid.*

4   This concept is beautifully and thoroughly described in Gammage, *The Greatest Estate on Earth: How Aborigines Made Australia*, 2012.

5   Gammage, *The Biggest Estate on Earth*, 2012, p. 2.

6   Viewed online, 6 May 2016, <http://www.williamdawes.org/patyegarang.html>.

7   Collins, *An Account of the English Colony in New South Wales*, May 1792.

8   *Ibid.*

9   Connor, *The Australian Frontier Wars 1788–1838*, 2002, pp. 39–40.

10   Sir William Macarthur, Notes on Aborigines, items 178–189, Volume 39: Sir William Macarthur letters and miscellaneous papers, 1824–1882, Mitchell Library, State Library of NSW.

11   Karskens, *The Colony: A History of Early Sydney*, 2009, p. 537.

12   Elizabeth Macarthur letter to England, extract, 22 August 1794.

13   Hadlow, *The Strangest Family: The Private Lives of George III, Queen Charlotte and the Hanoverians*, 2015, p. 200.

14   Elizabeth Macarthur to Bridget Kingdon, 1 September 1795 (incorrectly dated, should be 1798).

15   *Ibid.*

16   Atkinson, *The Political Life of James Macarthur*, PhD thesis, 1976, p. 20.

17   T.W. Plummer to Colonel Macquarie, 4 May 1809, *Historical Records of New South Wales*, Vol. 7, p. 120, as cited in Summers, *Damned Whores and God's Police*, 1994, p. 315.

18   *Ibid.*, p. 321.

19   Elizabeth Macarthur letter to England, extract, 22 August 1794.

20   *Ibid.* Elizabeth claimed the dogs killed about 300 pounds of meat per week (136 kilograms)—the equivalent is 2–3 kangaroos (at 50 kilograms each) and dozens of ducks (1 kilogram each).

21   Broadbent and Hughes, *Elizabeth Farm, Parramatta: A History and a Guide*. Sydney, 1984, p. 75.

22   Clarke, *A Colonial Woman: The Life and Times of Mary Braidwood Mowle*, 1986, p. 220.

23   Elizabeth Macarthur to Edward Macarthur, March 1827.

24   Yarwood, *Samuel Marsden: The Great Survivor*, 1977, p. 30.

25   *Ibid.*, p. 41.

26   Judge Advocate Ellis Bent, as cited in Whitaker, 'Mrs Paterson's Keepsakes: The Provenance of Some Significant Colonial Documents and Paintings', 2004.

27   Ralph Clarke, as cited in Macmillan, 'Paterson, William (1755–1810)', *Australian Dictionary of Biography*, viewed online, 20 June 2013 <http://adb.anu.edu.au/biography/paterson-william-2541/text3455>.

9. Babies, Bluster and Boasting

1   Auchmuty, 'Hunter, John (1737–1821)', *Australian Dictionary of Biography*, viewed online, 22 June 2013, <http://adb.anu.edu.au/biography/hunter-john-2213/text2873>.

2   Harris Papers, as quoted in Ellis, *John Macarthur*, 1978, p. 37.

3   The writer was Surgeon Balmain. See Ellis, *John Macarthur*, 1978, pp. 89–91.

4   Steven, 'Macarthur, John (1767–1834)', *Australian Dictionary of Biography*, viewed online, 15 November 2017, <http://adb.anu.edu.au/biography/macarthur-john-2390/text3153>.

5   Ellis, *John Macarthur*, 1978, p. 107.

6   As cited in Ellis, *John Macarthur*, 1978, p. 107.

7   *Ibid.*, p. 112.

8   *Ibid.*, p. 124.

9   Elizabeth Macarthur to Bridget Kingdon, 1 September 1795 (incorrectly dated, correct date 1798).

10 *Ibid.*

11 Ellis, *John Macarthur*, 1978, p. 139.

12 Bassett, *The Governor's Lady*, 1992, p. 114.

13 Elizabeth Macarthur to Bridget Kingdon, 1 September 1795 (incorrectly dated, correct date 1798).

14 *Ibid.*

15 *Ibid.*

16 Bridget Kingdon to Elizabeth Macarthur, 15 September 1799.

17 *The Australian*, 2 December 1831, as cited in Hirst, *Freedom on the Fatal Shore: Australia's First Colony*, 2008.

18 Elizabeth Macarthur to Bridget Kingdon, 1 September 1795 (incorrectly dated, correct date 1798).

19 Massy, *The Australian Merino*, 1990, pp. 26–27.

20 Elizabeth Macarthur to Bridget Kingdon, 1 September 1795 (incorrectly dated, correct date 1798).

21 *Ibid.*

22 Carruthers, *The Horse in Australia*, 2008, p. 5.

23 Yarwood, *Samuel Marsden*, 1977, pp. 93–94.

24 Elizabeth Macarthur to Bridget Kingdon, 1 September 1795 (incorrectly dated, correct date 1798).

25 *Ibid.*

26 *Ibid.*

27 *Ibid.*

28 Bridget Kingdon to Elizabeth Macarthur, 15 September 1799.

29 *Ibid.*

10. Pistols at Twenty Paces

1   As cited in Ellis, *John Macarthur*, 1978, p. 134.

2   Ellis, *John Macarthur*, 1978, p. 169.

3   *Ibid.*, pp. 178–82.

4   Bassett, *The Governor's Lady*, 1992, pp. 91–92.

5   Matthew Flinders, as quoted in Bassett, *The Governor's Lady*, 1992, p. 78.

6   Bassett, *The Governor's Lady*, 1992, p. 65.

7   *Ibid.*, p. 36.

8   Harriet Abbott was buried in the cemetery of St John's, Parramatta, index viewed online, 30 April 2017, <http://austcemindex.com/?cemid=789>.

9   Ellis, *John Macarthur*, 1978, p. 198.

10 *Ibid.*, p. 200.

11 As cited in Ellis, *John Macarthur*, p. 202.

12 *Ibid.*, p. 203.

13 Governor King to Christopher Lethbridge, 30 June 1802.

11. Managing Alone

1   Wright, *Beyond the Ladies Lounge: Australia's Female Publicans*, 2003, p. 20.

2   For entire paragraph, see Atkinson, *The Europeans in Australia: A History*, Vol. 1, 1998, pp. 199–200.

3   Levi and Bergman, *Australian Genesis: Jewish Convicts and Settlers 1788–1850*, 1974, pp. 19–29.

4   Elizabeth Macarthur to John Piper, 15 April 1804, as cited in King, *Elizabeth Macarthur and Her World*, 1980, p. 30.

5   Massy, *The Australian Merino*, 1990, p. 27.

6   *Sydney Gazette*, 26 March 1803.

7   Ellis, *John Macarthur*, 1978, p. 225.

8   *Ibid.*, p. 243.

9   Elizabeth Macarthur to John Piper, 15 April 1804, as cited in King, *Elizabeth Macarthur and Her World*, 1980, p. 30.

10 Davidoff and Hall, *Family Fortunes*, 1987, p. 274.

11 Matthew Flinders to Elizabeth Macarthur, 7 July 1803. Matthew Flinders—Private letters, Vol. 1, 1801–1806, Safe 1/55, p. 50, letter No. 46, Mitchell Library, State Library of New South Wales, viewed online, 14 May 2014, <http://acms.sl.nsw.gov.au/_transcript/2013/D17747/a050.html>.

12 Elizabeth Macarthur to John Piper, 15 April 1804, as cited in King, *Elizabeth Macarthur and Her World*, 1980, p. 30.

13 Matthew Flinders to Mrs Kent, 28 July 1803. Matthew Flinders—Private letters, Vol. 1, 1801–1806, Safe 1/55, pp. 55–56, letter No. 49, Mitchell Library, State Library of New South Wales. viewed online, 14 May 2014, <http://acms.sl.nsw.gov.au/_transcript/2013/D17747/a050.html>.

14 Atkinson, *The Europeans in Australia*, 1998, p. 270.

15 *Ibid.*, p. 269.

16 Yarwood, *Samuel Marsden*, 1977, p. 93.

17 Dyer, *The French Explorers and Sydney*, 2009, p. 59.

18 Matthew Flinders to Elizabeth Macarthur, 28 July 1803. Matthew Flinders—Private letters, Vol. 1, 1801–1806, Safe 1/55, p. 51, letter No. 47, Mitchell Library, State Library of New South Wales, viewed online, 14 May 2014, <http://acms.sl.nsw.gov.au/_transcript/2013/D17747/a050.html>.

19 Cooper, 'Flinders, Matthew (1774–1814)', *Australian Dictionary of Biography*, viewed online, 22 August 2014, <http://adb.anu.edu.au/biography/flinders-matthew-2050/

text2541>.

20 John Macarthur to Elizabeth Macarthur, 3 August 1810, as transcribed in Macarthur-Onslow, *The Macarthurs of Camden*, 1973, p. 201.

21 Macarthur Papers, Vol. 39: Sir William Macarthur letters and miscellaneous papers, 1824–1882. William Macarthur's memories noted by his niece, 18 March 1870, Items 240–43.

22 *Ibid.*

23 Atkinson, *The Europeans in Australia*, 1998, p. 251.

24 *Ibid.*

25 Elizabeth Macarthur to Captain Piper, 15 April 1804, Mitchell Library, Microfilm : CY A 256, Captain John Piper papers and Correspondence, 1790–1845, Call # A 256, pp. 419–30.

26 *Ibid.*

27 *Ibid.*

28 *Ibid.*

29 Flannery, *The Birth of Sydney*, 1999, p. 199.

30 Elizabeth Macarthur to Captain Piper, 15 April 1804, Mitchell Library, Microfilm : CY A 256, Captain John Piper papers and Correspondence, 1790–1845, Call # A 256, pp. 419–30.

31 Atkinson, *The Europeans in Australia*, 1998, p. 270.

32 Elizabeth Macarthur to Captain Piper, 15 April 1804, Mitchell Library, Microfilm : CY A 256, Captain John Piper papers and Correspondence, 1790–1845, Call # A 256, pp. 419–30.

33 *Ibid.*

34 *Sydney Gazette*, 27 January 1805.

35 Hill, *Paper Houses: John Macarthur and the 30-year design process of Camden Park*, PhD Thesis, 2016, p. 72.

36 Sir William Macarthur—Notes on Aborigines, Items 178–189, Vol. 39: Sir William Macarthur Letters and Miscellaneous Papers, 1824–1882, State Library of NSW.

37 Karskens, *The Colony*, 2009, p. 537.

38 Sir William Macarthur—Notes on Aborigines, Items 178–189, Vol. 39: Sir William Macarthur Letters and Miscellaneous Papers, 1824–1882, State Library of NSW.

39 William's fragment of reminiscence does not provide a date for the activities he describes. But he does say that at the time his father 'was absent in England'. Over the course of his life John Macarthur was absent in England only twice, and the second time he took William with him, so the event described here must have happened during his first absence, between 1801–05. And given that William wasn't born until December 1800, it seems more likely he would remember events occurring later during that period. As well, the article in the *Sydney Gazette* that notes that Gogie, or Goguey, had previously been involved in a ceremonial spearing and had been responsible for the subsequent death is dated 17 March 1805.

40 *Sydney Gazette*, 17 March 1805.

41 *Ibid.*, 28 April 1805.

42 Richard Atkins to Governor King, 8 July 1805, *Historical Records of New South Wales*,

Vol. V, No. 654.

43 Bassett, *The Governor's Lady*, 1992, p. 92.

44 *Sydney Gazette*, 31 March 1805.

12. The King's Merinos

1 King, *Elizabeth Macarthur and Her World*, 1980, p. 36. For a similar list see also Ellis, *John Macarthur*, 1978, p. 235.

2 Davidoff and Hall, *Family Fortunes*, 1987, p. 223.

3 Viewed online, 12 September 2014, <http://www.merinos.com.au/merinos. asp?pageId=16>.

4 Massy, *The Australian Merino*, 1990, Ch. 1.

5 *Ibid.*, p. 34.

6 *Ibid.*, p. 22.

7 *Ibid.*, p. 30.

8 Hughes, *John Macarthur and the Wool Industry*, 1984, p. 5. O'Brian, *Joseph Banks, A Life*, 1993, p. 271.

9 Massy, *The Australian Merino*, 1990, p. 30.

10 Ellis, *John Macarthur*, 1978, pp. 227, 234.

11 Atkinson, *Camden: Farm and village life in early New South Wales*, 1988, p. 10.

12 Copy of a letter received by John Macarthur from Henry Waterhouse, 12 March 1804, viewed online, 21 April 2017, <http://archival.sl.nsw.gov.au/Details/archive/110578994>.

13 Ellis, *John Macarthur*, 1978, p. 235.

14 *Ibid.*, p. 234.

15 King to Banks, 21 July 1805, as quoted in King, *Elizabeth Macarthur and Her World*, 1980, p. 38.

16 As cited in Bassett, *The Governor's Lady*, 1992, p. 92.

17 As cited in Ellis, *John Macarthur*, 1978, p. 242.

18 Macarthur Papers Vol. 39: Sir William Macarthur Letters and Miscellaneous Papers, 1824–1882, William Macarthur's memories noted by his niece, 18 March 1870, Items 240–43.

19 Ellis, *John Macarthur*, 1978, p. 240.

20 *Ibid.*, pp. 242–43.

21 *Ibid.*, p. 250.

22 *Sydney Gazette*, 8 December 1805.

23 Viewed online, 30 April 2017, <https://en.wikipedia.org/wiki/Mak_Sai_Ying>.

24 Marsden Online Archive, *Journal: Reverend Samuel Marsden's First Visit to New Zealand in December 1814*, viewed online, 3 October 2014, <http://www.marsdenarchive.otago. ac.nz/MS_0176_001>.

25 Walsh, 'Huon de Kerillieu, Gabriel Louis Marie (1769–1828)', *Australian Dictionary of Biography*, viewed online, 31 August 2015, <http://adb.anu.edu.au/biography/ huon-de-kerilleau-gabriel-louis-marie-2215/text2877>.

26 Atkinson, *The Political Life of James Macarthur*, 1976, p. 21.

27 Dyer, *The French Explorers and Sydney*, 2009, p. 59.

28 Kohen, 'Pemulwuy (1750–1802)', *Australian Dictionary of Biography*, viewed online,

23 June 2013, <http://adb.anu.edu.au/biography/pemulwuy-13147/text23797>.

29   *Ibid.*

30   Elder, *Blood on the Wattle: Massacres and Maltreatment of Aboriginal Australians since 1788*, 2003, p. 11.

31   Connor, *The Australian Frontier Wars 1788–1838*, 2002, p. 39.

32   Karskens, *The Colony*, 2009, 'Pemulwuy's War' pp. 474–481.

33   Macarthur Papers, Vol. 39: Sir William Macarthur Letters and Miscellaneous Papers, 1824–1882, A few Memoranda Respecting the Aboriginal Natives, Items 178–189.

34   *Ibid.*

35   'Told me by Sir William Macarthur, my great uncle', *Recollections by JW Macarthur-Onslow*, AIATSIS Library.

36   Atkinson, *The Europeans in Australia*, 1998, p. 167.

37   While each of the three rectangular grants remained twice as long as they were wide, united they ran for some seven miles (twelve kilometres) along the river, but only four miles (seven kilometres) inland.

38   Atkinson, *Camden: Farm and village life in early New South Wales*, 1988, p. 11.

39   'Davidson, Walter Stevenson (1785–1869)', *Australian Dictionary of Biography*, viewed online, 24 July 2015, <http://adb.anu.edu.au/biography/davidson-walter-stevenson-1960/text2361>.

40   Ellis, *John Macarthur*, 1978, p. 263.

41   As cited in Ellis, *John Macarthur*, 1978, p. 264.

42   Evatt, *Rum Rebellion*, 1975, pp. 19–20.

13. Malignant Falsehoods

1   'Death of Admiral Lord Viscount Nelson', *Sydney Gazette*, 3 August 1806.

2   Evatt, *Rum Rebellion*, 1975, p. 68.

3   *Historical Records of New South Wales*, Vol. IV, p. 189.

4   Ellis, *John Macarthur*, 1978, p. 261.

5   Elizabeth Macarthur to Eliza Kingdon, 29 January 1807.

6   Macarthur Papers, Vol. 39: Sir William Macarthur Letters and Miscellaneous Papers, 1824–1882, A few Memoranda Respecting the Aboriginal Natives, Items 178–189.

7   William Macarthur to Edward Macarthur, 4 July 1840.

8   As cited in Macarthur-Onslow, *The Macarthurs of Camden*, 1973, p. 472.

9   Edward Macarthur to his father John Macarthur, 19 November 1809.

10   *Sydney Gazette*, 19 October 1806.

11   As cited in Ellis, *John Macarthur*, 1978, pp. 269–270.

12   Elizabeth Macarthur to Eliza Kingdon, 29 January 1807.

13   Dando-Collins, *Bligh's Other Mutiny*, 2007, pp. 3–4.

14   Edmund Griffin's evidence at the trial of John Macarthur, 4 February 1808, *Historical Records of Australia* Vol. I, p. 323.

15   *Sydney Gazette*, 21 Dec 1806.

16   Bassett, *The Governor's Lady*, 1992, p. 95.

17   Elizabeth Macarthur to Eliza Kingdon, 29 January 1807.

18   Ellis, *John Macarthur*, 1978, p. 356.

19 Viewed online, 11 December 2015, <http://www.mayoclinic.org/diseases-conditions/polio/basics/symptoms/con-20030957>.

20 Karskens, *The Colony*, 2009, pp. 171, 186.

21 As cited in Ellis, *John Macarthur*, 1978, pp. 299–301.

22 As cited in Karskens and Waterhouse, *Journal of Australian Colonial History*, Vol. 12, pp. 13–14.

23 As cited in Ellis, *John Macarthur*, 1978, p. 304.

24 *Ibid.*, p. 305.

25 Atkins to Macarthur, 14 December 1807, *Historical Records of Australia* Vol. I, No. 6, p. 307.

26 As cited in Ellis, *John Macarthur*, 1978, p. 309.

27 *Ibid.*

28 *Historical Records of Australia* Vol. I, No. 6, p. 315.

29 Ellis, *John Macarthur*, 1978, p. 316.

30 As cited in Ellis, *John Macarthur*, 1978, p. 317.

31 *Ibid.*, p. 328.

32 *Historical Records of Australia* Vol. I, No. 6, pp. 225–227.

33 As cited in Ellis, *John Macarthur*, 1978, p. 346.

34 *Ibid.*

14. Rebellion and Consequences

1 Karskens, *The Colony*, 2009, p. 187.

2 Dando-Collins, *Bligh's Other Mutiny*, 2007, p. 73.

3 Elizabeth Macarthur to Edward Macarthur, 27 December 1830, as transcribed in Macarthur-Onslow, *The Macarthurs of Camden*, 1973, p. 463.

4 As cited in Dando-Collins, *Bligh's Other Mutiny*, 2007, p. 90.

5 John Macarthur to Elizabeth Macarthur, likely date 30 January 1808, as transcribed in Macarthur-Onslow, *The Macarthurs of Camden*, 1973, p. 153.

6 *Ibid.*

7 *Ibid.*

8 As cited in Dando-Collins, *Bligh's Other Mutiny*, 2007, p. 98.

9 *Ibid.*, p. 101.

10 *Ibid.*, p. 103.

11 *Ibid.*, p. 104.

12 *Ibid.*, p. 107.

13 John Macarthur to Captain Piper, 24 May 1808.

14 Hughes, *The Macarthurs: A Brief Family History*, 1984, p. 11. See also King, *Elizabeth Macarthur and Her World*, 1980, p. 51.

15 *Sydney Gazette*, 22 January 1809.

16 As cited in Dando-Collins, *Bligh's Other Mutiny*, 2007, p. 181.

17 *Ibid.*, p. 194.

18 John Macarthur to Elizabeth Macarthur, 30 July 1809, as transcribed in Macarthur-Onslow, *The Macarthurs of Camden*, 1973, p. 181.

15. Alone Again

1   Description of Parramatta in *Naval Chronicle,* Vol. XXII, July–December, 1809, pp. 478–481.

2   Macquarie's diary, viewed online 3 May 2017, <http://www.mq.edu.au/macquarie-archive/journeys/1810/1810a/nov6.html>.

3   Karskens, *The Colony*, 2009, p. 248.

4   Description of Parramatta in *Naval Chronicle,* Vol. XXII, July–December, 1809, pp. 478–481.

5   Cameron, 'Parramatta's General Hospital,' in *The Old Parramattan*, 2016, viewed online, 18 August 2016, <https://theoldparramattan.wordpress.com/2016/08/17/parramattas-general-hospital/>.

6   As cited in Karskens, *The Colony*, 2009, p. 340.

7   Edward Macarthur to his mother, Elizabeth Macarthur, 15 January 1809.

8   *Ibid.*

9   *Ibid.*

10 *Ibid.*

11 Edward Macarthur to Thomas Thompson, 5 December 1809.

12 John Macarthur to Elizabeth Macarthur, 28 November 1809.

13 Edward Macarthur to his father, John Macarthur, 19 May 1809.

14 John Macarthur to Elizabeth Macarthur, 28 November 1809.

15 Edward Macarthur to Walter Davidson, 28 February 1809.

16 Edward Macarthur to his father, John Macarthur, 17 November 1809.

17 Edward Macarthur to his mother, Elizabeth Macarthur, 15 November 1809.

18 Edward Macarthur to his father, John Macarthur, 29 November 1809.

19 Letter from Governor Macquarie to his brother Charles, as cited in Walsh (ed), *In Her Own Words, The Writings of Elizabeth Macquarie*, 2011, p. 45.

20 Walsh, *In Her Own Words*, 2011, p. 44.

21 Dando-Collins, *Bligh's Other Mutiny*, 2007, p. 244.

22 As cited in Dando-Collins, *Bligh's Other Mutiny*, 2007, p. 216.

23 *Sydney Gazette*, 14 April 1810.

24 *Ibid.*

25 Whittaker, *Distracted Settlement: New South Wales After Bligh*, 1998, p. 123.

26 Ellis, *John Macarthur*, 1978, p. 394.

27 Macarthur Family Papers, 1789–1930 [First Collection], State Library of NSW, Call # A 2909, pp. 9–11.

28 Lancaster, *The First Fleet Piano: A Musician's View*, 2015, Ch. 13.

29 Viewed online, 29 April 2016, <http://www.colonialdance.com.au/piano-of-the-first-fleet-29.html>.

30 As cited in Ellis, *John Macarthur*, 1978, p. 406.

31 King, *Elizabeth Macarthur and her World*, 1980, p. 62.

32 Macquarie's diary, viewed online, 27 May 2016, <http://www.mq.edu.au/macquarie-archive/journeys/1810/1810a/nov16.html>.

33 *Ibid.*

34 *Ibid.*

35 *Ibid.*

36 *Ibid.*

37 Presumably from the Aboriginal word *benkennie*, meaning high, dry land.

38 Macquarie's diary, viewed online, 27 May 2016, <http://www.mq.edu.au/macquarie-archive/journeys/1810/1810a/nov16.html>.

39 Elizabeth Macarthur to Eliza Kingdon, March 1816.

40 Elizabeth Macarthur to John Piper, 13 November 1811, Piper Papers, A 256, Mitchell Library.

16. Bad Debts and Sharp Words

1 Macarthur-Onslow, *The Macarthurs of Camden*, 1973, p. 186.

2 Ellis, *John Macarthur*, 1978, pp. 405-06, 411.

3 John Macarthur to Elizabeth Macarthur, 11 November 1810.

4 John Macarthur to Elizabeth Macarthur, 14 May 1812.

5 *Ibid.*

6 *Ibid.*

7 John Macarthur to Elizabeth Macarthur, 11 December 1809.

8 As cited in Evatt, *Rum Rebellion*, 1975, p. 212.

9 John Macarthur to Elizabeth Macarthur, 3 May 1810.

10 John Macarthur to Elizabeth Macarthur, 3 August 1810.

11 As cited in Dando-Collins, *Bligh's Other Mutiny*, 2007, p. 230.

12 John Macarthur to Elizabeth Macarthur, 18 November 1812.

13 John Macarthur to Elizabeth Macarthur, 4 March 1812.

14 John Macarthur to Elizabeth Macarthur, 26 July 1814.

15 As quoted in Hughes, *John Macarthur and the Wool Industry*, 1984, p. 8.

16 John Macarthur to Elizabeth Macarthur, 18 November 1812.

17 *Ibid.*

18 *Ibid.*

19 Ellis, *John Macarthur*, 1978, p. 411.

20 *Ibid.*, p. 416.

21 *Ibid.*, p. 411.

22 John Macarthur to Elizabeth Macarthur, 14 May 1812.

23 Mrs E., *Advice to a Young Lady in the Colonies*, 1979, p. 70.

24 John Macarthur to Elizabeth Macarthur, 14 May 1812.

25 Dunlop, 'Oxley, John Joseph (1784–1828)', *Australian Dictionary of Biography*, viewed online, 10 June 2016, <http://adb.anu.edu.au/biography/oxley-john-joseph-2530/text3431>.

26 *Ibid.*

27 Elizabeth Macarthur to Edward Macarthur, 31 May 1828.

28 Hannibal Macarthur to John Macarthur, 10 November 1812.

29 Karskens, *The Colony*, 2009, p. 137.

30 Kercher, *Debt, Seduction and Other Disasters: The birth of civil law in convict New South Wales*, 1996, p. 73–75.

31 Ellis, *John Macarthur*, 1978, pp. 426–427.

32 Elizabeth Macarthur to Eliza Kingdon, March 1816.

33 Hannibal Macarthur to John Macarthur, 3 July 1813.

34 As cited in King, *Elizabeth Macarthur and Her World*, 1980, p. 90.

35 For details of Thomas Herbert and his family see <http://australianroyalty.net.au/individual.php?pid=I62450&ged=purnellmccord.ged>, viewed online, 22 July 2016.

36 Atkinson, *Camden: Farm and village life in early New South Wales*, 1988, pp. 16–17

37 As quoted in Ellis, *John Macarthur*, 1978, p. 430.

38 Elizabeth Macarthur to Eliza Kingdon, March 1816.

17. Frontier Bloodshed

1 William Macarthur, 'Observations upon the Various Objections Urged in England upon the State in which Australian Wool is usually Sent to Market, Together with Some Account of an Improved Mode of Washing Sheep Practiced at Camden.' As transcribed in Macarthur-Onslow, *The Macarthurs of Camden*, 1973, pp. 441–47.

2 Roberts, ed. *Miss D & Miss N an Extraordinary Partnership: The Diary of Anne Drysdale*, 2009, p. 101.

3 *Ibid.*, p. 102.

4 *Ibid.*, p 100.

5 Hannibal Macarthur to John Macarthur, 3 July 1813.

6 John Macarthur to Elizabeth Macarthur, 26 July 1814.

7 John Macarthur to Elizabeth Macarthur, 31 August 1813.

8 John Macarthur to Elizabeth Macarthur, 26 July 1814.

9 From Blake, 'And did those feet in ancient time', 1808.

10 Macquarie's diary, viewed online, 19 August 2016, <http://www.mq.edu.au/macquarie-archive/journeys/1815/1815b.html>.

11 John Macarthur to Elizabeth Macarthur, 26 July 1814.

12 *Ibid.*

13 John Macarthur to Elizabeth Macarthur, 8 December 1814.

14 *Ibid.*

15 *Ibid.*

16 John Macarthur to Elizabeth Macarthur, 30 June 1814.

17 John Macarthur to Elizabeth Macarthur, 8 December 1814.

18 *Ibid.*

19 Elizabeth Macarthur to Eliza Kingdon, March 1816.

20 Hannibal Macarthur to John Macarthur, 16 August 1813.

21 Hannibal Macarthur to John Macarthur, 16 May 1814.

22 *Ibid.*

23 *Sydney Gazette*, 28 April 1805.

24 As cited in Karskens, *The Colony*, 2009, p. 493.

25 *Ibid.*, p. 505.

26 Governor Macquarie, as cited in Connor, *The Australian Frontier Wars 1788–1838*, 2002, p. 51.

27 Connor, *The Australian Frontier Wars 1788–1838*, 2002, p. 51.

28 Elizabeth Macarthur to Eliza Kingdon, March 1816.

29 *Ibid.*

30 As cited in Karskens, *The Colony,* 2009, p. 510.

31 Governor Macquarie, as cited in Connor, *The Australian Frontier Wars 1788–1838,* 2002, p. 52.

18. Prosperity

1   Elizabeth Macarthur to Eliza Kingdon, March 1816.

2   *Ibid.*

3   John Macarthur to Elizabeth Macarthur, 14 May 1812.

4   As cited in King, *Elizabeth Macarthur and her World,* 1980, p. 87.

5   John Macarthur to Walter Davidson, 3 September 1818.

6   Atkinson, *The Political Life of James Macarthur,* 1976, p 29.

7   John Macarthur to Elizabeth Macarthur, 29 April 1815.

8   *Ibid.*

9   John Macarthur to Elizabeth Macarthur, 23 April 1816.

10 Ellis, *John Macarthur,* 1978, p. 432.

11 John Macarthur to Elizabeth Macarthur, 28 July 1816.

12 *Ibid.*

13 Goulburn to John Macarthur, as quoted in Ellis, *John Macarthur,* 1978, p. 434.

14 John Macarthur to Elizabeth Macarthur, 18 February 1817.

15 John Macarthur to Elizabeth Macarthur, 24 March 1817.

16 John Macarthur to Elizabeth Macarthur, 18 November 1812.

17 John Macarthur to Elizabeth Macarthur, 18 February 1817.

18 John Macarthur to Elizabeth Macarthur, 30 September 1817.

19 Postscript from James Macarthur; John Macarthur to Elizabeth Macarthur, 30 September 1817.

20 Elizabeth Macarthur to Eliza Kingdon, 11 December 1817.

21 *Ibid.*

22 *Ibid.*

23 John Macarthur to Walter Davidson, 3 September 1818.

24 *Ibid.*

25 *Ibid.*

26 Yarwood, 'Johnston, George (1790–1820)', *Australian Dictionary of Biography,* viewed online, 3 May 2017, <http://adb.anu.edu.au/biography/johnston-george-2278/text2927>.

27 Elizabeth Macarthur to Eliza Kingdon, 17 May 1818.

28 King, *Elizabeth Macarthur and Her World,* 1980, p. 194.

29 Hill, *Paper Houses,* 2016, p. 216.

30 John Macarthur to Lord Bathurst, 1 August 1816.

31 In 1825 James and William attempted, unsuccessfully, to have Aboriginal men Bundle and Johnny appointed as constables on the Camden Park side of the Nepean, on full pay and rations. Viewed online, 20 May 2013, <www.lib.mq.edu.au/all/journeys/people/profiles/bundle.html>

32 As cited in Atkinson, *Camden: Farm and village life in early New South Wales,* 1988, p. 23.

33 Graham, *A Treatise on the Australian Merino*, 1870, p. 10.

34 Viewed online, 17 April 2017, <http://www.populstat.info/Oceania/australc.htm>.

35 Robert Scott to his mother, May 1822. As quoted in Broadbent, *The Australian Colonial House: Architecture and Society in New South Wales 1788-1842*, 1997, p. 269.

36 Elizabeth Macarthur to son John Macarthur, 7 June 1824.

37 *Ibid.*

38 Miss Elizabeth Macarthur to Eliza Kingdon, 8 March 1818.

39 Miss Elizabeth Macarthur to Eliza Kingdon, 15 July 1818.

40 *Ibid.*

41 Elizabeth Macarthur to Bridget Kingdon, 1 September 1798.

42 'Life at Government House in the Macquarie Era', viewed online, 16 December 2017 <https://sydneylivingmuseums.com.au/stories/life-government-house-macquarie-era>

43 Walsh, *In Her Own Words*, 2011, p. 224–25.

44 Macquarie's diary, June 1816, viewed online, 26 August 2016, http://www.mq.edu.au/macquarie-archive/lema/1816/1816june.html.

45 *Sydney Gazette*, 13 November 1823.

46 Elizabeth Macarthur to Eliza Kingdon, 7 June 1824.

47 *Ibid.*

48 Elizabeth Macarthur to Eliza Kingdon, 6 February 1825.

49 *Ibid.*

50 Elizabeth Macarthur to Eliza Kingdon, 7 June 1824.

51 Isabella's bible, inscribed with the names of her daughters and grandchildren, is to this day treasured by her Canadian descendants. Viewed online, 27 January 2017, <http://www.islandregister.com/bibles/ehenry.html>. It is also worth noting that Elizabeth Macarthur *did* name her second daughter Mary Isabella, perhaps in honour of her sister.

52 Helenus Scott to his mother, August 1824, as cited in Broadbent and Hughes, *Elizabeth Farm Parramatta*, 1984, p. 40.

53 John Macarthur to Walter Davidson, 3 September 1818.

54 *Sydney Gazette,* 25 March 1826.

55 Ellis, *John Macarthur*, 1978, p. 477.

19. Headaches and Public Humiliations

1   Elizabeth Macarthur to son Edward Macarthur, 17 December 1826.

2   *Ibid.*

3   Elizabeth Macarthur to son John Macarthur, 29 June 1826.

4   John Macarthur to son John Macarthur, 10 April 1830.

5   Elizabeth Macarthur to Eliza Kingdon, 4 February 1826.

6   Elizabeth Macarthur to Eliza Kingdon, 4 September 1822.

7   Elizabeth Macarthur to Eliza Kingdon, 28 June 1825.

8   Elizabeth Macarthur to Edward Macarthur, 25 March 1827.

9   Elizabeth Macarthur to Edward Macarthur, 4 March 1827.

10 *Ibid.*

11 Governor Darling to Under-Secretary Sir Robert Hay, 2 September 1826; as cited in Hill, *Paper Houses*, 2016, p. 102.

12 Darling to Under-Secretary Hay, 1 May 1826, as cited in King, *Elizabeth Macarthur and Her World*, 1980, p. 129.

13 Darling to Under-Secretary Hay, 24 May 1826, as cited in King, *Elizabeth Macarthur and Her World*, 1980, p. 130.

14 Elizabeth Macarthur to Edward Macarthur, 5 June 1832.

15 Elizabeth Macarthur to Edward Macarthur, 17 December 1826.

16 Elizabeth Macarthur to Edward Macarthur, 4 March 1827.

17 Elizabeth Macarthur to Edward Macarthur, 17 December 1826.

18 *Ibid.*

19 Elizabeth Macarthur to Edward Macarthur, 27 December 1830.

20 Why the cottage was named Hambledon is not clear. There are two villages called Hambledon in England, another called Hambleden (with an *e*), and a fourth place called Hambledon Hill. Several British naval vessels also bore the name Hambledon. If Penelope Lucas had ties to any one of them, they have since been lost to history.

21 James Macarthur to his brother John Macarthur, 17 May 1827.

22 *Sydney Gazette*, 14 and 16 May 1828.

23 As cited in Ellis, *John Macarthur*, 1978, p. 513.

24 *Sydney Gazette*, 14 and 16 May 1828.

25 For details regarding the Australian Agricultural Company see Atkinson, *The Political Life of James Macarthur*, 1976, pp. 63–65.

26 James Macarthur to his father John Macarthur, 24 June 1829.

27 *Sydney Gazette*, 18 February 1828.

28 Gray, 'Bowman, James (1784–1846)', *Australian Dictionary of Biography*, viewed online, 22 October 2016, <http://adb.anu.edu.au/biography/bowman-james-1812/text2067>.

29 Hart v Bowman 1828, NSW SupC 104, viewed online, 4 November 2016, <http://www.law.mq.edu.au/research/colonial_case_law/nsw/cases/case_index/1828/hart_v_bowman/>.

30 Hirst, *Convict Society and its Enemies*, 1983, p. 105. See also <http://sydneylivingmuseums.com.au/stories/mr-butler-macarthurs-butler> viewed online, 17 April 2017.

31 *Sydney Monitor*, 22 December 1832.

32 Ellis, *John Macarthur*, 1978, p. 492.

33 Marsh & Ebsworth to John Macarthur, 17 August 1821, cited in Atkinson, *The Political Life of James Macarthur*, 1976, p 42.

34 Harriet King to her husband, Phillip Parker King, 3 November 1828, as transcribed in Walsh, *The Admiral's Wife*, 1967, p. 103.

35 American Psychiatric Association's *Diagnostic and Statistical Manual of Mental Disorders* (5th Edition), p. 124. See also Hill, *Paper Houses*, 2016, Ch. 4.

36 *Sydney Gazette*, 25 April 1828

37 As transcribed in Walsh, *The Admiral's Wife*, 1967, p. 86.

38 Elizabeth Macarthur to Edward Macarthur, 31 May 1828.

39 Joseph Faringdon, as cited by Dr Marion Diamond, viewed online, 24 December 2016, <https://learnearnandreturn.wordpress.com/tag/history-of-sexuality/>.

40 Elizabeth Macarthur to Edward Macarthur, 21 December 1830.

41 *Ibid.*

42 Massy, *The Australian Merino*, 1990, p. 77.
43 Elizabeth Macarthur to Edward Macarthur, 21 December 1830.
44 *Ibid.*
45 *Ibid.*
46 Elizabeth Macarthur to husband John Macarthur, 1830.
47 *Ibid.*
48 *Ibid.*
49 Elizabeth Macarthur to son John Macarthur, 23 April 1831.

20. The End of a Marriage

1   William Macarthur to Edward Macarthur, September 1831.
2   John Macarthur to Edward Macarthur, March 1833.
3   Elizabeth Macarthur to Edward Macarthur, March 1832.
4   Elizabeth Macarthur to Edward Macarthur, May 1832.
5   Elizabeth Macarthur to Edward Macarthur, 31 May 1828.
6   Elizabeth Macarthur to Edward Macarthur, 4 March 1827.
7   Edward Macarthur to John and Elizabeth Macarthur, 25 April 1831.
8   *Ibid.*
9   Elizabeth Macarthur to Edward Macarthur, May 1832.
10 *Ibid.*
11 Elizabeth Macarthur to Edward Macarthur, 30 June 1832.
12 Elizabeth Macarthur to Edward Macarthur, 3 July 1832.
13 *Ibid.*
14 Elizabeth Macarthur to Edward Macarthur, 9 June 1832.
15 Elizabeth Macarthur to Edward Macarthur, 3 July 1832.
16 *Ibid.*
17 Elizabeth Macarthur to Edward Macarthur, 25 May 1833.
18 Elizabeth Macarthur to Edward Macarthur, 2 November 1832.
19 Letter in the *Australian* from 'An Observer', letter dated 14 May 1833, published 17 May 1833.
20 Elizabeth Macarthur to Edward Macarthur, 25 May 1833.
21 *Ibid.*
22 Elizabeth Macarthur to Edward Macarthur, 25 May 1833. Elizabeth Macarthur to Edward Macarthur, 23 January 1834.
23 Elizabeth Macarthur to Edward Macarthur, 23 January 1834.
24 *Ibid.*
25 Elizabeth Macarthur to Edward Macarthur, 31 May 1828.
26 Elizabeth Macarthur to her daughter Elizabeth, November 1830.
27 Papers of Sir Thomas Mitchell, Journal, November 1831, as cited in King, *Elizabeth Macarthur and Her World*, 1980, p. 119.
28 Elizabeth Macarthur to Edward Macarthur, 29 September 1833.
29 Elizabeth Macarthur to Edward Macarthur, 23 March 1832.
30 *Ibid.*
31 Elizabeth Macarthur to Edward Macarthur, 12 May 1831.

32 Elizabeth Macarthur to Edward Macarthur, 23 March 1832.

33 Elizabeth Macarthur to Edward Macarthur, 23 March 1834.

34 *Ibid.*

35 Elizabeth Macarthur to Edward Macarthur, 23 March 1832.

36 Elizabeth Macarthur to Edward Macarthur, 25 May 1833.

37 Elizabeth Macarthur to Edward Macarthur, 17 May 1834.

38 Hill, *Paper Houses*, 2016, p. 252.

39 Lord Aberdeen's secretary to Edward Macarthur, 5 January 1835.

40 Postscript by daughter Elizabeth Macarthur, added to a letter from her mother Elizabeth Macarthur to Edward Macarthur, 11 September 1835.

41 Elizabeth Macarthur to Edward Macarthur, October 1834.

42 Elizabeth Macarthur to Edward Macarthur, 20 February 1835.

43 Captain Phillip Parker King's son (named Phillip Gidley King after his grandfather) was also aboard the *Beagle*, as a junior officer. Governor King's grandson and Darwin had entered into a friendship that would continue their whole lives, even after Phillip Gidley King married one of Hannibal's daughters and retired from the navy to live and work in New South Wales. Years later, in 1842, another of Hannibal's daughters, Anna, would also marry one of the officers from Charles Darwin's *Beagle* voyage, a man called John Clements Wickham. They moved to Brisbane, and lived in a property as fine as the Vineyard, called Newstead.

44 Viewed online, 6 Jan 2016, footnote 197 <www.asap.unimelb.edu.au/bsparcs/covingto/chap_7.htm#note>.

45 *Ibid.*

46 Flannery, *Birth of Sydney*, 1999, p. 256.

47 Elizabeth Macarthur to Edward Macarthur, 11 September 1835.

48 Anne Deas Thompson to her brother Dick Bourke, 11 November 1835, as cited in King, *Elizabeth Macarthur and Her World*, 1980, p. 165.

49 Elizabeth Macarthur to Edward Macarthur, 1 March 1836.

50 *Ibid.*

51 James Macarthur to his father, John Macarthur, 7 April 1829.

52 Elizabeth Macarthur to Edward Macarthur, 30 December 1836.

21. Family Feuds

1 Sibella Norman to G.W. Norman, 15 June 1838, as cited in Atkinson, *The Political Life of James Macarthur*, 1976, p. 213.

2 Rev T.H. Scott to Elizabeth Macarthur, 14 June 1838, as cited in King, *Elizabeth Macarthur and Her World*, 1980, p. 171.

3 Elizabeth Macarthur to Edward Macarthur, 27 April 1838.

4 *Ibid.*

5 Elizabeth Macarthur to Edward Macarthur, January 1842.

6 Gray, 'Bowman, James (1784–1846)', *Australian Dictionary of Biography*, viewed online, 21 April 2017, <http://adb.anu.edu.au/biography/bowman-james-1812/text2067>.

7 Elizabeth Macarthur to Edward Macarthur, 28 November 1838. Elizabeth Macarthur to Edward Macarthur, 5 May 1838.

8　Elizabeth Macarthur to Edward Macarthur, 28 November 1838.

9　Patrick Leslie to his father William Leslie, 29 November 1839, as quoted in an email to the author from Dr Marion Diamond, received 29 January 2016.

10　As cited in Massy, *The Australian Merino*, 1990, p. 288.

11　Massy, *The Australian Merino*, 1990, p. 77.

12　William Macarthur to Edward Macarthur, 4 July 1840.

13　*Ibid.*

14　*Ibid.*

15　*Ibid.*

16　*Ibid.*

17　Elizabeth Macarthur to Edward Macarthur, 5 October 1841.

18　Elizabeth Macarthur to Edward Macarthur, January 1842.

19　*Ibid.*

20　*Ibid.*

21　Elizabeth Macarthur to Edward Macarthur, 12 October 1842.

22　Elizabeth Macarthur to Edward Macarthur, 28 August 1842.

23　*Ibid.*

24　*Ibid.*

25　William Macarthur to Edward Macarthur, 6 May 1848.

26　Elizabeth Macarthur to Edward Macarthur, 25 December 1842.

27　Elizabeth Macarthur to Edward Macarthur, 26 May 1832.

28　As cited in Hughes, *The Macarthurs: A Brief Family History*, 1984, p. 9.

22. The 'Dear Old Lady'

1　Elizabeth Macarthur to Edward Macarthur, 12 October 1842.

2　Emmeline Macarthur to Edward Macarthur, 1829, as cited in Hughes, *The Macarthurs: A Brief Family History*, 1984, p. 21.

3　Elizabeth Macarthur to Edward Macarthur, 4 March 1827.

4　As cited in King, *Elizabeth Macarthur and Her World*, 1980, p. 183.

5　*Ibid.*, p. 184.

6　Auction Catalogue: ML Series 02: A 4240/Item 3: Papers Concerning Stock and Wool: Extensive Sale of Australian Horses. Catalogue of Seventy One Valuable Horses...To Be Sold At Public Auction, by Messrs. Tulloh and Co...Monday, 16th December and Saturday, 21st December 1844, viewed online, 21 April 2017 <http://archival.sl.nsw. gov.au/Details/archive/110368563>.

7　Elizabeth Macarthur to her son Edward Macarthur, 17 October 1845.

8　*Ibid.*

9　Isabella Hacker's Bible. Viewed online, 27 January 2017, <http://www.islandregister. com/bibles/ehenry.html>.

10　As cited in King, *Elizabeth Macarthur and Her World*, 1980, p. 193.

11　*Ibid.*

12　Emmeline Parker to Edward Macarthur, 1844, as cited in Hughes, *The Macarthurs: A Brief Family History*, 1984, p. 9.

13　Elizabeth Macarthur to Edward Macarthur, 14 December 1844.

14 Elizabeth Macarthur to Edward Macarthur, 30 August 1846.

15 Elizabeth Macarthur to Edward Macarthur. As cited in King, *Elizabeth Macarthur and Her World*, 1980, p. 194.

16 As cited in Atkinson, "The Moral Basis of Marriage' in *Push from the Bush* 2, 1978.

17 As cited in King, *Elizabeth Macarthur and Her World*, 1980, p. 197.

18 As cited in Atkinson, "The Moral Basis of Marriage' in *Push from the Bush* 2, 1978.

19 As cited in King, *Elizabeth Macarthur and Her World*, p. 196.

20 Hughes, *The Macarthurs: A Brief Family History*, 1984, p. 21.

21 As cited in King, *Elizabeth Macarthur and Her World*, 1980, p. 199.

22 *Ibid.*, p. 200.

23 *Ibid.*

24 *Ibid.*

25 *Ibid.*, p. 201.

26 Arthur Phillip to Lord Sydney, 15 May 1788, *Historical Records of New South Wales* Vol. 1, p. 122.

27 Badger, 'The Lamentable Death of Lady Mary Fitzroy' *Journal of the Royal Australian Historical Society*, 1 December 2001.

28 Nairn, 'Macarthur, Hannibal Hawkins (1788–1861)', *Australian Dictionary of Biography*, viewed online, 29 January 2017, <http://adb.anu.edu.au/biography/macarthur-hannibal-hawkins-2388/text3149>.

29 As cited in King, *Elizabeth Macarthur and Her World*, 1980, p. 203.

30 *Ibid.*

31 *Australian Town and County Journal*, 13 May 1903, p. 31, viewed online, 5 May 2017, <http://trove.nla.gov.au/newspaper/article/71481134/5333997>.

32 Elizabeth Macarthur to Edward Macarthur, 1 August 1849.

33 Elizabeth Macarthur to Bridget Kingdon, 7 March 1791.

34 Elizabeth Macarthur to Edward Macarthur, as cited in King, *Elizabeth Macarthur and Her World*, 1980, p. 193.

35 Death Notice, *Sydney Morning Herald*, 16 February 1850, viewed online, 22 December 2017. <https://trove.nla.gov.au/newspaper/article/12915786?searchTerm=elizabeth%20macarthur&searchLimits=dateFrom=1850-01-01|||dateTo=1850-12-31>.

36 Emily Macarthur to Aunt Martin, 10 July 1850, as cited in 'The Macarthur Collection: Its Contribution to Australian Historiography', Joy Hughes, Elizabeth Farm Bicentennial Seminar, 24 October 1993.

Epilogue

1 Viewed online, 3 Feb 2017, <http://familypedia.wikia.com/wiki/James_Kinghorne_Chisholm_(1830-1912)>.

2 See Broadbent, *Elizabeth Farm Parramatta: A History and a Guide*, 1984, for examples.

Illustrations

Elizabeth Macarthur (reputedly), dated from clothing 1785–90: State Library of New South Wales

John Macarthur: Sibella Macarthur-Ownslow, *The Macarthurs of Camden Park*, 1914.

Lodgeworthy: the author

Edward: Camden Park, photographed by Jane McKenzie

John: Camden Park, photographed by Jane McKenzie

William: Camden Park, photographed by Jane McKenzie

Elizabeth: State Library of New South Wales

Mary: State Library of New South Wales

James: Camden Park, photographed by Jane McKenzie

James's wife, Emily: Camden Park, photographed by Jane McKenzie

Hannibal: State Library of New South Wales

Anna Maria: State Library of New South Wales

Anna Josepha King: State Library of New South Wales

Elizabeth Paterson: William Owen, Art Gallery of New South Wales

Elizabeth Macquarie: State Library of New South Wales

Betsy Marsden: State Library of New South Wales

Daringa: Thomas Watling, National History Museum, UK

Elizabeth Farm: Sydney Living Museums

Clovelly: State Library of New South Wales

Elizabeth Macarthur, aged seventy-nine: Camden Park

Map of Port Jackson: compiled and published by W. Meadows Brownrigg, land surveyor and Estate Agent, c 1850, State Library of New South Wales

Index